THE MURDER OF DR. CHAPMAN

THE
MURDER OF
DR. CHAPMAN

The Legendary Trials
of Lucretia Chapman
and Her Lover

Linda Wolfe

HarperCollins*Publishers*

FIRST EDITION

Designed by Laura Lindgren

Printed on acid-free paper

Library of Congress Cataloging-in-Publication Data

Wolfe, Linda.
    The Murder of Dr. Chapman: The Legendary Trials of Lucretia Chapman and Her Lover / by Linda Wolfe.—1st ed.
        p. cm.
    Includes bibliographical references and index.
    ISBN 0-06-019623-8 (hardcover)
    1. Murder—United States—Case studies. 2. Chapman, Lucretia.
3. Estradas de Mina, Carolino, 1809–1832. I. Title.

HV6239.W65 2004
364.15'23'0974821—dc21   2003050833

04 05 06 07 08 09 NMSG/RRD 10 9 8 7 6 5 4 3 2 1

To Larry Weisman

O, what may man within him hide
Though angel on the outward side.

—WILLIAM SHAKESPEARE
Measure for Measure

Contents

Acknowledgments

I would like to thank the many institutions and individuals whose help I received during the course of writing this book. Chief among the institutions is the Library Company of Philadelphia, whose impressive collection of nineteenth-century Pennsylvania newspapers is available to researchers not on microfilm but in the flesh, so to speak—that is, in bound volumes. This made an enormous difference to me, for turning the papers' well-preserved pages and letting my eye fall at will, I was able to make unexpected and important discoveries about the Chapman case.

I had some of this joy-in-print at the American Antiquarian Society, where researchers are permitted to read actual print if the newspapers they wish to study have not yet been microfilmed. Fortunately some of the papers I needed had not yet suffered that awful fate.

The Allen Room at the New York Public Library was another special place. The library's trove of early nineteenth-century books is a marvel, and the Allen Room, where I was kindly granted permission to read for a year, is a researcher's paradise.

I'd also like to thank Yaddo, where the voice of David Paul Brown seemed to enter into me, and the Bucks County Historical

Society. This book would truly not have been possible without the society's exceptional collection of Bucks County books and papers, and especially without the generous help of librarian Donna Humphrey.

It might not have been possible, too, without the assistance of my bright and dogged researcher Jasmine Park, at the time a mere junior at the University of Pennsylvania. She was wise many years beyond her age.

There are many other people I want to acknowledge: Dr. Lawrence Alpert for providing me with information about arsenic poisioning; Oliver Allen for allowing me to examine the remarkable Philadelphia watercolors of his ancestor George Albert Lewis; Rebekah Ambrose of the Onondaga Historical Association for information about early nineteenth-century Syracuse, New York; General Ray Bell for tips about soldiering during the War of 1812; Brett Bertolino of the Eastern State Penitentiary Historic Site for information about the prison; Kellee Blake of the National Archives Mid-Atlantic Division for telling me about William Chapman's baggage; Norman Brower of the South Street Seaport Museum for enlightening me about what it was like to sail to America in its earliest days; Cintra Jones Browse and Eithne Ross for familiarizing me with the family history of prosecutor Thomas Ross; Kit Campbell for information about early nineteenth-century costume; Al Clark of the Barre Historical Society for his entertaining stories about Lucretia Chapman's youth and family history; Mignon Geliebter of the Philadelphia College of Pharmacy for sending me material about Elias Durand; Judy Keenan and Ellen Saxon for accompanying me on site visits to some of the Bucks County locations mentioned in the text; Bonnie Lassen for her heroic wrestling with the endnotes; Dr. Richard Layman of Bruccoli Clark Layman, Inc., for information about early nineteenth-century publishing; David Moore of the Genealogical Society of Pennsylvania for helping me trace the genealogical history of various individuals mentioned in this book; Mary Sicchio of the William Brewster Nickerson Memorial Room for information about the Winslow family; and Rachel Winslow for perambulating around Philadelphia with me in pursuit of my characters' old haunts.

Last but very far from least, I want to thank those who read early drafts of the manuscript and made astute comments, among them Deborah and Jude Pollack, Daniel Pollack-Pelzner, and Lois Rosenbaum. My debt to them is great. But my greatest debts are to my husband, Max Pollack, who kept me going during the four years it took to write this book, and my daughter, Jessica, whose brilliant editorial suggestions and extraordinary spirit have sustained me always.

THE MURDER OF DR. CHAPMAN

One

❧

Bucks County, Pennsylvania
June 1831

ᴇARLY ON THE MORNING of June 19, 1831, Dr. John Phillips, one of the most highly regarded physicians in Bucks County, Pennsylvania, was awakened in his Bristol home by a persistent banging on his front door. Phillips arose reluctantly. It was a Sunday, and he'd hoped to sleep until it was time for church. God knew he needed some rest. But he wasn't like some of the doctors who were practicing nowadays, the kind who put their own needs first and turned away patients when being called upon didn't suit them. Some of those shirkers didn't even have diplomas. Others had them, but from places he'd never heard of, and as far as he was concerned, if a doctor hadn't been trained as he was, at the University of Pennsylvania Medical School, he had no use for him, none whatsoever.

Still sleepy, he threw off his covers and peered out the bedroom window to see who was making the commotion. It was Mina, that Spanish or Mexican fellow who was boarding at the home of his good friend Dr. William Chapman. A handsome fellow, with olive skin and deep-set anthracite eyes. Tiny, though. But many men looked small to the six-foot-tall Dr. Phillips.

Bounding downstairs on his long legs, he let the foreigner in and, hoping the clamor hadn't disturbed his wife and children, asked him who was sick. One of the Chapmans' children? One of their students? William and his wife ran a boarding school at which Lucretia taught reading, writing, and comportment, mostly to young ladies, though she had a few male pupils, too, and William gave speech lessons to stammerers who sought him out from all over the country, and even from Europe.

In a torrent of garbled English, the foreigner began answering Phillips's questions. He was difficult to understand, but after a while the doctor was able to gather that it was William who was sick. He'd been throwing up since Friday night.

Nothing unusual about that, Phillips thought. It was almost summer. Cholera morbus time. In the warm months people frequently came down with that nasty stomach affliction that made them regurgitate all they ate and turned their stool to water. There wasn't much a doctor could do—just wait till it subsided, which it almost always did.

Still, according to the Mexican, Lucretia Chapman was insisting he come over and have a look at William. So Phillips dressed himself, got into his carriage, and followed the voluble man over to the Chapman house, which was ten miles away in the town of Andalusia.

When he arrived, Lucretia and William's brood of five children and half a dozen or so of their students were just finishing breakfast. Lucretia, looking harried, was serving them herself. Her housekeeper, she explained, had recently quit.

She was a striking woman, buxom and almost as tall as Phillips himself, with pleasing features and a cascade of fashionably bobbing reddish-brown curls, a head of hair that belied her profession.

She offered him some food, but he declined and went upstairs to look at the patient.

William was pale, his corpulent body so flabby and white that, lying in the middle of the big marital bedstead, he looked like a beached whale, and the bedstead itself like an island in an archipelago of beds. It was surrounded by a scattering of the trundle beds the Chapmans used to accommodate very young students.

He felt weak, William said to Phillips. He'd been vomiting copiously. Could it be because of the pork he'd had for both dinner and supper on Friday?

William wasn't a medical doctor. He was a scientist, but he'd taken a few courses at the University of Pennsylvania's medical school. Phillips respected him. He told Chapman it could have been the pork, but most likely it was cholera morbus, the cause of which no one could say precisely.

Cholera morbus wasn't the same ailment as cholera, the virulent bacterial disease of the intestinal tract that was, even as William lay sick, advancing relentlessly from its birthplace in India across the European continent. Phillips had heard about that deadly Asiatic cholera, which in a year would reach the shores of America and produce one of the most frightening epidemics the young country had ever known. But on this bright June morning in 1831, cholera, with its notorious ability to kill within hours after delivering its first symptoms, had yet to cross the Atlantic, and cholera morbus was not a killer. Indeed, it generally got better in just a few days. After examining William, Phillips prescribed a light diet.

His plump friend was well enough to be annoyed by that recommendation. "A beefsteak," William said testily, "would do me more good than anything else."

But Phillips was adamant that he eat lightly. He directed

Lucretia to feed William rice gruel. And chicken soup. He might even have a little of the chicken with which she made the soup. "Not much," he advised. But the broth would be very good for him. "He may eat plenty of that."

Phillips was busy the next few days. He had a great many patients, spread out over the entire area of lower Bucks County, and he was the consultant of choice among the county's medical men, the doctor they turned to when they had particularly difficult cases. But on Tuesday, after hearing that William Chapman was still sick, he made up his mind he'd drive to Andalusia the next day and check on him again.

When he got there on Wednesday Lucretia informed him, to his surprise, that William had been so violently ill the night before that she'd called in another doctor, his colleague Allen Knight. Knight had given the Chapmans the same diagnosis Phillips had: cholera morbus. He'd also given them a prescription for calomel drops. But she and William had objected to the drops, Lucretia said. Calomel was a purgative, and William didn't need any more purging. What he needed was for the purging to stop. And it hadn't. He was purging himself constantly now.

Phillips went upstairs to have a look for himself, and he realized at once that William was considerably worse. His limbs felt cold and clammy. His pulse was barely perceptible. His skin was discolored—a rash of dark spots had sprouted under his eyes and alongside his ears. More, he seemed to have gone entirely deaf. He kept asking anxiously, his brow a web of taut lines, whether he was going to recover. But when Phillips tried to explain his condition to him, he couldn't understand a word.

Get me a slate, Phillips directed Lucretia.

She brought him one from a classroom, and he chalked out an

opinion. William couldn't read the words. He couldn't get his eyes to focus.

Worried about the dire turn his friend had taken, Phillips decided to remain at the Chapman house. He ate a quick supper in the dining room, then returned to the sickroom. So did Lucretia. Her boarder and one of William's older students, a Vermonter, had volunteered to assist with the nursing chores, to apply cold vinegar compresses to William's aching head and to empty his foul-smelling sick basins. Nevertheless, Phillips noticed, Lucretia was doing most of the chores herself.

Phillips felt sorry for her. She was one of the best educated women in the county. She knew literature, history, even a smattering of science. Knew how to sing and accompany herself on the piano, too. Yet here she was, spending her time bathing a dying man's clammy limbs, sponging the vomit from his lips, wiping feces off his body and bedclothes. She didn't seem to mind. She was doing everything most attentively, he noted. Most tenderly.

At midnight she was still up and in the sickroom with him when a neighbor, a crusty farmer, came over to lend a hand. "I'm drowsy," Lucretia confided to the man, "drowsy from waiting on Mr. Chapman." Phillips heard her, and when, shortly after she spoke, Dr. Knight stopped by again, Phillips took advantage of the younger doctor's presence by announcing that he would like to rest for a while and recommending Lucretia do the same.

She accepted his suggestion gratefully, said, "Call me if I'm wanted," and went into another room to lie down. Phillips lay down, too, stretching out on a mattress in a spare room and falling asleep as soon as his head touched the pillow. But around three in the morning he awakened abruptly and hurried into William's room. What he saw was dismaying. William had fallen into a coma, and his bowels were emitting a bloody discharge.

The end was in sight, Phillips realized. He summoned Lucretia, who woke the children, and the six of them gathered around William's bedside. In hushed voices the family prayed, while Phillips bent over his friend to monitor his passage from earthly travail. The coma, he noticed, had brought a peaceful look to William's face. Gone were the traces of anxiety that had marked it earlier. As to his breathing, it was shallow—barely a breath at all. Then, as the first faint grays of the June dawn began to light up the room, he saw that William had stopped breathing.

Straightening up, Phillips glanced worriedly at Lucretia. The poor woman was a widow now. Just forty-three years old and a widow. A widow with five fatherless children to look after. What would become of her? As gently as he could, he told her that her husband was dead.

But dead of what? he wondered. Of cholera morbus? Now that he'd witnessed the appalling progression of William's disease, he wasn't entirely sure.

Two

Cape Cod and Philadelphia

1804–1818

𝒯HE FIRST TIME LUCRETIA fell in love, she was sixteen. It was up on Cape Cod, where her parents had been born and many of her aunts and uncles still lived. She herself was from Barre Plains, in an inland part of Massachusetts, but she adored the Cape, its gilded northern light, long beaches, and wild ocean that washed the very wharves of the villages and the seaside gardens of her relatives, and her parents often allowed her to spend the warm months there. The spring in question, the spring of 1804, she was visiting her aunts and uncles in Harwich when a boy named Mark Holman began courting her and telling her how comely she was.

She *was* comely, auburn-haired, tall, and with the erect bearing of her father, Zenas, who'd been a militia colonel in the Revolution, so pretty that Harwich had chosen her to be its Queen of the May.

As for Mark, he was bright and bold and seventeen. In the middle of the Maypole festivities, the two of them slipped off into the piney woods. They stayed there, blissfully alone, for several hours, and when they returned, there was a terrible commotion among Lucretia's aunts and uncles. They were Winslows, descendants of the pious Edward Winslow who had helped found America's first permanent settlement, and the Winslows were famously upstanding. Lucretia's great-grandfather Kenelm Winslow had been the keeper of the Sabbath peace in Harwich. Her grandfather Thomas Winslow had been both a physician and a judge. Her father had been a justice of the peace, at least before he'd moved to Barre Plains and taken up land surveying. The Winslows didn't approve of girls going off unchaperoned into the woods. But when Lucretia told the family that she and Mark were figuring to get married, she was forgiven her transgression. Her relatives gave her their blessings, and she went home to her parents and began planning her wedding.

She was grappling with whom to invite, and whether to wear the traditional wedding dress of gray or brown silk, and whether to hold the ceremony up on Cape Cod or in the local Congregational church where Zenas and her mother, Abigail, worshipped, when at summer's end Mark changed his mind. He sent her a letter saying he didn't want to get married after all, that instead he wanted to go to college. And he went off to Yale and left her in the lurch.

She was a figure of disgrace after that, not so different from the girl one of her neighbors in nearby Worcester had written about in a book, a girl who was so ashamed at being jilted that she went out and hanged herself. Lucretia wasn't the type for such a desperate, depressive measure. She lived with her shame, remaining at home, in sight of the twisty road she'd imagined would carry her far away, looking after her younger siblings, and hoping that sooner or later she'd find another young man to love and marry.

But she didn't, and finally, when she was twenty, an age well past that at which most of the girls she knew were not just already married but already mothers, she realized that, married or not, she wanted to leave Barre Plains. She also realized that if she was going to do so, she'd best have some way to support herself. Fortunately, there was newly a way. All over the fledgling country, schools were mushrooming. There weren't enough educated men to teach the press of pupils, so unmarried women, provided they had some education, were suddenly in demand to fill the gap. Lucretia had received an education, had even shown a particular aptitude for reading and writing. She took a job as a schoolteacher. Up at the Cape.

She taught there for five years, correcting numbers and alphabet letters on the slates of a roomful of children, most of them boys, some just out of their cradles, others great gangly fifteen-year-olds. But Mark never again asked her to marry him, nor did any other young man, and in 1813, when she was twenty-five and well on her way to being a spinster, she decided to go to Philadelphia and take a teaching job there.

Philadelphia! Lucretia had been jouncing for nearly a week along log-lined corduroy roads and crudely surfaced turnpikes when, in September, she caught her first sight of the prosperous city on the Delaware. Steamboats had recently begun to ply their way down the river, and she could have boarded one in New Jersey and gone at least part of her way on the water. But it was wartime. British ships were stationed downstream. Lucretia had chosen a stagecoach company that advertised overland routes that were safe despite the war, then endured such a rattling and shaking that, at times, she'd feared she and her fellow passengers would be hurled to the bottom of their cramped carriage or tossed up against the roof so hard their skulls would be crushed. But they'd made it to Philadelphia without calamity, and now, through the carriage's tall, leather-shaded windows, Lucretia started seeing gleaming white marble buildings; wide, regular avenues; and an extraordinary crush of people—merchants in frock coats, women in stylish high-waisted gowns, soldiers in blue and scarlet uniforms.

The vision excited her, and when the driver reined the horses to a stop, she stepped eagerly from the coach, ready to start what she was certain would be a new and better life. How could it not be? She would be living in Philadelphia, the largest, wealthiest, and most culturally vibrant city of the new American republic, and she would be teaching at a new French school, an evening school for adults. Her French was rudimentary. But she'd taught herself enough to be able to instruct beginners, and Jean Julien Bergerac, the man who had hired her, had been happy to offer her a job. Everything French, from the couture to the quadrille to the language, was in fashion now that France had allied itself with America in the war against the English. Indeed, so popular had France become that it seemed as if everyone wanted to learn the country's language—four new French schools were due to open in Philadelphia that very autumn. Bergerac had been hard-pressed to find teachers with any French at all.

He was there to meet her. He kissed her hand, inquired after her health in heavily accented English, and told her he'd rented elegant and spacious quarters for his academy on an excellent corner, New Market Street and Stamper's Alley. Then he accompanied her to the baggage shed to retrieve the luggage she had sent on ahead.

It wasn't there—not her bundle of bedding, or her case of toiletries, or her trunks, the two trunks she had packed so carefully with all her dresses, cashmere shawls, and lamb's wool petticoats and drawers. Somewhere en route, all her possessions had disappeared.

Distraught, Lucretia asked Bergerac what she should do, and he told her not to worry. He'd advertise her loss in the local papers, he said, and with luck the bags would turn up. With luck they'd not been stolen, but had merely fallen off the baggage wagon; whoever had found them would happily return them once he knew their rightful owner.

Lucretia doubted it. She had reason to distrust the honesty of her fellow men and women. But she kept this to herself and accepted Bergerac's offer to pay for an ad for her, several ads if necessary.

A short while later, ensconced in a room on Pine Street the Frenchman had arranged for her to occupy, she unpacked the meager few things she had carried with her and made ready to start her new and better life. Her teaching duties were not due to commence for another few weeks. She would have time to prepare her lessons. Time to explore her new city. Time to get used to the idea that she would be starting her new and better life considerably poorer than she had hoped and planned.

During the next few weeks Lucretia got to know Philadelphia. She sauntered from her quiet neighborhood down to the bustling port, where the river was thick with three-masters under sail, and over to Center Square, where the waterworks were disguised by a little Greek temple, and out along Market Street, where so many wagons and horses were tied up, it looked as if some vast caravan out of Asia had just arrived. The city was astir with war activity, and nearly every day she encountered soldiers on parade or marching toward the wharves to board ships bound for battles in Canada. But civilian life was not much disrupted. On the brick-lined sidewalks, chimney sweeps and sidewalk scrubbers were still yodeling their services, and streetcorner food peddlers were touting their pepperpot soups, roasted corn, and molasses-drenched pears. Head shielded in a plumed bonnet and feet sheathed in thin-soled embroidered walking shoes, the provincial Lucretia took in the cacophony of sounds and gazed with ever-widening eyes at the city's profusion of theaters, music schools, and professional offices—the chambers of doctors boasting that their consulting rooms were *private,* the chambers of dentists offering high fees for human teeth so that they could try to transplant them.

She passed luxury, three-story houses that were rumored to possess flushing toilets and bathtubs that could be filled with hot running water. She passed squalor, too, waterside streets that were ankle-deep in mud, crowded alleyways where pestilential odors wafted from overtaxed privies, and tiny yardless houses draped with so much drying laundry they resembled tents.

It was the luxury that most impressed her, the things that money could buy in Philadelphia. Fine velvet cloth and leather boots from England, perfumes and rouge from France, shawls from India, vases from China, even lion skins from Africa. You could buy just about anything in Philadelphia, and you could fill every spare moment with something interesting to do—see a circus, hear a concert, watch a great actor perform Shakespeare.

One day Lucretia went to Peale's Museum to see the fabled mastodon skeleton that had been dug up in the mountains of New York, and one night—it was just before she started her teaching duties—she saw the town at its most glorious, its public buildings and even many of its private mansions ablaze with a brilliant fiery light. The spectacle had been arranged to honor Commodore Perry, who two weeks earlier had routed the British in the Battle of Lake Erie. No Philadelphian—no American, for that matter—had ever seen so much light, so much banishing of night's gloom. For Lucretia and all who witnessed it, the illumination of Philadelphia was at once both sight and symbol: the future would be boundlessly bright.

On the day of the illuminations a thirty-five-year-old Englishman named William Chapman opened an office on Arch Street. The office would specialize, he announced, in arranging clients' financial records and collecting overdue debts. A short, heavy-set man with a severe stammer, William had immigrated to the United States twelve years earlier, sailing from Bristol to Philadelphia on a vessel called the *Roebuck*, a three-master with a tiny crew, and undergoing numerous hardships on the voyage. The *Roebuck* wasn't built to accommodate passengers—it was a cargo ship that took on voyagers only when it needed some extra ballast. William and a half-dozen other travelers had been given a place to sleep on a small wooden platform in the hold. They'd had to bring their own bedding, and even their own food—the only sustenance the captain promised to provide was bread and water from emergency supplies, should his vessel be shipwrecked. William had equipped himself with a barrel of biscuits and a few other foodstuffs, and taken turns with his fellows at cooking simple meals on a brick hearth on the deck. But a tumult always ensued around the fire, with the weak being pushed out of the way by the strong, and William, whose garbled speech made it difficult for him to assert his rights to a turn, had frequently found himself shoved aside. Still, like so many immigrants before and since, William had suffered his hardships gratefully. He had been poor in England, but was expecting to be rich in America.

After six long weeks his fortitude had been rewarded. On October 3, 1801, he'd stepped off the *Roebuck*'s swaying boards onto the firmness of a Philadelphia wharf and made his way into town, his feet unsteady and his arms clutched tightly around his sparse posessions—his bedding, the single box of clothing he had brought with him, and a little portable writing desk. The writing desk was his prized possession. It was through that desk that, somehow, he intended to become rich.

An educated man, he'd worked first as a schoolteacher. But

because of his stammer schoolboys often taunted him. And eventually, although still listing himself on official documents as a schoolmaster, he'd begun to pursue bookkeeping, a more behind the scenes occupation.

Even that proved a struggle for him in the beginning. Although he was skilled with numbers, many people declined his services, finding his way of speaking tiresome, or worse, unintelligible. He couldn't blame them. When he spoke, his arms would flail, his head would jerk, his lips would twist into fearsome grimaces. Some who met him even viewed his stammering as a sign that he was a man of low intelligence—"A stammering tongue signifies a weak understanding, and a wavering mind," Americans had been warned by a prominent physician of the time. Still, William was a man of great persistence, and gradually a few merchants had placed their accounts in his care and come away impressed by his precision, orderliness, and ability to keep a closed mouth about business secrets. He was still considered, William would later write, a subject of "painful commiseration." But even so, by the time he opened his new office, he had garnered numerous clients, enough to make him advertise proudly on the day Philadelphia was illuminated that he could provide "the most respectable references."

He had also applied to become a citizen of America. Naturalization was in some ways a less formal process than it is now—Philadelphia's Committee on Naturalization sometimes interviewed prospective citizens in a popular local tavern—but then as now it was a slow-moving one. Those who wanted to become Americans had to reside in the country at least five years before filing papers indicating they intended to become citizens and had subsequently to wait another three years before they could achieve that goal. William had applied in 1811. But in 1812, when the war with England broke out, he was still officially an alien, and as such, forced to register and to endure the constant suspicion that he might be a spy. Then, as the war continued, Pennsylvania offered its so-called friendly aliens the opportunity to prove their loyalty to America— they could enroll as volunteers in the militia. William promptly signed up.

In the summer of 1814, almost a year after he had opened his new office, he was called to an onerous duty. The war had been going badly. The British had captured Washington, burning many of its principal buildings. Now they were heading north toward Baltimore. Philadelphia's officials, afraid that if Baltimore fell, the British would march on their city, mobilized the volunteers, and William and hundreds of other unlikely soldiers—shopkeepers and silversmiths, lawyers and laborers—were dispatched to encampments south of Philadelphia to help the regular army protect the imperiled metropolis.

For the next few weeks the untried soldiers engaged in fatiguing marches up steep rough hills and, guns in arms, endured interminable drills. Sometimes they hefted their weapons for eighteen hours a day, becoming so exhausted they fell asleep the moment they lay down on their straw pallets. Soon they were sleeping through the booming of the cannon that was used to awaken them, its ear-shattering sound, at first so electrifying, no longer even penetrating their dreams.

The weather, too, oppressed the men. It was a rainy autumn. "Not a stitch of dry clothing in the camp," one soldier wrote in his diary. "Never rained harder since the flood." Worse, food rations were short. Sometimes the men, even the regulars, received nothing but a thin, eight-inch-long slice of beef and a single loaf of bread for an entire day's sustenance. But the situation of the volunteers was particularly desperate. One day they were given no rations at all. Nor were they fed the day after that.

On the third day the volunteers mutinied. Starving and dizzy, they gathered in the center of their camp and refused to do any further duty. After all, they shouted, the men of the regular army were being fed. Why were *they* being left to drill and march on empty stomachs? Were they not American soldiers, too?

The protest grew rowdy and vehement. Some volunteers merely milled about, cursing their officers and declining to form ranks, others said they were leaving and began packing their knapsacks. Their superiors tried to quell the mutiny, insisting the officers of the regular army would soon learn of the protest and send supplies. But no food wagons appeared. Instead, troops from the regular army came marching on the double toward the volunteers' camp, their gaze forward and their muskets at a tilt. Seconds later they surrounded the volunteers and their commanding officer demanded that the mutineers lay down their arms. The volunteers panicked, sure they were about to die, for the regulars were lowering *their* weapons and taking aim.

At that moment a general came striding into the midst of the rebellious soldiers. He was Brigadier General Cadwalader, the man in charge of the entire encampment. He called out to the mutineers that they were behaving absurdly, that the failure to provide them with food had been merely a quartermaster's oversight. Return to your duty, he commanded. If you return to duty, you'll be fed.

The volunteers heard the words as if through a deluge. Their hearts were beating as loudly as thunder. Then suddenly one of them backed down and yelled, "Three cheers for Cadwalader," and quickly others joined his capitulation. They shouted hurrahs, they clapped and cheered, and they began to fall into formation. At this the soldiers who had been aiming at them put down their weapons. The unruly volunteers were part of the army again, not mutineers, not rebels.

Perhaps it was on that frightening day, certainly it was some-time during 1814, the year he was a soldier, the year he'd had orders hurled at him and been in danger of losing limbs or even life if he stalled at indicating compliance or at least comprehension, that something altogether extraordinary happened to William. He began to speak without stammering. For the rest of his life he would revere that year, mark it as a turning point. Somehow words had stopped stumbling madly over one another in his throat, making him crow with the pain of their collision. Somehow he had taught himself to move his mouth without hawing and croaking, without twisting his lips all the way over to his ears or all the way down to his jaw, and had found himself complaining, cursing, *talking*, just like all the other soldiers.

Lucretia's life also took a turn for the better in 1814. She had not been sheltered from the war. The same threat of British invasion that had driven William into soldiering had taken a toll on the civilian population. Philadelphia's administrators had issued an edict warning the population that as soon as the enemy began marching toward the city, all citizens would be required to destroy their provisions and disable their water pumps, so that the British would be unable to get food or drink. Some people had decided not to wait for a potential invasion and its ensuing hardships. Wealthy Philadelphians packed their silver and silks into Conestoga wagons and sent them out of the city. Less affluent citizens followed suit, packing their carts with more ordinary goods, with blankets and chickens and hoarded food, then climbing aboard themselves. In the exodus, merchants suffered. Theaters went unattended. Evening schools like Lucretia's lost students.

Lucretia didn't flee. But like all who remained behind, she was frightened, and frequently she hurried over to Chestnut Street to join the throngs of men and women who gathered there to glean the latest war news. On the fifteenth of September, 1814, a particularly dense crowd assembled and began exchanging dire rumors, when all at once a panting horse and rider came galloping down the street. The rider reined to a stop and, too out of breath to speak, sat his horse in silence. For an awful few seconds the crowd heard nothing but his heavy breath rising and falling. Then he shouted exultantly, "The damned British have been defeated and their general killed!" Moments later the details of the battle for Baltimore spread like a warming blaze through the crowd. The British had viciously shelled the city's Fort McHenry. They'd bombarded it for forty-eight hours. But the Americans had held out, their striped and star-spangled banner still waving victoriously over the fort as the British began to retreat. The Americans had triumphed.

For Lucretia, as for all the other Philadelphians who had stayed in the edgy city, while fear of the British didn't altogether disappear after that feverish day, it became muted, faint, for as the fall progressed, each day brought better and better news. In New York the American navy defeated the British in the Battle of Plattsburg. In Florida General Andrew Jackson broke their alliance with the Creek Indians at the Battle of Pensacola. Lucretia also received good news of a more personal nature.

It concerned her older brothers, Mark and Edward, who were quite unlike their law-abiding ancestors. The brothers had joined a ring of counterfeiters, and a court in Worcester had learned of their activities and begun to investigate them. The good news, conveyed to Lucretia by her concerned parents, was that the court's chief witness against Mark and Edward had disappeared. He'd been bribed to run away, the prosecuting attorney had railed, but absent that witness, the prosecutor had been forced to drop his charges.

Relieved for her parents and no longer dreading a British invasion, Lucretia mobilized herself to make a change in her circumstances. Bergerac's school, despite her initial hopes, had not done very well. It was time to leave. Saying goodbye to her first Philadelphia employer, she took a position with one of his competitors, a Monsieur Charles LeBrun.

LeBrun's establishment, a boarding school on Spruce Street that he ran with his wife, was highly regarded, for LeBrun was famous. He had translated a number of important French and Spanish works; had published a book of his own, *Bienfait d'un Philosophe;* and written a popular textbook on how to teach French to the young. The children who boarded with the LeBruns, boys from some of Philadelphia's wealthiest families, studied French by LeBrun's method, which entailed not just learning French grammar and literature, but doing basic arithmetic in the unfamiliar tongue. Nevertheless, they were also expected to master their native language, and Lucretia, whose French was still not proficient, was hired to teach English to these upper-crust youngsters. She taught them to read simple stories, like the one about a bee who so surfeited himself on nectar that he could no longer fly, and the one about the good little boy who broke his family's best mirror but confessed to his misdeed because, as he told his father, he could not tell a lie. She built their vocabularies with hectoring homilies like "Without frugality, none can be rich," and "Diligence, industry, and proper improvement of time are material duties of the young." And at night, alone in the boardinghouse to which she'd moved, Mrs. Blayney's big place on South Eighth Street, she began to think about improving on her own use of time.

Madame LeBrun was cultivated and artistic. She knew how to sing and accompany herself on the piano. Lucretia decided to use her association with the accomplished Frenchwoman to become a more cultured person herself, and she started taking lessons from Madame LeBrun in advanced French, singing, and the piano.

Only a small minority of American families, fewer than one in a hundred, owned a piano—an expensive instrument cost as much as a small house, while even an inexpensive one could set an average worker back a half year's wages—and possession of a piano had become a badge of gentility. "To beautify the room by so superb an ornament," one music teacher of the time declared, is "the only thing that distinguishes 'decent people' from the lower and less distinguished." This was true whether those who owned a piano could play it or not. Being able to play conveyed even higher distinction. The woman who knew how to do so—and at the time Lucretia learned the instrument it was almost exclusively the province of females—was signaling as soon as she sat down at the keyboard that she was a well-to-do, refined person. Lucretia knew this and attended to her music lessons avidly, and in time her ability to sing and play the piano, plus the fact that she was teaching the offspring of highly placed Philadelphians, gained her entry into sophisticated circles. She was invited to cotillions, dinners, and tea parties, and introduced to men.

But despite all her new skills, none of the men she met offered what she still desired but increasingly suspected she would never obtain—a marriage proposal. Perhaps the men were put off by her height—at five feet, ten inches tall, she towered over many men of her day—or perhaps they found her, with her independence and broad knowledge, insufficiently womanly. Years later a journalist would do so, and would brand her for all time with the condemnatory term "masculine." In the meantime, single, she remained with the LeBruns for the next three years, years during which the war ended in victory for America, patriotism reached a new high, and a surge of interest in educating female students arose.

Girls needed to be educated, went the thinking of the day, not because education would benefit girls, but because their being educated would benefit the country. They were vessels that could early pour into the next generation of men principles of virtue and freedom—provided they could be made to understand these. They were vehicles that could produce, as the journalist Frances Wright was shortly to put it, "a new race," a breed of men who would see to it that America's national character became the envy of "any nation on earth."

In 1817 Lucretia became an early champion of the new trend. She took the bold step of leaving the LeBruns to open a school of her own—a girls' school. "Miss Winslow most respectfully informs her friends and the public," she advertised in the fall of the year in *Relf's Philadelphia Gazette,* that come November she would be opening a seminary on South Second Street "where YOUNG LADIES will be instructed in all the useful and ornamental branches of a polite education."

Lucretia's seminary for young ladies was not the first such school. Ambitious and idealistic female instructors had been opening girls' schools, often in their own homes, sometimes with but a single pupil or two, ever since the 1790s. But there weren't many of these pioneers, and until the 1820s there weren't many girls' schools; Lucretia's Young Ladies Seminary in Philadelphia, which antedated by several years such eventually famous female seminaries as Emma Hart Willard's in Troy, New York and Catharine Beecher's in Hartford, Connecticut, was among the country's first.

At the time she opened it, she had no access to textbooks written specifically to cater to the interests of girls. In a few years publishers would begin putting out many such works. In the meantime Lucretia contented herself with schoolbooks that, while written for boys, made an effort to include at least some material that might strike a girl's fancy—books like John Hamilton Moore's *Young Gentleman and Young Lady's Explanatory Monitor,* which contained an essay on beauty and a critique of girlish habits like giggling and whispering, and Susanna Rowson's *An Abridgement of Universal Geography,* which included observations on the status of women in countries throughout the world. Rowson was one of Lucretia's favorite authors. Lucretia had read with tearful eyes and racing heart the writer's *Charlotte Temple,* the story of a young woman who was seduced and abandoned by a handsome stranger, and she would always remember that book and allude to it in her later years.

Still, despite her own fondness for fiction, Lucretia didn't encourage her pupils to read novels, for the educational ethos of the day frowned upon girls' reading made-up stories. Rather, schoolgirls were expected to apply themselves in their spare time to the kind of reading that would develop their moral fiber. In the ad for her seminary, which touted her years of teaching experience and her fine references, Lucretia promised prospective parents that at *her* school they might "rely on the most scrupulous attention being paid to [teaching their daughters] morals and improvement."

She left no record of how she taught these matters. But the handwritten notes of a schoolgirl at a comparable seminary in Litchfield, Connecticut suggest the nature of that education. "Have you rose early enough for the duties of the morning," wrote the Litchfield girl in a list of questions she had been taught to ask herself each day. "Have you read a portion of scripture by yourself. . . . Have you wasted any part of holy time by idle conversation, light reading, or sloth. . . . Have you shown decent and respectful behaviour to those who have charge over you. . . . Have you torn your clothes, books, or maps. Have you wasted paper, quills, or any other articles. Have you walked out without liberty. Have you combed your hair with a fine tooth comb, and cleaned your teeth every morning."

Lucretia ran her school for both day and boarding students, providing the boarders with beds, linens, and meals. She didn't do much cooking herself—she employed a cook for the tedious business of preparing meals over an open fire. But she often did the shopping. She chose plump vegetables at farmers' stalls, selected fish from innovative dealers who brought their wares to market on sloops loaded with ice, and decided what meat to purchase by watching the city's parades of "show" meat, farm animals decked out in garlands and bright ribbons, that were driven through the streets prior to slaughter.

In a short while she acquired the knack of running an establishment that was more than simply a schoolhouse, and began putting by enough money to hire a few auxiliary teachers for the school and even to spend some on herself.

There were all sorts of new things on which to spend money— gory waxwork displays, breathtaking balloon ascensions, shocking exhibitions featuring men and women cavorting together uninhibitedly after inhaling nitrous oxide gas, as well as myriad new stores selling ever fancier and fancier goods. Around the corner from Lucretia's school there was a particular mecca for luxury shoppers. She had only to step out of her door and walk along Second Street to see shops selling imported fruit and expensive clothing, tableware and books, all ranged, according to a writer of the day, along great stretches of pavement filled with "crowds upon crowds of buyers, sellers, and gazers." When Lucretia had first come to

Philadelphia, she had been a mere gazer. Now, only three years after her arrival, she could afford to be a buyer. But for all the good fortune of her present life, she still had a nagging unhappiness— she was a spinster, she was nearing thirty, and chances were she would never marry.

William Chapman, the teacher and bookkeeper, had become interested in science. In this he resembled many members of his generation, for early Americans idealized science, considered it not just a prestigious but even a sublime pursuit. Moreover, situated as he was in Philadelphia, William was living in the country's scientific capital, home to a great hospital, a renowned medical school, and numerous scientific societies. But William had a special and personal reason to be interested in science. For centuries the prevailing wisdom had held that the ailments that plagued mankind, including mental retardation, deafness, muteness, and William's personal scourge, stammering, were God-given and therefore immutable. But, in the wake of the revolutions that had swept both America and France in the late eighteenth century, a dramatic shift in thinking had occurred, a growing conviction that the human condition was amenable to correction, not just through political change but through science. And indeed some of the once seemingly unalterable afflictions had begun to yield to the discoveries of scientists. Philippe Pinel had developed techniques for treating the insane; the Abbé Sicard had taught the deaf and dumb to communicate through sign language. William, himself able to communicate relatively normally at last, conjectured that stammerers could also be helped—if only proper techniques could be devised—and while still making his living as a bookkeeper, began to study medicine at the University of Pennsylvania and to learn as much as he could about blocked speech.

Working on the problem, he developed a method for correcting stammering, and soon became convinced that it was foolproof. He told others that he'd found such a method. But he kept the details secret.

Lucretia met William around this time. He was older than she was—forty to her thirty—and he was shorter, a good few inches shorter. But she found him intriguing—he talked passionately about his discovery and his hopes of aiding stammerers. More importantly, he found her appealing, and his interest in her enabled her to overlook his bulky body and the grimaces, a leftover from his earlier years, that occasionally wracked his features.

The two of them had a number of things in common—an interest in education, an appreciation of the struggles that newcomers to Philadelphia faced in trying to make a place for themselves in the city, and above all a lust, that enduring American lust, for money and success. When William asked Lucretia to be his wife, she said yes, and in August 1818, happy to have found a husband after all her years of being single, she married him.

Three
❧

Marriage
1819–1828

𝒲ILLIAM HAD TRIED OUT his method for curing stammering on a young man with serious speech hesitancy and, working with him for nearly a year, succeeded in getting him to express himself clearly. It was time, he decided soon after he married Lucretia, to test his method on other stammerers, time to teach as many as he could how they, too, could speak properly.

He wasn't the only person working on the problem of stammering. Throughout Europe and America physicians and pedagogues alike were experimenting with ways to alleviate or cure the difficulty, each practitioner asserting the supremacy of his own favorite technique. A few employed harsh, mutilating, and occasionally fatal methods like surgically cutting the strings of the tongue or the nerves of the cheek. Others used less drastic methods: mechanical means that entailed placing a wad of cloth under a stammerer's tongue or encompassing the root of that organ with a tiny golden or ivory fork; rigorous diets that involved swallowing purgatives or consuming great quantities of salty foods; rhythmics that required marking the intervals between words with slight movements of the feet or strong movements of the arms. But whatever method they used, virtually all those who tried to cure stammering did so by also giving their clients breathing and vocalization exercises.

William's method and specific exercises are unknown. He never revealed his technique, and neither did any of those who came to him for treatment—he demanded they sign legally binding papers swearing that they would not "tell, reveal or communicate to any person or persons, either directly or indirectly, in any manner or form whatsoever, the Course of Application or any Rules thereunto belonging." Nevertheless, William began boasting that he had found a cure for stammering—"the" cure, he called it—and he was believed. No matter that the boast should have strained credulity, that even today there is no foolproof single cure for stammering. No matter that most stammerers, some say as high a number as eighty percent, eventually are cured with or without treatment, simply by outgrowing the condition. William, rather like a self-help guru of our own day, announced himself to be a miracle worker, and the afflicted, eager to believe in miracles, flocked to him. By 1820, a year that saw the establishment in Philadelphia of two institutions, one public, one private, for teaching sign language to the deaf and dumb, William was working as both an accountant *and* a speech therapist, and planning to open an institution of his own, the United States Institution for the Treatment of Defective Utterance.

That year, far from Philadelphia in the port city of Cartagena, Colombia, a man named Manuel Entrealgo was laying plans to transport his family—a wife, three sons, and two daughters—to the island of Cuba. Simón Bolívar had just been elected president of the Republic of Greater Colombia, a vast territory he had helped liberate from the rule of the Spanish crown, and Entrealgo, a royalist, preferred the idea of living in Cuba, where Spain's King Ferdinand VII still reigned, to living in the new democratic state that

Bolívar was patterning on that of the United States. In 1821 the disaffected Entrealgo succeeded in arranging passage for himself and the family, and by 1822 he was living in the city of Trinidad on Cuba's southern coast and working there as a city surveyor. One of his sons was a thirteen-year-old, a boy named Carolino Estrada Entrealgo.

Lino, as the boy was called, was an agile adolescent with coal-black eyes and thick wavy hair. Like many boys, he was a daydreamer, fond of inventing scenarios in which he won fierce battles, rescued the good from the clutches of evil, enjoyed the attentions of beautiful girls. He was also fond of pretending to himself that his father was not a mere civil servant but a Spanish grandee. And when, on occasion, he behaved badly, ignored his studies, stole from his mother or sisters, he told tall tales about why he had done so, tales that invariably exonerated him.

Lucretia had a child of her own by then, her first daughter, Mary. Eventually she would have two more daughters, little Lucretia and Abby Ann, and two sons, William Jr. and John.

She had started her family just at the time that Americans were beginning to say that being a mother was the most important and satisfying work any woman could do. Back when she was a girl, caring for children had been just another part of a mother's daily round of chores, a part no more or less important than boiling and baking and turning the spinning wheel. Now she kept hearing all about her that the very safety and security of the country depended on a woman's ability to shape the character of her children. More, she began reading in literary anthologies poems and stories that idealized mothers, and encountering in bookstores a new kind of publication, the child-rearing manual.

Part and parcel of her time, Lucretia was deeply influenced by the new status of motherhood, but she wasn't about to abandon her career as a teacher. She and William had bought themselves a roomy house on Pine Street. She ran her school from the house, and rather as a modern woman might do, incorporated her children into her work life, encouraging them to attend classes with her pupils and play alongside them during recreation periods.

She was happy enough during those early years of her marriage, happy even though William, often engaged in scholarly tasks, left most of their chores to her. She was the one who cared for their children, supervised the servants, handled the bills, corresponded with the parents of prospective students and speech patients. Some people noticed, said William was passive and Lucretia the spark of their household. But she didn't seem to mind William's passivity. Or if she did, she didn't show that she did. William's first stammering patient, the one he had taught to speak properly after a year's worth of work, became good friends with the couple, visited them regularly, and found Lucretia to be even-tempered and content. One of Lucretia's many nieces, a young woman who came to live with the Chapmans for a few years, observed that Lucretia was always "tender" to her husband, and that the couple "seemed to enjoy an uninterrupted happiness in each other's society."

They were in that society more and more, for as the 1820s advanced, William relied increasingly on Lucretia, even drafting her to assist him in the dull work of putting the stammerers through their breathing and vocalization drills.

In 1823 Lucretia's brother Edward returned home to Barre Plains after a three years' absence.

He was a broken man. Back during the War of 1812, when the state of Massachusetts had tried to indict him for counterfeiting, he'd beaten the rap. There'd been no witnesses bold enough to testify against him. There'd been none to testify against his brother Mark, either. So after the war the two of them had just continued to engage in counterfeiting, a trade that was profitable and easy because currency was not yet uniform. State banks issued their own money—bills with unique and disparate designs—and the public, unfamiliar with much of the cash that came its way, could be readily fooled about a note's authenticity. Mark and Edward bought forged bills, hid their stash in the old stone walls that marked the Winslow property, and passed the fakes off to strangers and neighbors alike. But one day Edward had made the mistake of boasting to a neighbor about how well made his Gloucester Bank tens, twenties, and fifties were. "The bills are true," he'd pointed out, "except for the signature of the bank's president." He'd also made the mistake of condemning a sheriff who'd arrested his supplier. "Here I stood to make some money," he'd cussed, "but there must always be some damn fool in the way." The neighbor had ratted on him, the state had come after him again, and this time he'd been convicted and sentenced to life imprisonment doing hard labor.

They'd put him to work breaking rock. That's what had broken *him*. He'd gotten as weak as his aging parents. Unable to do any labor anymore. That's why they'd let him go free. That, and the letter his parents wrote to the governor, begging to see their son "in the land of the living, and enjoy his society, in the few remaining days there may be allotted to us to continue in this world of trouble and anxiety."

He'd been pardoned, and he'd gotten down on his knees—he did a lot of that in the jailhouse—and thanked God for His mercy and promised never to pass counterfeit again. And he didn't.

Which was more than he could say for Mark. Mark refused to change his ways. Counterfeit was his career. He'd go on trading in false bills till the day they locked *him* up.

For Lucretia, having black sheep like Edward and Mark in the family was a trial, something for her and William to keep hidden from their friends and discuss only in private, for more and more they were moving in the most elevated and respectable circles of Philadelphia life. Among their friends were such dignitaries as William White, the bishop of the Protestant Episcopal Church; James Taylor, the pastor of the Unitarian church; William Tilghman, chief justice of Pennsylvania's Supreme Court; and Joseph Hopkinson, a member of the United States Congress. With these friends and others they participated in the ever more sophisticated life of the city, enjoyed plays at the striking new Chestnut Street theater, receptions for prize-winning inventors and mechanics at the Franklin Institute, and—the city's latest rage—elegant suppers devoted exclusively to scientific conversation. Women were welcome at some of these science soirées. A Scottish visitor to Philadelphia described attending one at which a woman familiar with the components of the atmosphere anticipated the approach of a period when oxygen would supersede champagne, and young gentlemen and ladies would hob and nob in gas, thus allowing "the vulgar term *drunk* [to] give place to *inflated.*" But women were generally not invited to the most prestigious scientific suppers of all, those of the Wistar Society. Still, William may have attended some, for Tilghman and Hopkinson were aware of his scientific work and, being members of the society, were entitled to bring guests.

Americans of the day were highly proper—"there is no country in which scandal, even amongst the fashionable circles, is so rare as in the United States," a German traveler observed—and Philadelphia, in the view of many foreign visitors, was particularly stuffy. The visitor from Scotland derided it as a place where the very atmosphere was pervaded by a spirit of quietism. Charles Dickens complained that after he walked about the town for an hour or two, its monotony made him feel as if he was metamorphosing into a Quaker: "The collar of my coat appeared to stiffen, and the brim of my hat to expand. . . . My hair shrunk into a sleek short crop, my hands folded themselves upon my breast of their own calm accord."

In such a city, and with friends like theirs, scandal was the last thing Lucretia and William wanted associated with their names.

In 1824 an old hero of the War of 1812, Andrew Jackson, ran for president of the United States but was narrowly defeated. On Cuba, young Lino Entrealgo turned fifteen. He had received minimal schooling—his handwriting was a scribble, a miserable scrawl, and would remain so throughout his life. Yet he had a certain brilliance. He could converse on all manner of subjects, even with his elders, and entertain his friends with stories of his own devising about pirates and princesses, shipwrecks and hurricanes, vivid accounts he filled with grisly details. He was musical, too, could play the guitar and sing mournful love songs.

The wealthier boys of his town, many with far less talent than he possessed, were continuing their education, going off to Havana to study at the university there. For Lino there were no such opportunities. His family was poor; he was expected to start working. Manuel Entrealgo pulled strings, called in favors, and got his son a job as a policeman.

Lino began his duties, but in a short while, unpleasant rumors about him began circulating. He was taking advantage of his position, people whispered. He was stopping the countryfolk on their way into town to sell their *plátanos* and *calabazas* at the market and demanding they give him money for the privilege. If they didn't voluntarily fork over some coins, he lay in wait for them when they made their way home and, in the cane-redolent twilight, roughed them up and robbed them.

William Chapman had a rival, a woman in New York. Her name was Jane Leigh, she had been treating speech problems since the early 1820s, and in 1825 she opened a clinic for stammerers on Manhattan's lower Broadway. Like William, she claimed to have discovered the single and only efficacious cure for stammering. But unlike William, she promised an exceedingly swift cure, one she contended she could effect in a few short days.

Across the country, Jane Leigh's promise caused consternation among practitioners of stammering therapy, for they generally made their money by treating clients for a long period of time, insisting that without lengthy treatment a patient, even if apparently cured, might have a relapse. In Philadelphia, Lucretia took the matter in hand. She changed William's treatment, made what the *Philadelphia Gazette* would eventually term a splendid "discovery," a way of helping stammerers in weeks rather than months.

Still, shortening the length of treatment didn't put an end to the threat posed by Leigh. For one thing, the New York woman began franchising her cure, establishing clinics in Baltimore, Boston, Charleston, Cincinnati, Pittsburgh, even Philadelphia, a development that incensed the Chapmans and prompted William to open a branch of *his* clinic in New York, just a few blocks from Leigh's. For another thing, in 1826 Leigh published a book, *Facts in Relation to Mrs. Leigh's System of Curing Stammering, and Other Impediments of Speech.*

The book didn't say what her technique was. Leigh was as secretive about her methods as William was about his. Nevertheless she had no qualms about stating that her undescribed system was the only reliable cure for stammering. Worse, she insisted that anyone other than herself who claimed to be able to alleviate stammering was an impostor, a charlatan, or a quack. "We are perfectly satisfied that no other person in the country possesses the *effectual* cure for stammering, but Mrs. Leigh and her accredited agents," she wrote. "Attempts have been made by persons in several places to palm upon the community a mode of cure which has no resemblance whatever to Mrs. Leigh's system. A very considerable number of individuals . . . have spent their time and money fruitlessly with such pretenders."

These were fighting words, and late the same year Lucretia and William took Leigh on by publishing a book of their own, one that took pains to position them as the most experienced people in the field. "Mr. and Mrs. Chapman respectfully inform the people of the United States," the work begins, "that they have conducted an Institution for upwards of NINE YEARS" and that theirs "is the first institution of the kind that has been established in the United States."

The book was a joint effort. Lucretia was given credit for her role in streamlining William's treatment, but he was termed "the inventor" and the "Original Discoverer" of a "secret" revealed to him by "an all-wise Providence."

Bearing almost the same name as William's clinic, the work was entitled *The United States Institution for the Treatment of Cases of Defective Utterance.* It listed the many types of speech impediments the institution treated, among them "Partial Speechlessness, Stuttering, Stammering, Hesitancy, Weakness of Voice . . . Lisping." And it contained some highly personal information about William, including the fact that he had once endured such intransigent speech problems that people found him "irksome" to listen to and worse to watch, for both his face and body underwent "violent contortions." But the bulk of the book consisted of glowing encomiums from patients, not the least of which was a letter to a physician written by a man convinced that William was a genius. "That numerous instances of cures have been effected by Mr. Chapman cannot longer be questioned," wrote the ardent admirer. "If a great and important discovery demands a tribute of admiration and a pledge of gratitude; if the archives of benevolence shall have deposited within them that which should be the boast of the present, as no doubt it will be the glory of succeeding ages, where will the name of WILLIAM CHAPMAN stand when nations shall fix the seal of immortality upon the authors of those discoveries the superlative benefits of which shall continue to be felt through the rounds of time?"

The boast of the present. The glory of succeeding ages. The seal of immortality. For William Chapman, the immigrant who had come to America with only a single box of clothing, a roll of bedding, and a portable writing desk, these were heady words indeed. In a short while, even though he had taken courses in medicine for merely two years, he would begin referring to himself as Dr. Chapman.

The same year the book was published the Chapmans started to look for a home outside Philadelphia. The Pine Street house had become too modest for their growing status. Besides, Philadelphia itself—increasingly a center of manufacturing—no longer appealed to them. Mills and factories were spewing fiber dust and chemicals into the once pure air, and rough-looking immigrants, most of them recent arrivals from Ireland, looking for industrial jobs, were crowding the streets. Sometimes fights erupted between the new immigrants and the already established workers. Sometimes rumors that the immigrants were spreading disease erupted. The Chapmans had come to think of Philadelphia as unwholesome. They wanted a place in the countryside, something airy and healthful.

They found precisely what they were looking for in the small Bucks County town of Andalusia, on the northern outskirts of Philadelphia. The town, located amid pristine farmlands and virgin woods, had taken its exotic name from a large estate in the region that had been dubbed Andalusia by its first owner, a Philadelphia importer-exporter who traded in sherry from the Spanish province of Andalusia. He and a few other well-to-do city dwellers, hoping to escape Philadelphia's torrid summer heat and periodic yellow fever epidemics, had started buying land and building summer houses up the Delaware back in the 1790s. By the time the Chapmans went househunting, Andalusia had attracted a number of professional people as well as a few highly successful merchants and bankers, including Nicholas Biddle, president of America's most important moneylending institution, the Second Bank of the United States. But its chief occupants were farmers, men and women of British, Irish, and Dutch descent, some of whom worked as tenant farmers on the properties of the affluent, others who farmed for themselves, growing crops and grazing livestock on their own, smaller tracts of land. Across the road from the place the Chapmans found was the property of one such farmer, a gruff-spoken man named Benjamin Boutcher, who raised poultry with the help of his wife and nine children and, to supplement his income, repaired and made wagon wheels.

The Chapmans knew that many of their neighbors would be unsophisticated country folk like the Boutchers. But they trusted that eventually they'd make friends comparable to the ones they'd had in Philadelphia.

As to shopping, they realized they wouldn't be able to buy much in Andalusia. The town proper consisted of a handful of mills, taverns, and general stores. To satisfy any but their most basic needs they'd have to go to Bristol, where once a week there was a country market, or else make a trip down to Philadelphia. But the city was only thirteen miles away, and thirteen miles, a daunting distance just a few years before, was no longer a formidable commute. Steamboats were frothing up the Delaware constantly now, and a wharf had been built just a mile from the center of Andalusia. There was also the Bristol Turnpike, a smooth and level toll road that passed right through town. They'd be able to get into Philadelphia relatively quickly and easily.

They could even get to the New York clinic relatively quickly and easily. A Philadelphia-to-New York mail coach stopped in Andalusia every afternoon about five o'clock.

Contemplating the move, the Chapmans considered maintaining their New York and Philadelphia clinics. But they decided to close them both and consolidate their teaching efforts in Andalusia, for the house they had found was perfect for a large institution.

It was a grand house, a three-story stone mansion with a slate-tiled mansard roof, tall French windows, an imposing front staircase, and a big rambling porch. It had commodious parlors, a large cellar kitchen, and numerous bedrooms, enough to sleep everyone comfortably: the family, Lucretia's pupils, and William's speech-impaired clients—they were coming to him from as far away as Europe now. The house also had four acres of land.

After the move Lucretia changed the name of her school to the Andalusia Boarding School for Young Ladies and enlarged her curriculum, offering classes in ancient and modern history, in biography and mythology, even in botany and chemistry, subjects that were newly becoming acceptable for girls to study. She also constructed a recreation area. Experts were advising that females, just as much as males, needed to engage in sports if they were to be healthy, and recommending that girls do archery, toss quoits, and play out-of-doors at vigorous games like blindman's buff and shuttlecock. Lucretia fenced in a whole acre of her land for athletics. Then, inspired by all the acreage still remaining, she began keeping cows so that she could serve her pupils fresh milk.

Soon she was advertising the school in newspapers and on handbills. She would take day as well as boarding students, she advised the public. Tuition for day scholars would be twenty dollars a year, with the use of globes, pens, and ink thrown in free; tuition plus room, board, and laundry, a hundred and twenty dollars a year; piano and French lessons could be had for an additional fifty dollars a year; dance instruction, for forty. Further, she advertised, she would pay careful attention to her pupils' health and conduct and would encourage academic excellence by giving weekly tests in every subject of her broad curriculum, rewarding the girl who scored highest with a silver medal. Not only that, but the child who won the medal could display it on her school dress for an entire week.

Her ads attracted parents, and before long the Andalusia Boarding School for Young Ladies began flourishing.

But although Lucretia and William had closed their other schools, they had not given up their Philadelphia property. Instead, they'd hired a manager to run the Pine Street building as a boardinghouse. This was to prove an unlucky decision. A year after the move to Andalusia, the police raided the boardinghouse. Some of its residents were involved in criminal activities, the police asserted, and they arrested several men who were subsequently convicted of counterfeiting.

Later in Lucretia's life people would gossip about this episode, say that the schoolmistress herself must have been involved with the counterfeiters, for after all, didn't she have brothers who had pursued that unsavory occupation? But no evidence that she was involved was ever produced, and despite the incident she became known in Andalusia as an exceedingly upright woman. Neighbors noted that she insisted on family prayers twice a day, parents that she paid keen attention to her students' acquisition of moral principles. The pastor of the church she joined—the All Saints Episcopal Church in nearby Hulmeville—told one and all that the youngsters in her care were exceptionally well-versed in the catechism.

The pastor had ample opportunity to discover this, for Lucretia and those in her care frequently attended his church, a pre-Revolution structure built of fieldstone and embellished with a high-pitched roof, tiny bell tower, and miniature flying buttresses. Lucretia, her tall figure matured now and stately, would come bustling in on her long legs, a cluster of clean-scrubbed girls swathed in Sunday best in her wake. She would seat them in the straight-backed pews, keep them from fidgeting, and encourage them to lift their high-pitched voices in the hymns. She herself would sing the hymns exquisitely, her well-trained voice soaring melodically to the eaves of the little church.

William only rarely came to church. He had begun to believe in his own reputation, to imagine himself as the boast of the present and a scientist who would be hailed even by future generations, and he preferred to stay at home and ensure his stature by furthering his studies. He had also become hard of hearing and very obstinate.

Increasingly, Lucretia found him trying. During the daytime he did almost nothing around their place, just left everything to her and sat all day long in his study. At times he didn't even do her the courtesy of coming to dinner when he was called. She and the children would wait for him, the food growing cold on the sideboard, and when she remonstrated with him, he would tell her he couldn't interrupt his work just because she said it was time to eat.

He wasn't around much in the evenings, either. He went to bed early, leaving her to sit alone in the drafty parlor, preparing menus, correcting tests, and doing the school accounts, and sometime after the move to Andalusia, whether because she felt overworked or because she felt dissatisfied with her life's lot in general, she ceased being the acquiescent, grateful wife she had been in the first years of her marriage. She began to pick on William, who was growing ever more overweight and sluggish, demanding he help out with domestic chores. He should make his own bed, she said. He should put in the potatoes. These complaints she voiced publicly, as if no longer able to hide not just from herself but from others her irritation with the famed "inventor" and "original discoverer."

Four
❧

Lino

1829–1830

*L*INO HAD GRADUATED FROM robbing farmers to stealing
from the rich, hooking up with a group of fellow thieves to
plunder the homes and storerooms of Spanish nobles. One day he
and his band attempted a particularly audacious theft—a raid on
the royal treasury in Havana.

They waited until darkness shrouded the white walls, climbed
over a lofty palisade, dropped on cats' feet into an arcaded court-
yard, and stealthily made their way to a subterranean chamber containing gold and jewels. But their movements attracted attention. A
group of royal guardsmen rushed toward them, guns blazing. Lino
had a gun, too. He fired into the guards' midst and fled.

He didn't get far. He was apprehended, jailed for murder as
well as attempted robbery, and warned that he would be a very old
man indeed before he would ever again set foot on the cobble-
stoned streets of Havana. He was nineteen.

His parents were distraught. Their son had committed a terrible crime, they told the authorities, but it was not his fault. He was
insane, and to punish the insane was wrong. They pleaded, peti-
tioned, begged, and finally bribed, and in the end succeeded in

obtaining clemency. The Crown agreed to pardon Lino, provided he accepted one condition: he must leave Cuba forever.

He wasn't happy about being banished. He would probably never again see his parents, he realized. But more importantly, he would probably never again see someone he cared for as much as, perhaps more than, his parents—his daughter. She'd been born to a young woman with whom he'd had an affair before his capture. He'd felt no strong attachment to the mother. When he made love he always pledged to love his women forever and always abandoned them afterward; it had been the same with the mother of his child. But the child was someone he didn't want to abandon, someone who inexplicably stirred his heart. He longed to see how his little girl would turn out, and knowing that he'd be unable to do so gnawed at him. Still, he accepted the pardon, chose America as his destination, and, borrowing passage money from one of his brothers, boarded a New England–bound brig.

The brig sailed into Boston harbor in September 1829, and Lino took a room at a local inn, the Sun Tavern. The Sun was a popular place—its setting, as its owner proudly advertised, elevated and healthful, and its manager a friendly, efficient fellow who did not ask many questions. Lino liked the sound of the manager. He was hoping to keep his past secret and had even decided to call himself by a new name, Don Amalia Gregoria Zarrier.

America was in the throes of a second revolution, a social revolution, that autumn. Six months earlier Andrew Jackson had at last succeeded in becoming president, swept into office on a tidal wave of votes cast not so much by the landholding men who had fashioned America but by new types of citizens—backwoods farmers and frontier trappers, shopkeepers and mill workers—most of whom were struggling hard to attain some modicum of prosperity. To these men, Jackson, who'd been born in a log cabin to immigrant parents but nevertheless became rich enough to acquire an estate, represented an ideal. When he was inaugurated they'd traveled from hundreds of miles away just to be able to see him. They'd swamped the White House, surging through the doors in their buckskin clothes, muddying the carpets with their dirty boots, breaking glasses, spilling punch, climbing clumsily onto fragile upholstered chairs, so many of them trying so hard to offer congratulations to the man they had elected that he was forced to flee through a back window. Jackson was more than a war hero and a president. He was what so many in the still-young country aspired to be: something other than what they had been born to be.

In a short while Jackson became a hero to Lino.

On December 31, 1829, a meteor flashed through the skies above Andalusia. It came from the north, and left a streak behind it that was like a brilliant rainbow. For Lucretia the spectacle in the sky that New Year's Eve offered a moment of splendor in what she had increasingly begun to view as a lusterless existence.

It was true she'd made a success of her school, and she'd done it despite stiff competition. Each year in the countryside outside Philadelphia, more and more girls' schools had been opening and established boys' schools had been adding female branches; one, in Germantown, was about to recruit the famed educator A. Bronson Alcott, father of Louisa May, to teach its youngest boys and girls. Lucretia had kept pace with her rivals and stayed abreast of new educational trends. She'd taught her girls how to use globes not just to learn geography but, with the aid of a quadrant, to solve calculation problems like finding the nautical distance between any two places on earth and translating it into miles. She'd taught them how to write a fine hand using the latest technology for writing, steel-nib pens. She'd taught them how to draw plants and trees, and in the process subtly introduced them to botanical nomenclature and classification. Indeed, she'd taught her girls so much, and so well, that even though there were several good boarding schools for boys in the vicinity, some parents had asked her to instruct their sons. This was flattering, as well as potentially remunerative, and she'd started taking in a few boys.

It was also true that she'd made friends—many more than William, who at times complained, "My friends are on the other side of the Atlantic." She was no snob, was on good terms with Ellenor Boutcher, from whom she bought her chickens, and Esther Bache, the seamstress who made her clothes, and on intimate terms with Sophia Hitchbourn, an intelligent widow who lived a half mile away, and Sarah Palethorpe, a neighbor who'd placed her bright young daughter in the school. Sometimes she invited Sophia or Sarah to tea, and they'd exchange confidences or gossip about juicy local scandals. And on occasion she entertained or was entertained by a schoolmaster brother of William's who'd landed a teaching job nearby, or by the wives of some of the local doctors and school proprietors she's managed to meet. But the truly interesting people in the neighborhood, the ones she might most have enjoyed knowing, were as yet outside her social circle.

She heard about them from time to time. Heard about Nicholas Biddle and how his bank was riling President Jackson. Heard about Sam Ingham, who was secretary of the treasury and knew all the latest intrigue about Peggy O'Neale—that infamous woman had gone behind her husband's back to have an affair with the secretary of war, and after her husband died a mysterious death, she'd upped and married her lover. Heard most of all about the neighborhood's most fascinating resident, a man who held a station so exalted Lucretia knew he was far beyond her reach.

He was Joseph Bonaparte, brother of Napoleon, and once—

before Napoleon's defeat—the king of Spain. He had come to America in 1815, lived for a time in Philadelphia, and ended up purchasing a vast tract of land in Bordentown, New Jersey, some twenty miles from Andalusia. His grounds, people said, were laid out in the style of the Spanish royal residence outside Madrid and were traversed by twelve miles of drives and bridle paths. His lawns were ornamented with statues. He had dammed a stream and created a lake two hundred yards broad and half a mile long on which a flock of white swans floated. He had built himself a home that was the finest in America, finer than the White House, a mansion overflowing with sculptures, drawings, and paintings by the likes of Rubens, Canaletto, Velázquez, even Leonardo da Vinci.

Some neighbors had seen Bonaparte's grounds. They'd skated on his lake and picked fruit in his orchards. Some local people, the truly important people, had even been invited into the mansion. Lucretia envied them. It was said the great man served his guests champagne, feted them with seventeen-course meals, toured them through his house, and even showed them the room in which he slept, a room hung with paintings of women in so little clothing that some visitors grew faint at the sight. Daydreaming about the ex-king of Spain, his wealth and sophisticated European ways, Lucretia became more and more dissatisfied with the less-than-glamorous man to whom she was married, and her entire life began to seem to her a disappointment, a life that was slipping by without her ever having truly ranged the world or tasted its passions and exotic pleasures.

Despite his lowly Hispanic origins, Lino was a man of grand American ambition. He meant to carve out for himself a comfortable, even luxurious, existence in his new country, and he took his first steps toward it in Boston. He told the manager of the Sun

Tavern that *his* money, Don Zarrier's money, wasn't that dubious paper stuff the Americans used, but gold, real Spanish gold. To prove the point, he produced a gleaming coin, a half doubloon, and asked the manager to change it into American bills for him.

The manager was unsure of the coin's value and declined to make the exchange. But his new guest *was* Spanish, and the half doubloon did seem to be gold. Perhaps, he speculated, the guest was a very rich man, one whose presence at the inn would lend the establishment a certain distinction.

In his gullibility, the manager was no different from hundreds of other Americans who were increasingly finding themselves the dupes of wily strangers—confidence men, they would soon come to be called. America's vast size, combined with the mobility of its population, made it easy for deceivers to practice their arts, and swindlers were beginning to turn up everywhere, not just in the large urban centers, but wherever money could be made by gambling, selling fraudulent goods, passing fake money, or using a self-created identity to gain financial or social advantage. In the next few years their predatory presence in the culture would spawn advice manuals that taught people, particularly the young, how to recognize tricksters—and eventually Americans would become more wary of strangers. But at the time of Lino's arrival in America, credulity was common. The manager of the Sun Tavern, impressed by Lino's foreign accent and his glittering foreign coin, agreed to let him stay at the inn on credit. Don Zarrier could pay him later, he said, once he'd changed his gold into proper American money.

After fooling the manager, Lino, who was to become a consummate con man, perhaps the greatest in the history of early America, continued his climb toward that distinction by playing to the hilt the role he had assumed—that of a Spanish gentleman. He played it not just at the inn, where he commanded for his table only the most costly wines and dishes, but in other venues, too. At a nearby tailor shop he used his half-doubloon ploy to persuade a tailor to make him a few suits in the latest fashion, with tight pants, cutaway jackets, and embroidered vests. At a stable he convinced the owner to rent him a fine carriage and sleek horses.

But he was still a novice in his new career, and one day he aroused the suspicions of both the owner of the stable and the manager of the Sun, who demanded he pay them immediately for the services they'd rendered. Lino promised he would give them their money the next day, and that night he packed up his wardrobe and fled.

He took to the road after that, living by his wits and slowly making his way down through New England, New York, and New Jersey.

Early in 1830 Lino fetched up in Philadelphia. There he adopted yet another name, Celestino Almentero, and rented a room in a reputable boardinghouse.

He was twenty-one years old now, and although he was short, he was striking, a small man whose stylish attire made the most of a less than imposing figure. More, his elegant outfits were matched by his remarkable face—a dark, handsome face, with fine thin lips, penetrating black eyes, a long straight nose, and a wreath of curly hair. But what was most notable about him was his personality. He was magnetic, full of energy. When he talked, his hands and arms made constant expressive gestures and his words flowed out in a tumbling quicksilver mix of Spanish and English. When he listened, his reckless beckoning eyes seemed to welcome the speaker's every word.

His personality drew his fellow boarders to him, and he quickly forged several friendships. But he wasn't at the boardinghouse very long before he began preying on his friends, sneaking into their rooms when they were out and helping himself to their belongings. One day he stole several quite valuable items, including a gold watch and musical snuff box. The owner of the objects complained to the police, and Lino was arrested.

In March he was tried and convicted of theft, receiving a sentence of eighteen months' imprisonment, and transported to Philadelphia's Eastern Penitentiary. There, with his head and face shrouded in a black hood, a symbol of the curtain that would separate him from now on from the rest of the living world, he was escorted through the fortresslike entrance and led to a cell—a private cell, for in the Eastern Penitentiary each prisoner received solitary confinement.

Solitary confinement was a new idea, and one intended to be humane. In the old and cruel world of Europe, went the philosophy behind the Philadelphia penitentiary, prisoners had been treated like animals, beaten, starved, herded together; here in the New World, in the City of Brotherly Love, they would be treated with respect, given work to do that would afford them dignity and quarters to live in that would afford them privacy. They would not be struck, they would not be denied nourishment. Indeed, they would receive no punishment whatsoever, except the punishment of being denied access to fellow human beings.

Unfortunately, however, solitary confinement was not truly beneficent. Charles Dickens noted, after paying a visit to the famed prison, "I am persuaded that those who devised this system of Prison Discipline, and those benevolent gentlemen who carry it into execution, do not know what it is that they are doing. I believe that very few men are capable of estimating the immense amount of torture and agony which this dreadful punishment, prolonged for years, inflicts upon the sufferers. . . . I hold this slow and daily tampering with the mysteries of the brain, to be immeasurably worse than any torture of the body: and because its ghastly signs and tokens are not so palpable to the eye and sense of touch as scars upon the flesh; because its wounds are not upon the surface, and it extorts few cries that human ears can hear; therefore I the more denounce it, as a secret punishment which slumbering humanity is not roused up to stay."

The garrulous Lino, with little idea in what part of the building he was, or what kind of men were near him, or whether in fact there *were* men near him, suffered during his confinement. His cell, with its two doors, one of oak, the other of iron, had heat and indoor plumbing, this at a time when even Andrew Jackson in the White House didn't have these amenities, but the plumbing pipes were housed on the outside walls of the cells, to prevent prisoners from communicating with one another by tapping. His cell had a window. But the window was high up in the ceiling, a small round circle that, because it faced only the heavens above, was known as the Eye of God. He was assigned to work at winding bobbins—other inmates spun thread and wove cloth—and allowed to exercise for an hour a day. But he worked alone, in his own cell, and he exercised alone, in his own tiny yard; all the exercise yards were private, each one a narrow, high-walled space attached to the back of a prisoner's cell.

Theoretically this arrangement kept prisoners from seeing any human movements other than those created by the hands of the guards who passed food to them through a grating in their inner doors and from hearing any human voice other than that of the clergyman who on Sundays led communal prayers at the head of each corridor. But in actuality the rules of solitary confinement were sometimes relaxed. Lino may have had occasional contact with fellow prisoners. Certainly he was permitted, after he'd been in the prison a year, to ask a fellow inmate to translate into English a letter he'd composed in Spanish, a letter begging prison inspectors to grant him a pardon.

He was born on Cuba, his letter said, and he'd traveled from there to Mexico as part of an expedition against General Santa Anna. But Santa Anna's men had arrested him as a spy and put him into prison. Eventually they'd pardoned him—"on account of my youth," he said—and slowly he'd been able to make his way up to New York to book passage home. Alas, though, he'd lost his money and travel documents while en route, so "the Spanish Consul would not assist me, and being utterly destitute and in great distress, I came on to [Philadelphia] in search of a countryman of mine, who, could I have found him, would have relieved me. . . . In the meantime I was arrested in this city for stealing a common breast pin, a very common silver watch, and a musical box. These things were given to me by another person of my own age, and what ought to convince others that I did not steal them is the fact that I gave them to another boy as a gift. As, however, the witness swore that the articles were not given to me, and I being unable to prove it, and ignorant of the laws, the customs, and the language of this country, I was convicted."

His imploring letter, which contained additional allusions to his youth as well as a promise to return immediately to Cuba if he was set free, brought a happy, swift result. He was granted an early release, and at dawn on May 19, 1831, four months short of the completion of his full sentence, a guard swung open the doors to his cell and walked him to the prison's formidable front gate. There, a free man once again, he was set loose in a landscape of deserted fields and pastures. In his pockets he had only four dollars, the money the prison allotted to departing prisoners. On his body he had only a worn pair of pants, a flimsy jacket, and a fraying shirt. But he was out.

In the gray early light he headed in the direction of the city, hurrying to put a distance between himself and the tomb from which he had just emerged. He would go to New York, he decided. He would take a steamboat up the Delaware.

When he reached Philadelphia he went at once to the wharf on Chestnut Street from which steamboats departed every morning for both Baltimore and New York. All around him carriages, wagons, and wheelbarrows were disgorging passengers and freight. All around him bells were clanging, steampipes were hissing, boiler fires were shooting fountains of crackling sparks up into the air, and travelers, behaving as if they were about to depart on a long ocean voyage, were noisily sobbing and bidding farewell to those who had come to see them off. Lino slipped unnoticed aboard a New York–bound boat.

Inside, where a harpist was entertaining in the ladies' cabin and a Scottish bagpiper was pumping out tunes in the men's quarters, Lino found himself amid the kind of luxury to which, but a year and a half ago, he had hoped to grow accustomed. He saw cabins whose carved wooden beds were covered in soft fabrics, public rooms adorned with paintings, and a salon in which a long table was set with breakfast foods: steaks and chops, ham, chicken and game, hot bread, omelets, fragrant coffee. Approaching the buffet, he ate the best meal he had eaten since his imprisonment. But when the boat was well up the river and approaching Bucks County, a ship's officer asked for his ticket, and when Lino said he had none, the officer directed him to purchase one immediately. Lino didn't want to. Reluctant to part with any portion of his four dollars, he told the officer he had no money. The officer was unsympathetic. He warned Lino he'd be put ashore if he didn't buy a ticket, and when Lino made no move to do so, the officer ordered several crewmen to seize him.

Lino resisted. The men held on. They held on so tightly they tore his shirt. He struggled against them. He begged and cajoled. But it was all to no avail. Near the tiny town of Andalusia, at a wharf that was the first stop for northbound steamboats, he was summarily thrown off the boat.

On shore he stood dazedly, gazing in dismay at the departing boat. Then he began to shuffle away from the river. After walking about a mile he reached the town itself, with its cluster of small shops and taverns. He went into one of the smoky taverns and asked the tavernkeeper if he could have a room for the night.

At twilight that evening Ellen Shaw, the Chapmans' elderly housekeeper, was out in the barn milking the cows when she saw a stranger approaching through the spreading gloom. The family's watchdog saw him, too, and began charging forward, his barks piercing the stillness of the countryside. Ellen called off the dog, and the stranger came nearer. "I need victuals," he said, his accent foreign and sibilant. "Victuals and lodgings for the night."

Ellen didn't like the looks of him. He was dirty, she noticed, his boots were muddy, and his shirt was a disgrace. Not worth anything, she thought. Still, the Chapmans were benevolent and kind to the needy. Sometimes they let them stay for a night or two in the cellar, in what they called the "beggar's room." Dutifully, she pointed out the way to the front door of the house.

The stranger didn't thank her, just sprinted toward the door and banged on it.

A boy named James Foreman answered his knock. Lino asked if he could see the master or mistress of the house, and James, nodding, showed him into a big parlor room. It was filled with desks and books, and in the center of the room was a group of children hovering around a stout man and a tall, auburn-haired woman.

Lino addressed the man, whom his guide indicated was called William Chapman. "I need a night's lodging," he said.

William told him there was a tavern down the hill.

"They refused me," Lino said.

William frowned. It was true that he and Lucretia kept a room for penniless travelers, and many people in Andalusia knew this. But he wasn't eager to have this ragged-looking fellow spend the night. "There's a tavern *up* the hill," he said.

Lino threw himself at William's mercy, said in as clear English as he could muster how very tired he was, how he'd come all the way from Philadelphia—he didn't mention that he'd been thrown off the steamboat—and how he hadn't had a bite to eat the entire time. Then he grew even more creative, said he'd have money tomorrow, *por cierto,* said he was on his way to Bonaparte's, where he had a friend who was a close companion of the former king, a friend who owed him money, and by this time tomorrow he'd be able to pay handsomely both for his room and for any food he might be allowed.

Lucretia's ears perked up at the mention of Bonaparte.

She asked Lino his name. "Carolino Amalia Espos y Mina," he said, the invented syllables rolling melodically off his tongue. Then, "My father's a Mexican general," he offered. "The governor of Upper California."

Lucretia was intrigued. She took William aside and suggested they let the man stay for the night.

William acquiesced. "My dear, if you think so," he said.

Eleven-year-old Mary Palethorpe was one of the children who was present in the schoolroom when Lino arrived. She and a handful of other young scholars, including the boy who had shown Lino into the house, as well as Huson Fassit from Philadelphia; Benjamin

Ash from New York; and John Bishop, a Vermonter who was studying stammering control with William, ate supper with Lino and the Chapmans. There was enough important news in Bucks County that night to sustain the usual animated dinner table conversation. Jackson had dismissed his original cabinet, including the county's own favorite son, Sam Ingham, and was trying to put together a new one. The Baltimore and Ohio Company was on the verge of opening the region's first set of railroad tracks. A local woman named Joanna Clue, who'd been on trial for poisoning her husband with arsenic, had just been set free because the jury couldn't agree whether the unfortunate Clue had died naturally or been murdered. But the conversation at the Chapmans' big wooden table focused chiefly on Lino, and little Mary Palethorpe would never forget the spellbinding tale that poured from his lips as he elaborated with sparkling detail on the story he had begun to fabricate in the parlor classroom.

His father was the governor of California, he said, and the owner of vast silver and gold mines in Mexico. He was the family's only son and heir, and so his father had decided to send him to Europe to gain the kind of polish that befitted a young man of his station and prospects. He'd given him a trunkful of money, some thirty thousand dollars it was, and assigned him a guardian, a friend of the family. His guardian and he had sailed for Europe and traveled about happily until one morning in Paris, in a church where they'd gone to pray, his guardian suddenly keeled over and died. He'd been distraught after that, sick with grief at losing his only friend, especially in that cruel city where he could hardly speak the language and where who knew what thieves and scoundrels lurked. He'd been so beside himself that in a moment of madness—he was given to such moments, he explained, for he suffered from fits—he had torn off his expensive cape and suit and tried to make himself less conspicuous by dressing in workman's clothes.

That had been a terrible mistake, he went on. For soon some French police—they *said* they were police—had come to his rooms and informed him that they'd been assigned to confiscate the trunks of the dead man. They aren't *his* trunks, Lino had protested. They're mine. But the French, seeing that he looked merely like a servant, refused to believe him. They carted off everything. *Todo,* Lino said. My good clothes. My jewelry. My thirty thousand dollars.

Mary was fascinated by this harrowing tale. She listened with wide eyes, etching into memory the poignant particulars, while Lino, only occasionally pausing for a bit of sustenance, proceeded to embroider further.

I was *muy pobre,* he said, so poor I could not even pay my passage home. I knew no one. *Ninguno.* I was desperate. And then *un estranjero,* a good Samaritan, took pity on me and lent me one hundred dollars, and with that I sailed at once for Boston. For I had *un amigo* there I was sure would help me out. But when I arrived in that cold, cold city *mi amigo* was gone. Gone south, they told me at his house, south to Philadelphia. So I came down to Philadelphia. But he's left there, too, gone I don't know where. Still, all is not lost. Because *mañana* I shall go to Joseph. Joseph Bonaparte is also my friend. Or at least he is the friend of my father and of a friend of mine, Señor Casanova, who also owes me money and who is staying with Joseph. *Mañana* Joseph and Casanova will rescue me. For the sake of my father. The governor of California.

After supper the Chapmans went to pains to make their unfortunate and apparently well-connected visitor as comfortable as they could. William lent him a fine linen shirt, and when it was time for bed, Lucretia took him not to the beggar's room below but to an upstairs bedroom where the mattress was stuffed with feathers. Lino slept well in the comfortable bed and in the morning didn't go to Bonaparte's, or anywhere else for that matter. He just lounged around the house.

Lucretia talked to him at one point. She may have advised him to clean himself up before attempting to visit the ex-king. Certainly she took his grooming in hand. She brought to his room a selection of William's shirts.

William was irritated by her raid on his wardrobe. "What am I to do for shirts," he complained, "if this Lino has them all?" But the next morning, upon learning that their visitor was indeed going to Bonaparte's that day, he got over his pique. "Suppose you go with this gentleman and get someone to drive you," he suggested to Lucretia, as intrigued as she was by the foreigner's presumed eminence.

Right after breakfast Lucretia, Lino, and Ben Ash, who'd been recruited to do the driving, set out in the Dearborn carriage. Lucretia was excited. Lino had said Bonaparte was a friend of his father's and of his own friend Casanova, and that Casanova was not just an ordinary companion of the great man, but his intimate. She imagined that today she would surely see the fabled house, perhaps even meet the former king.

As to Lino, he was scheming. He had no friend Casanova, but he was banking on Bonaparte's reputation. The ex-king of Spain was known as an unusually charitable man, and one who was particularly generous to emigrants from France, Spain, and Mexico, whose crown he had once been offered. He gave work to the poorest emigrants and lodgings and loans to impoverished aristocrats and merchants. His kindness had often been imposed upon, in some cases

quite flagrantly, and the onetime ruler was said to be learning cir-
cumspection, but Lino was hoping he was still an easy mark.

En route to Bordentown Lucretia urged Ben to make haste on
the long drive, and by midafternoon she was experiencing at first
hand the legendary grounds of the Bonaparte estate and the views
she had heard so much about, the swans gliding on the glistening
lake, the miniature forests of oak and pine, the dazzling flower
beds, and the profusion of marble gods and goddesses scattered
about the lawns—naked, each and every one of them. The carriage
progressed for miles through this wonderland of landscaping, until
at last it pulled up at the entrance to the grand mansion, where
Lucretia and Lino descended. At once they were greeted by a servant dressed in impeccable livery. Without hesitation, Lino asked
the imposing retainer to show them to Señor Casanova, the gentleman from Spain who was staying at the mansion.

The servant replied that no Spanish gentleman was in residence, although two had been there recently and left two days ago.

Lino was unfazed. He coolly suggested that since his friend had
departed, perhaps he and Lucretia could be received by His Royal
Highness.

"Count Bonaparte has company," the servant replied. "He cannot be seen for two or three hours."

Lucretia did some quick calculations. They could wait two or
three hours until the servant informed the count of their presence.
But there was no guarantee that they would be received, and by the
time they got word, it would be close to evening. "I have to return
to my school tonight," she said to Lino, and, unwilling to risk getting home late, suggested they go back.

They did. They drove straight home to Andalusia, and everything was the same for Lucretia as it had been before, except that
she'd finally been to Bonaparte's, even if she'd been just to the

entryway. And except for the fact that while they were driving Lino said he wished he could stay at her house and study English with her. When he did, it was as if some darkness within her lifted, as if the oil lamps that lit her school had suddenly been replaced with those new gas lamps that flickered light even into the corners of rooms.

Back home that night, she gathered the children for evening prayers, beseeching God to bless them all and keep them from sin, and after the prayers, told William what Lino had said about staying on.

He'd speak to their visitor about the matter, William offered, and he went and had a private talk with Lino. When he returned he reported that their visitor had offered to pay them a handsome sum for the privilege of staying on—two thousand dollars a year for room, board, and tuition—and that he had given his approval.

Lucretia passed the exciting news on to Ellen before she went to bed that night. Señor Lino would be studying English with her and William, she said, and staying for an indeterminate period of time, perhaps as long as three years.

Ellen didn't approve. "You'd best let him alone," she snapped. "He's a Spaniard. A body don't know what he might do."

"He's a fine young man," Lucretia burst out. "I'm going to treat him like one of my own sons."

If Lucretia's interest in Lino was, at first, maternal, William's was financial. Lino had not only offered to pay munificently for the Chapmans' services, but he'd assured William that he'd have no problem obtaining the money. His father, the governor of California, would happily foot the bill, he'd said. All that was necessary was for William to write to his father explaining the arrangement.

Accordingly, a week after the newcomer took up residence in

the house, William penned at Lino's direction a letter addressed to "His Excellency, the Governor of the Province of California, Don Antonio Mara Esposimina."

"Sir," William wrote, "I have the pleasure of addressing you on a subject that will doubtless be very interesting to you. On the 9th instant your son Lino Amalio Esposimina came to my house. He has a great desire to learn the English language, finding that travelling in the United States is attended with considerable difficulty without a ready knowledge of that language. He writes to you by this conveyance, and will acquaint you with his circumstances. He will continue here until he hears from you, during which time it is his intention to exert himself in acquiring such an addition to his English education as the time may admit of."

Then William appended one of his publications, suggesting that the governor read it and give publicity to the cures that he had effected with the speech impaired, adding proudly that he had had "four hundred and eleven [such] pupils, of both sexes, and all ages and conditions in life: of that number, several have come to me from Europe, the West Indies, and great distances in the United States."

He signed it, "Your most obedient servant, William Chapman."

When he was done he directed Lino to write to his father, too, and inform him of where he was and why he proposed to stay.

Lino, who was hoping to obtain as many copies of William's signature as he could in order to practice forging his flourishes, said he didn't want to have to write to his father because he was ashamed of his poor handwriting. Would William write his letter for him? And sign it for him, too?

William saw nothing wrong with *endorsing* a letter from Lino to his father. But he felt it was only proper for the esteemed governor to receive word of their arrangement not just in English but in

Spanish, and he himself didn't know any Spanish. "Lino," he told his prospective student, "you know I do not understand your language. If you will write the letter, I will sign it."

Satisfied, Lino wrote something out in Spanish, and William autographed the bottom, remarking as he scrawled his name, "I have done for you what I never did for anybody in the world. It shows the confidence I have placed in you, for I have signed what I do not understand."

Lucretia also wrote a letter that day. She wrote to a Doña Maria de Calme Mirones in Mexico City—Lino's mother, or so she believed. Her letter was less formal than William's, a mother-to-mother sort of note, praising Doña Maria for having brought up such a fine son as Lino and expressing pleasure at how much that son delighted her own children. "Dear Madam," she wrote, "I am happy to inform you that it will be the pleasure of my husband and myself to treat your son as OUR own child, while he remains in our house, and I sincerely hope he will not soon leave us, as myself and family are already much attached to him. Though he speaks the English language but imperfectly, yet he is very intelligent, and has given us interesting accounts of his family, in the English language. His manners are so mild and engaging that he wins the affections of everyone in our house; even our youngest child (a little boy three years old) is delighted to remain by him while taking our meals at the table."

When the letters were finished Lino said he would take them to the Mexican consul in Philadelphia and ask him to send them by diplomatic pouch to the American consul in Vera Cruz, who would forward them on.

She'd like to go with him to Philadelphia, Lucretia volunteered. She could pay a call on her old employers, the LeBruns. She could also introduce Lino to William's tailor. If he was going to be visiting people like the consul of his country, he ought to start getting himself some decent suits.

William's tailor, Richard Watkinson, had a shop on Chestnut Street. The street was the most fashionable in Philadelphia and its tailors the most expensive—they produced suits that were renowned for making men look as elegant as Parisian boulevardiers. Lucretia, accompanied by Lino and two of her children, drove the Dearborn to Watkinson's, hitched the horse to a post, and went into the shop alone. Lino's clothes were so ill-fitting—he was wearing not only a shirt of William's but a pair of William's oversize pants—that she wanted to prepare the fastidious tailor for the sight of him.

Inside, she told Watkinson that she'd brought him a new customer, a young man who had been very unfortunate. "He has no money," she said, "having lost upward of thirty thousand dollars somewhere in France. He wants to go to see his consul, but hasn't a suit fit to visit in." Then she asked Watkinson to make the young man a suit on credit, assuring him that the consul would be forwarding a letter requesting funds from his father, a prominent general, who would send the money directly.

Watkinson, a shrewd businessman, wasn't so sure. He told Lucretia that he couldn't undertake any tailoring without the certainty of payment. She tried to persuade him that the money would absolutely be forthcoming. But there was no reasoning with the man, and in the end she said, "Make the clothes and charge them to me." After that she called in Lino, and Watkinson measured him, stretching his tape around Lino's small waistline and down his slender arms and legs.

His new customer was diminutive, Watkinson saw. Only a few inches over five feet. He looked like a little bantam cock. Especially standing alongside the gangly Mrs. Chapman. And the outfit he had on! That nasty little jacket. Those ghastly pants. They were so loose, the tailor would later say, the little fellow "could hardly hold them up."

It was nearly one o'clock when Lucretia, her children, and the still atrociously attired Lino pulled up at the Union Street office of the Mexican consul, Colonel Estanislao de Cuesta. Leaving the children in the carriage, Lucretia and Lino went inside and were shown into the colonel's presence. "I am an unhappy Mexican," Lino said at once, without pausing for formalities. "My name is Carolino Amalia Espos y Mina. I beg you to hear my misfortunes." Then promptly he told Colonel Cuesta that he was the son of General Mina, the governor of California.

Cuesta's curiosity was piqued. He knew of General Mina, one of Mexico's most famous military heroes. The general had once even been to Philadelphia—back in 1817 he'd been the one who'd led a delegation of Spanish and Mexican revolutionaries to Joseph Bonaparte's home and offered to make him king of Mexico. Intrigued, Cuesta offered Lino and Lucretia seats, and Lino, addressing the consul in Spanish, proceeded to relate his tale of woe, the same tale he had told the Chapmans.

Lucretia didn't know Spanish, but she sat through the recital anyway. Had she known the language, she might have heard things that would have awakened her from the dream to which she was more and more succumbing—the dream that the handsome Lino was precisely what he claimed to be and was going to make her and her family extremely wealthy. But her Spanish was minimal, and as Lino chattered on, his account interrupted at times by questions from Cuesta, she began thinking about the LeBruns and how she'd promised the children that they'd visit them today. Could she leave, she wondered, leave and go pay her call? Lino, who'd gotten through the lengthy narrative of his disastrous visit to Paris, was explaining how he'd happened upon the Chapmans, and how they'd offered to take him in and to write letters to his parents. Distracted, she sat on.

Cuesta, however, was listening attentively. A diplomat of no mean accomplishment, he wore a sympathetic look on his amiable face. But his expression belied his inner thoughts. Strange fellow, Cuesta was thinking. Looks more like a beggar than the son of a Mexican nobleman. He was so skeptical that when Lino finished his story and asked him to forward the Chapmans' letters to the American consul in Vera Cruz, he decided to lay his cards on the table. "Your manners," he said, "your way of speaking. These do not show you to be such a man as you would have me believe."

If Lino was taken aback, he didn't reveal it. "It's true," he acquiesced, and while the uncomprehending Lucretia continued to consider excusing herself, quickly amended his story. "I am an ignorant man without any kind of education," he said. "But the reason is that my grandfather, by whom I was raised, was without education and neglected me in that particular and therefore sent me to travel, to improve my manners."

"I did not know there was any governor by the name of Mina in Mexico," Cuesta persisted.

Perhaps his father wasn't the governor, Lino hedged. Perhaps he was wrong about his title. "I only heard it from my grandfather." Still he was sure his father was an important figure in Mexico's province of California. "He is in some high employment, and I thought it was governor."

Cuesta wasn't sure whether to believe the young man or not. "Where in Mexico did you reside?" he asked.

This time Lino fumbled for an answer, and Cuesta frowned. "You're lying to me," he said. "You've never been in Mexico."

"I have," Lino protested. "All I've stated is true. But I have been suffering so much from the loss of my friend and my money that I am almost out of my senses."

"Give me some proof that you're Mexican," Cuesta commanded. Lucretia, oblivious to the direction the interview had taken, was planning the rest of her day.

"What proof?"

"Your passport."

"I have none," Lino mumbled.

"Your certificate of baptism, then."

"Lost." But the loss of the documents was not his fault, Lino insisted. The papers had been in the trunk of the friend with whom he'd traveled to Europe, and the friend had died, and the police had confiscated his trunk.

The man has an answer for everything, Cuesta thought. But perhaps, who knows, maybe he's telling the truth. After all, the woman with him looks quite respectable. She's got her own carriage. Brought him here in it.

Observing her dignified demeanor, he decided to do as the fellow requested and forward the letters. But as soon as he said he would, the stranger asked for still another favor. He asked if he could write another note, one to his mother, and have it included in the packet.

Cuesta said yes, and handed him a pen and some paper. At this Lucretia finally stood up. "If you'll excuse me," she said, "I have some business in town. I'll come back for him in an hour."

The consul bowed. Lucretia left. And Lino eyed Cuesta and asked for even a third favor. Would the consul write the letter to his mother *for* him? "I'm ashamed to write in front of you," he explained. "Because my handwriting is very bad."

It was too much for Cuesta. "I'm busy," he snapped. "Write to your mother yourself—particularly as it's rather her fault that you write badly, isn't it?"

With that, he leaned forward at his desk and began doing his own work. He was still at it—and his visitor was still penning his letter—when his servant arrived and called him to dinner.

Cuesta did the polite thing. He invited Lino to join him. Not that he expected him to accept. "It is a custom in my country," he would later say, "that when a person is called to dinner, he invites the stranger with him; but it is customary also that the stranger never accepts such an invitation, because it is understood merely as an act of politeness."

This stranger's manners were so bad that he accepted.

Lucretia was late getting back to Colonel Cuesta's after her visit to the LeBruns. The family was at table, a servant informed her. But he showed her into a parlor and sent up word of her arrival, and a few minutes later the consul appeared. "We are just beginning to eat," he greeted her. "Won't you join us? I'd feel much honored if you would."

She said no, she'd dined with her friends, and besides, her children were outside, looking after the horse.

No need for that, the gracious diplomat replied, and, dispatching a servant to take care of the horse, went outside himself and brought the children into the house. "Would they like a sweet?" he asked Lucretia. "And you? Would you care for a drink?"

She said that she'd take a glass of water. But he brushed aside her modest request. "Cold lemonade," he suggested, and before she could reply, or so it seemed, a servant was handing her a glass of icy lemonade and passing around a tray of sweetmeats.

These little attentions to her and her children delighted Lucretia. Even more pleasing was Cuesta's suggestion that he send one of his sisters downstairs to talk to her until he and Lino were finished with their meal. "Romania speaks a little English," he said. "She can keep you company while you wait for Señor Mina."

Romania proved as delightful as her brother. She chatted with Lucretia on a variety of subjects, and then began talking about Lino, whose tragic story she had learned while in the dining room. She spoke sympathetically of Lino's plight and said his family was a prosperous one in Mexico. Indeed, "In his own country," she confided, "he's very rich."

So it's true, Lucretia thought. So it's all true.

By the time Lino and the consul came downstairs, she and Romania had become fast friends. "You must come and see me at *my* house," she said to the Mexican woman as she prepared to leave. "And you must come and see me here again," Romania said. They hugged each other and the consul escorted his visitors outside and personally handed Lucretia into the Dearborn.

If a suspicion of Lino's true character had ever flashed across Lucretia's mind, that suspicion was now, or so she would one day say, altogether dispelled. From this moment on, she would say, she was certain that Lino was every bit the Mexican nobleman he had represented himself as being. Otherwise Romania wouldn't have talked about his being wealthy back home. Otherwise Colonel Cuesta would never have invited him to dinner.

Five

♋

Bucks County, Pennsylvania
June 1831

OON AFTER THE VISIT to the Cuestas, Lucretia's maternal
affection for Lino blossomed into a different kind of love. She
stepped across some forbidding Gobi desert deep inside her and
like a traveler arriving at an oasis, found herself ready to gorge on
whatever was offered. First it was conversation, never a strong suit
of William's. Lino chattered, spouted stories, made the dinner hour
come alive. Then it was music, long Lucretia's favorite pastime.
Lino asked her to entertain him, and when she did, playing the
piano and caroling the hymns that were her specialty, he responded
with his repetoire—love songs. Next it was touching. When they
went out on errands in the carriage, Lino would sometimes say he
had a headache and, laying his mop of black curls down in her lap,
ask her to stroke his throbbing forehead. When they were surrounded by others in the house, he would sometimes say he could
feel a fit coming on and beg her to keep him from flailing about
when the shakes gripped him. To spare him embarrassment, she
would send the others out of the room and hold and soothe him
until he felt better. Finally it was sexual relations—she began going
up to his attic room regularly.

Ellen noticed. One evening she saw her mistress, dressed in nothing but a flimsy nightgown, perching on the edge of Lino's attic bed. One morning, at dawn, she saw her tiptoeing down from his room.

If Lucretia was aware of Ellen's spying, she didn't seem to care, for by the end of May she was fully in love with the handsome stranger. And he with her—if he could be believed. At times it crossed her mind that he couldn't, shouldn't be believed, that given the disparity in their ages—she was forty-three, he a mere twenty-two—it would have been more credible and more appropriate for him to have fallen in love with her daughter Mary, now a strapping girl of twelve. But when Lino insisted that despite Lucretia's being old enough to be his mother, he loved her, and that he loved her because she *was* like a mother, because she'd nurtured him and given him refuge when he was down and out, she accepted his explanations, took what was offered.

Lino's protestations, and the passion he had kindled in her, made her more and more irritable with William. She flew off the handle at the least provocation. One morning she asked William to help Mary turn over a mattress, and when he ignored her, she told him that in that case she wouldn't serve him any breakfast. Another day she asked him to call everyone to the table for morning prayers, and when he procrastinated, she told him that in that case there wouldn't *be* any prayers, and got so mad that she locked up the prayer book. Yet a third day, she was so irked by the sight of William's homely face and rotund aging body that she shouted at him that she wished to God he was gone, for she was tired of him, and even gave him a little kick with her foot.

On a clear cool morning in early June, Lucretia's friend Esther Bache came to the house to make Lucretia a new dress. Soon after she had cut and pinned the fabric they'd selected and was ready to begin the sewing, Lucretia asked to be excused, explaining that Lino, her new boarder, was subject to fits, and she needed to attend to him. Esther nodded and took up her needle. She stitched away dutifully, but occasionally she was distracted by the sound of conversation coming from the room above. She could make out the voices, Lucretia's high-pitched tones and the deeper tones of the boarder. The two were chatting animatedly, and sometimes they burst into laughter, the boarder's guffaws and Lucretia's silvery trills drifting merrily down the stairs.

The sound made Esther think that the boarder couldn't be very sick, not so sick that Lucretia couldn't come down and let her do some fitting.

She kept on sewing, but after a while she told Mary Chapman she needed her mother and asked the girl to go fetch her. To her astonishment, Mary refused to do so.

Esther was puzzled. Later that morning she was even more puzzled, for when Lucretia finally did turn up, she said darkly that the boarder was no better. In fact, "We fear for his life," she sighed.

Still, when the household was called to the midday meal, the boarder appeared and took a seat at the table. Right beside Lucretia, Esther observed. She observed, too, that he seemed perfectly well. He ate his food heartily and after emptying his plate was in such fine fettle that he suggested taking Lucretia and ten-year-old little Lucretia out for a carriage ride.

At that they disappeared, leaving Esther to work on the dress, and they didn't return till evening. When they did, Lucretia invited Esther to come sit in the parlor with her, and William and Lino joined them. Lino was in high spirits and started telling a story. Esther understood the tale well enough—it was about his voyage from Mexico. But William, she observed, didn't quite get the drift.

A perplexed look clouded his face, and he interrupted with a question.

Lino didn't answer, just gave the elderly man a dirty look.

Esther glanced at Lucretia, who acknowledged that the boarder had been rude and quickly apologized for him. But she seemed to feel her husband was responsible for the boarder's display of bad manners. "Mr. Chapman hardly understands anything," she complained.

The next morning the dressmaker left, Lino hitched up the horse, and Lucretia and the housekeeper climbed into the Dearborn. Ellen had asked Lucretia for the day off so she could visit relatives, Lino had offered to drive her, and Lucretia had said she'd like to go along.

It was a hot morning. Ellen was glad she was sitting beside Lucretia in the back of the carriage, where her head would be protected from the sun. But Lino, who was sitting on the exposed driver's seat, began to fuss that he was getting a headache, and after they'd gone just a few miles he asked Ellen to change places with him.

She came up front. She took the reins, clucked the horse forward, and trained her aging eyes on the road. But from time to time she glanced resentfully back at Lino.

He'd made himself mighty comfortable, she saw. He'd put his head down in the mistress's lap!

A few moments later she heard him start to sing. It was, she thought, a love song. The words sounded odd, what with his broken English and all, but from the sound of it, she was sure it was a love song. Holding her back stiffly, she tried not to listen, but next thing she knew, Mrs. Chapman was singing, too. What she was singing didn't sound much like a hymn. No, what she was singing sounded like a love song, too.

Ellen turned her head and shot a disapproving look at her mistress and the flirty, flighty Lino. He saw her stern expression, but instead of sitting up straight and stopping his nonsense, he offered teasingly to put his head in *her* lap. Ellen glowered at him. Then, "Who wants to be troubled," she snapped, "with a butterfly like you."

At last they arrived at her relatives' place. But it wasn't the kind of visit she'd hoped to have—the family was getting ready to white-wash the house and had piled up all the furniture. Mrs. Chapman suggested that since there wasn't a decent place to sit down, they leave her relatives to their efforts and go for a walk in the woods. But Ellen said no, she'd rather stay by the house, so the mistress and Lino strolled off into the forest by themselves. Ellen didn't mind at first. She was sitting under a shade tree, and it was cool enough. But then she ended up sitting there for two or three hours—that's how long it took Mrs. Chapman and that butterfly of hers to come back.

I'm going to quit working for Mrs. Chapman, Ellen decided. She isn't the same woman she was when I came to her a year ago. She isn't the same woman she was just a month ago, before that Lino turned up.

But she didn't give notice that night. She had arrangements to make, family members to consult, and by the following Monday she still hadn't told the mistress she was leaving. So she was still with the Chapmans when out of the blue Mrs. Chapman announced that she was going into Philadelphia for the day and that she'd asked Ben, the student who was so good at managing the horse, to drive her. They'd be taking Lino and William Jr. along, Mrs. Chapman said, and they'd be back in the evening.

Ellen nodded and went about her work. But in the evening when the first fireflies began twinkling in the yard, the mistress wasn't yet home. Nor was she home when full dark descended. Ellen felt sorry for poor Mr. Chapman. He was running around the house like a crazy man, worrying aloud where his wife was and what on earth was keeping her.

"Maybe they've run off to Mexico," Ellen said.

"I wouldn't be surprised," the old man steamed. "The way they've been going on." But afterward his eyes filled with tears and he said with a sigh that cut right through her, "I wish the ship that brought Mina from Mexico had sunk."

It isn't easy to face up to the defection of a spouse. William, like many a husband whose wife is being unfaithful, was at once both aware and yet not aware of what was happening with Lucretia. He knew and didn't know. He knew and didn't want to know. Part of him liked to think that she was just flirting with Lino, trying to flatter the young fellow so he'd be sure to make them all rich when the money from his father arrived. But part of him didn't trust Lino, didn't think he was what he said he was. And that part, a part of himself he hated, told him that maybe Lino was having sexual congress with his wife, that maybe he was getting her to sneak up to his room at night. Would she do a thing like that? He'd never caught her at it. But after all, he was an old man, given to nodding off well before she did. Who knew what went on when he was asleep?

On Tuesday evening, when Lucretia still hadn't returned, William gave vent to his apprehensions in front of a new friend. The friend was Edwin Fanning, a door-to-door book salesman whom William had invited to stay at the house. After the children went to bed, William asked Fanning, who was occupying a spare room in the attic, to sit with him in the parlor for a while. He poured him a brandy. He talked to him about buying some volumes of an encyclopedia the salesman was touting, and then he began to unburden himself. He told his new friend that Lino had promised to give him and Lucretia a large sum of money in exchange for room, board, and English lessons, but that he thought Lino might be an impostor. "A rogue," he said, adding that even if Lino wasn't a rogue, even if he was really going to make him and Lucretia rich, he didn't care anymore. No, "I'd rather be poor," he fumed, "than have my peace disturbed the way it's been since this fellow came here."

Fanning was a good listener. So William continued his diatribe, and after a while he got to what was really on his mind, which was his suspicion that Lucretia and Lino wanted everyone to be asleep when they came home so that what they did next wouldn't be noticed. "In all probability," he declared, "their object is to tarry until the family has retired, and perhaps then to engage in improper conduct."

Fanning didn't say anything, and William went on fiercely, "If I know of their going together to Mina's lodging room, I will be in there, and by God I'll kill him."

He felt better after that. Tired out, too. And why not? It was nearly eleven. Way past his bedtime. "I'm going to bed," he announced. But he couldn't stop himself from imploring the salesman to serve as his surrogate. "You stay up," he said, "You stay up, and if they come home and go to that rogue's room, you let me know."

Fanning did as he was bid. He stayed up till past midnight. But Lucretia didn't come home, and finally Fanning went to bed, too.

The next morning Lucretia still wasn't home. Nor was she home by afternoon. William was beside himself. Then at last he heard the horse's hooves clattering up the driveway, and saw William Jr.

bound out of the carriage and Lino saunter onto the porch and Lucretia come gliding through the front door, her voluminous skirts rustling and her coppery curls flying. As soon as he saw her, William was sorry for the way he'd spoken about her to Fanning, and he felt sorrier still when Lucretia told him why they'd been so delayed in Philadelphia. Almost as soon as they'd arrived there, she explained, Lino had received word that his sister had died. He'd become distraught, too distraught to make the trip home.

Listening to her, William shook his head sympathetically. Poor Lino. Poor, poor Lino. The Mexican had gone into the parlor and crumpled onto the sofa. William turned from Lucretia, sat down beside the grieving man, and tried to comfort him, reciting to him several consoling verses from the Bible.

As William recited, Lino cried, and afterward he began speaking passionately about how much he'd loved his sister and how devastated he felt by her sudden death. William cried a little, too. It was partly out of sympathy, partly because he was feeling guilty, ashamed of himself for having spoken ill of Lino to Fanning and especially for having done so at a time when the poor man was suffering a death in his family. William felt so bad that he asked Lino if there was anything he could do to help. Buy him some mourning clothes? A fine suit that would show his respect for his dear departed sister?

When Lino accepted his suggestion, William went to his desk and immediately wrote a letter to Watkinson, authorizing him to make Lino a good mourning outfit and to charge it to his account.

Lino requested black trousers, a vest, and a costly black frock coat from Watkinson, and on Thursday, June 16, he went into town with Lucretia to pick up the clothes. After he got them, he put them on, then he and Lucretia separated. She went to attend to some personal chores, and he went into a pharmacy on Chestnut and Sixth, across the way from Watkinson's.

It was the handsomest drugstore in the city, the creation of Elias Durand, an émigré from France. Durand had studied his profession in Paris and served Napoleon as a pharmacist in the Grand Armée, and he still bought all his medications and chemicals from France, which led the world in the manufacture of drugs. His taste for things French was also evident in his shop's sophisticated decor, its array of polished mahogany cabinets, marble-topped counters, and etched-glass windows and doors.

Lino had a friend at at the fancy shop, a clerk named Alfred Guillou. He'd met Guillou a few weeks earlier when he'd stopped in the pharmacy to ask for street directions. The young clerk, who knew some Spanish, had considerately supplied the directions in that language, and since that time Lino had paid him several other visits. He'd chatted with Guillou about his origins and told him he was the son of the governor of California, but he hadn't given him either his true name or his adopted name of Espos y Mina. Instead he'd said he was called Estanislao de Cuesta, just like Mexico's consul to Philadelphia.

Today he dawdled among the shiny cabinets and finally mentioned to Guillou that he was planning to stuff and mount some birds. Arsenic was a principal ingredient in taxidermy. Lino followed his statement by asking if the shop had any of the popular arsenical soap he wanted to use.

"We haven't," Guillou said. "But we might prepare it."

That wouldn't be necessary, Lino demurred. "If you have plain arsenic powder, that would answer."

Guillou wasn't sure whether he ought to sell Lino arsenic itself. He said he'd ask the boss, and called over Durand.

Durand was a clever man, the inventor of an apparatus for

carbonating water who would soon open the first soda bottling company in America. More, he was scientifically astute, so knowledgeable about drugs that Philadelphia's top physicians were in the habit of asking *his* advice before they prescribed medicine to their patients. But he was a poor judge of intent. After peering down his long Gallic nose at his clerk's impeccably dressed friend, he averted his gaze, turned his heavy-lidded eyes toward his shelves, and took down one of his French porcelain jars. Then he scooped some powdery salt onto his brass scale and sold Lino two ounces of arsenic.

The following night William was seized with stomach cramps and nausea. He wasn't worried about it. Assuming that something he'd eaten had been a little spoiled, he reviewed what he'd had. Roast veal, hot boiled pork, and green peas at the midday meal. Cold pork in the evening, topped with smearcase, the creamy cottage cheese that he relished. No one who'd dined with him had a stomachache, not Lucretia or Lino or any of the children or boarding students. But none of them had eaten any of the pork, his favorite, even though he'd urged it on them, told them how very tasty it was. It must be the pork that was making him feel so bad.

A little brandy would calm his stomach, he decided, and asked Lucretia to fetch him the bottle. But even though he drank a hearty swallow, his stomach continued to feel queasy, so he asked her to get him the peppermint. Alas, she couldn't find it, which was unfortunate, because without the mint, he stayed up most of the night vomiting, and the next morning, Saturday, he still felt sick.

That was when Lucretia suggested they send for Dr. Phillips. William didn't want Phillips. He didn't want any doctor. "The doctor will only give me medicine," he grumbled. "I have drops for stomachache in the house. I'll take those."

Lucretia gave him the drops, but he continued to throw up. He threw up all day, and all night, too, and on Sunday morning Lucretia insisted on getting Dr. Phillips. She didn't consult William, just sent Lino over to Bristol, and next thing William knew, Phillips was there examining him. "You've had a mild attack of cholera morbus," he said when he was done, and advised eating lightly for the next few days.

Doctors! "A beefsteak would do me more good than anything else," he'd groused at Phillips.

After Phillips left, Lucretia went into the kitchen. She'd hired new help to replace Ellen, who'd finally quit. She'd hired Juliann, a local woman, as cook, and Ann Bantom, a black woman from Philadelphia, as part-time housecleaner and laundress. But it was Sunday, and neither Juliann nor Ann was in that day. She herself would have to cook William a meal, a light meal as Dr. Phillips had recommended. She decided on rice gruel, boiling the grains until they were soft and letting little Lucretia, who liked helping out in the kitchen, pound them in the mortar until they formed a smooth, gluey porridge.

The next morning Ann came to work but Lucretia still had no cook—Juliann had sent word she was sick. There was nothing for it but to do the cooking herself again. What to make for William? Going across the road to the poultry farm of her neighbors, the Boutchers, she bought a chicken, then hurried home and set about making the chicken soup Dr. Phillips had recommended.

She made a bland concoction, simmering the bird merely in salted water. But by the time the chicken was cooked through, its flavor had transformed the liquid into a rich broth. She added some seasoning, poured her soup into a pretty blue bowl, placed the fowl on a separate plate, carried both dishes to the parlor, and asked Mary to take the meal upstairs to her father.

Little Lucretia was keeping William company when Mary arrived with the food. The two girls got him up, sat him in the rocking chair, and made his bed. Then Mary took advantage of her position as elder sister and assigned Lucretia to help their father eat.

Lucretia didn't mind. Her father was feeling a bit better, the little girl noticed. He wasn't vomiting anymore.

Still, he ate slowly at first. He started with the gizzard—he was partial to gizzard. But he said this one was tough, so he gave the rest to her, and soaking a cracker in the soup the way her little brother John used to do when he was a baby, gummed the broth-drenched biscuit. The sucking made his appetite return and soon he was ignoring the soup and tackling the chicken again. He seemed very hungry—he ate all of the breast and part of the back.

When he was done with his meal little Lucretia hefted the heavy blue bowl and the plate of leftover chicken, carried her burden gingerly down the stairs, and set it on the kitchen table. Then she skipped back upstairs to her father.

He didn't seem so well now, she thought when she scuttled into his room, not so well as he'd been before he'd eaten. He was vomiting again.

Downstairs, a few hours later, the cleaning woman was having a hard time. The children, all five of them, had been running in and out of the kitchen all day, and Ann had hardly had a minute to straighten up. Now it was nearly teatime. She'd best get started, Ann realized, and picking up the bowl of soup and plate of chicken bones that had been sitting out on the table since midday, tossed them into the yard.

After tea, when she'd done all her work, Ann thought maybe she'd take the liberty of looking in on poor Dr. Chapman. She wasn't supposed to go up to the bedrooms, just stay below stairs or out in the yard. But under the circumstances, she hoped, surely she'd be forgiven if she broke the rules and offered her sympathies to the invalid. So tiptoeing upstairs, she peeked into the sickroom and asked the doctor how he was feeling.

"Not so well as in the morning," he lamented. "I have a misery at my stomach. It feels very much like fire."

Edwin Fanning, the book salesman, was still staying at the Chapmans', and that evening he came home from his rounds with the volumes of *The Family Encyclopedia* William had agreed to order. Fanning wanted to show the books to William, but Lucretia said her husband was too sick. With a candle, she lighted the salesman's way to the sickroom, and as soon as they entered he saw what she meant. William was vomiting profusely into a basin.

"Tarry with me through the night," William said when he lifted up his head.

Fanning said he would.

He had terrible pains, William moaned, pains that were not just in his stomach, but in his head and chest, too.

Fanning pulled the rocker close to William's bed and sat down, and Lucretia left him to look after William for a while. Seeing her go made William bitter. "When Don Lino is sick," he railed, "all attention must be paid to him. But now that I am sick, I am deserted. I am left."

Lucretia stayed away almost a whole hour. While she was gone, Fanning did his best to comfort William, and when she returned he talked worriedly to her about her husband's condition. She seemed to think his trouble had been caused by some bad beef she'd inadvertently served—didn't Fanning recall, she asked, that beef dinner they'd had a while back? The meat had been stale, spoiled. The rest of them had hardly touched it, but William had consumed a great deal.

Fanning didn't think it was the beef that was making William so sick. That beef dinner had been more than two weeks ago! Besides, he'd seen William after he ate the beef dinner, and William had been fine.

Maybe she ought to get Dr. Phillips again, he suggested. He'd be willing to go to Bristol to fetch him, even at that late hour.

Lucretia said it wasn't necessary. "Then give him some salt and water to stop his vomiting," Fanning urged. "I've heard it recommended."

Lucretia went out, returned with a teacup, and began spoon-feeding something to William—the salt and water that he'd suggested, Fanning assumed.

Despite this, William went on vomiting. Or at least trying to, for he wasn't really bringing anything up, just heaving, gagging, convulsing. He was in agony. He was in so much agony that he seemed to prefer death to the continuation of his ordeal. "I cannot," he groaned, "live so."

Fanning sat with him until eleven o'clock, and he would have stayed up longer, except that he had an appointment early the next morning to show textbooks to the principal of a boys' academy, and he needed his rest. So he decided he'd best go to bed.

He climbed up to the attic, and there he ran into Lino. The Mexican was chatty, expansive. He offered Fanning *his* bed, the feather bed, a far more restful affair than the bed in Fanning's room.

Still, Fanning declined the offer. He hadn't forgotten the things William had said about the boarder. That he thought he was an impostor. A rogue. Fanning didn't want to sleep in such a man's bed, however comfortable it might be.

The next afternoon Benjamin Boutcher noticed that his ducks, which had gotten into the unfortunate habit of wandering off his property into the Chapmans' yard, were at last starting to waddle home. They were parading single file, one behind the other. Boutcher watched them as they traversed a patch of lawn between the Chapmans' house and shed. The Chapmans' boarder, Lino, was watching them, too. He was standing, Boutcher observed, underneath a buttonwood tree, right close to the flock. Then, just as the ducks reached the road, one of the ducks fell over dead.

The poultry farmer shook his head in annoyance. He'd only recently begun keeping ducks, and they were proving more difficult to raise than chickens. Their constitutions were delicate—they got sick if it rained too hard. They were stupid, too. If you were building a shed and happened to leave a bucket of lime water around, they'd find it and drink it, and if you threw any pickled food into the garbage, they'd scratch it up and swallow it and the salt would stick in their craws. Swiveling, Boutcher continued to study the nuisancy birds as they headed across the road. They were walking oddly, he saw, tottering like toys. Seconds later the first few ducks made it back onto his own property, entering it through a hole in the fence near the drainage ditch. But as soon as they were in the yard, another bird collapsed and fell over.

Boutcher was disgusted. He called one of his sons to come outside and look after the birds and slammed into his workshed. But in a few minutes he heard his son shout that another duck was dead.

A laconic man, in as few words as possible Boutcher told the boy to get rid of the dead ducks. "Bury them," he ordered. But later he found himself talking obsessively to his wife about what had happened. Because he'd had some twenty ducks, and they'd all died. All except four fat ones that hadn't been able to get to the Chapmans' yard because they hadn't been able to squeeze through the fence.

Ellenor figured that what was wrong with the birds was that they'd eaten some of the kitchen waste in the drainage ditch. She'd been cleaning fish that morning, and she'd flushed the guts into the ditch. "Fish water can kill ducks," she reminded him. But Boutcher didn't think his wife was right about the salty fish water. "They've been poisoned," he insisted.

In the Chapman house that Tuesday afternoon the family grew more alarmed about William's condition, and toward evening Lucretia asked Lino to fetch Dr. Allen Knight. He was a younger man than Dr. Phillips, and she didn't know him quite as well, but Knight lived only a quarter of a mile away. He could be at the house quickly.

Dr. Knight arrived at about seven o'clock. William spoke to him huskily, told him he had a burning sensation in his stomach and that he'd been vomiting and having diarrhea. Knight began to examine him. The patient's mouth was terribly dry, he noted. His legs were frigid. He had no fever.

Cholera morbus, Dr. Knight decided. The disease was usually accompanied by fever. But he'd seen some cases of it where the temperature stayed normal, the way William's was. Prescribing calomel, and extricating from his bag a supply of the tasteless compound, he mixed the calomel with a little water and portioned it into several small convenient doses.

Dr. Knight returned several times on Wednesday. William was much sicker. His mouth was even dryer than it had been the day before. His mind was wandering with delirium. His pulse was barely perceptible. Knight told Lucretia to make mustard plasters for his hands and feet, which felt even colder than they had yesterday, and he sent word to the local drugstore to deliver some tincture of opium.

Dr. Phillips also came by that day, and this time he remained in the house, sometimes resting, sometimes attending to the increasingly debilitated William.

Many of the neighbors knew by now that the speech doctor was desperately ill—Lucretia had asked the members of her congregation to pray for him—and at around ten P.M. Boutcher, the closest neighbor, decided that he ought to volunteer his services to the afflicted family. Entering the house unannounced, he clambered upstairs to the sickroom, where he saw Dr. Phillips hovering over William. He saw the boarder, too. Lino was holding a pocketwatch and taking the sick man's pulse.

"Fifty-five beats in the minute," Boutcher heard him announce. to Dr. Phillips. Then, a few moments later, "Now it's forty-five."

The poultry farmer was surprised that the Mexican knew how to take a pulse and told him so. "I studied medicine for two years," Lino informed him huffily.

Ignoring the man's prickliness, Boutcher looked down at the anguished face of his neighbor and whispered that he didn't think William was going to live until sunrise.

Lino started to cry. Or at least he seemed to be crying. His shoulders shook and sobbing sounds issued from his throat. But there were no tears in his eyes, Boutcher noticed. None at all.

Around midnight Dr. Knight stopped by again, and Dr. Phillips and Lucretia retired. By dawn, William was dead. Phillips gave Lucretia the news and commiserated with her over the terrible case of cholera morbus, the worst he'd ever seen, that had taken away her husband.

It didn't occur to him that William might have died unnaturally, might have been poisoned with arsenic. But even if such a thought had crossed Phillips's mind, there would have been no way for him to be certain, not even if he had autopsied the body, for even upon post-mortem examination, arsenic poisoning could not be conclusively detected. Not then. Not for another five years, when in 1836 an English chemist named James Marsh published a method of convert-ing arsenic in body tissues into a poisonous gas that could be turned back into solid arsenic. Before that, arsenic was the preferred choice of poisoners, for unlike other lethal substances, it was altogether taste-less and thus didn't arouse suspicion in prospective victims when sprinkled into their food or drink. In ancient Rome it had been widely employed for assassinating political enemies, and in early nineteenth-century France it had proved so useful for dispatching rich relatives that it had been dubbed *poudre de succession*—inheritance powder. But one of its most common uses, throughout the world and through-out history, was getting rid of an unwanted spouse—particularly a male spouse, or so the public believed, on the theory that women were the primary handlers of food.

Before Marsh's accomplishment, there were numerous criminal trials in both England and America of women suspected of flavoring their husbands' meals with arsenic. Some were accused of adminis-tering the poison in small doses over a long period of time, causing the men to die after a few years of prolonged stomach discomfort. Some were accused of administering it in a large dose or two, bring-ing their spouses to a swift and harrowing end. But these women were rarely convicted, for although physicians and chemists tried doggedly to find a means of identifying arsenic in victims' organs and occasionally even gave evidence asserting they had done so, their efforts and testimony were at best inconclusive and at times ludicrous. Juries, having little to go on but circumstantial evidence, were prone to accept that victims had died of gastroenteritis—albeit a gastroenteritis accompanied by certain peculiar signs: nerve pain, loss of reflexes, and a rash or skin discoloration.

Dr. Phillips would have been familiar with some of these cases, most probably with that of Joanna Clue, the Bucks County woman who had been acquitted of poisoning her husband the very week Lino had arrived at the Chapmans'. But, consoling Lucretia and telling her to prepare her husband for burial, he wrote down cholera morbus as the cause of William's death.

Lucretia said farewell to William the following day in the dandelion-strewn graveyard of All Saints Church. There were quite a few Chapmans already buried in the yard. One was William's brother John—William had had a falling out with John's family and hadn't wanted them to know he was sick. There were also Chapmans from other families. Anne Chapman, dead since 1790. John Barrett Chapman, dead since 1796. Esther, dead since 1815. So many dead Chapmans. And now her husband. Lucretia, dressed all in black, stood at his gravesite and listened somberly to the prayers of the Reverend Scheetz.

She was standing alongside Dr. Knight. He'd been the one to escort her from her carriage to the grave. She'd wanted Lino to do it. But her friend Sarah Palethorpe had come by the night before to take the boarding students away, and when Lucretia mentioned having Lino walk alongside her at the funeral, Sarah said he wouldn't do.

"Why would Don Lino not do?" Lucretia had asked. Upstairs, William's body was being washed by his devoted student John Bishop, but the house was permeated with his odor.

"Because he's a stranger," Sarah, a handkerchief pressed to her nose, had said. "A stranger, and undersized."

Was he really so short? Lucretia rarely thought about Lino's height. Only about that other great difference between them—their ages—and how he was closer in years to her daughter Mary, who was standing next to him now.

She'd asked Sarah if *that* was all right, if Lino could be Mary's escort—she'd wanted him at the funeral, even if he couldn't stand beside *her*—and Sarah had said, "Yes. I see no impropriety in that."

Impropriety—as if Sarah knew something about her and Lino. Or suspected something. But no, if she did, she'd have withdrawn her daughter from the school.

Reverend Scheetz had finished speaking. The coffin was being lowered into the newly dug grave. A very deep grave. Scheetz had scolded the sexton for digging his graves too shallow, and he'd gone to the opposite extreme this time. Dug right through the loamy clay to the sandy soil beneath. Lucretia heard terrible sounds, the harsh grating of ropes as the coffin descended deeper and deeper, the hard smack of earth on the wooden lid as the grave was closed up. Back home in New England it had all been so different. In the graveyards they put straw on the coffin lids. You didn't have to hear the smash of soil on wood. In the houses they covered the mirrors with white cloth. You didn't have to see yourself in mourning. She missed New England. She missed her mother. She even missed Lino, standing so far away from her.

She didn't miss William.

Six

※

Betrayal

July 1831

*I*N THE MONTHS TO come Lucretia's friends and neighbors would obsessively ask themselves if the schoolmistress knew that William had been poisoned and even whether it was possible that she herself had poisoned him. But on the day of William's funeral they had no idea that the man they called Dr. Chapman had been murdered, let alone any suspicions of his widow. Those who had been at the graveside ceremony returned to Lucretia's home, where a big funeral supper was laid out, and consoled her in the most affectionate terms. Later, more friends and neighbors arrived, and a few, occupying the beds that had been emptied by the departure of the boarding school students, stayed on for several days to comfort the grieving woman. For her part, she continued to dress in black, albeit topping her outfits with her lilac-trimmed white turban, and at times stared disconsolately out the parlor windows and remarked that even the sun looked gloomy to her.

Seven days passed. Eight. And then abruptly, covertly, nine days after the funeral, she married Lino. It was a startling thing to do, for it was exceedingly rare to marry so soon after a spouse's death.

According to Lucretia, it was Lino who proposed, telling her that William on his deathbed had suggested the boarder marry his widow so that he could die knowing his family would be looked after. Lino had told Lucretia this, then offered marriage in return for her past charity to him. "Lino never forgets a favor," he'd said. "If you will marry me, I will take you to Mexico. And my mother will never forget what you have done. She has gold mines there, and you shall share a part of them." Still, those words and the glittering promise they held hadn't persuaded her. At least not at first. She'd rebuffed Lino, said to him, "Would it not be more proper for you to marry my daughter Mary?" But he'd declared, "No, it is you, Mrs. Chapman, that I wish to possess—it was you that took me in your door, not knowing who I was." And when she'd continued to resist, pointing out the impropriety of her marrying *anyone* so soon after her husband's death, he'd brushed away her reluctance by saying, "It would be thought nothing of in Mexico."

According to Lino, it was Lucretia who proposed, saying simply but demandingly, "Lino, I want you to marry me." He'd demurred and replied, "Not till I ask my father." But she hadn't wanted to wait, and she'd wheedled, "I love you so much" and hugged and kissed him so fervidly that finally, moved by her ardor, he'd agreed.

Whichever of the two did the importuning, on July 5, 1831, they were married in New York City in a secret ceremony performed by an Episcopalian bishop and witnessed by two strangers. Then, oddly, they parted. Lino took a steamboat south to Pennsylvania. Lucretia took one north to upstate New York. She was heading for the Syracuse home of her sister, Mercy Winslow Green, hoping to persuade Mercy to return with her to Andalusia and run the school while she and Lino made a wedding trip to Mexico to claim his riches.

She was deeply in love with Lino at the time. That very night, just after arriving in Albany and just before boarding an overnight mail coach that would take her from Albany to Syracuse, she wrote him a breathless letter, one of many passionate communications she would eventually send him. "My Dear Lino," she wrote, "Very pleasant are the sensations which vibrate through my soul, when thus addressing you ('My dear Leno [*sic*]') for the first time to call you *mine*! and till death shall separate us! how pleasing, how delightful! And you, *dearest* Lino, so young, so fond, so noble, and so truly grateful to your Lucretia! My soul would gladly dwell upon *you* till the time for writing would pass away.

"The stage is to be ready to leave here at half past ten this evening, so I have but half an hour to say all I wish to my *dearest dear* as it was nearly 10 o'clock when the boat arrived at Albany. . . . I would rest myself here for the night, but I recollect your particular request, to return as quick as possible, which I cheerfully comply with, and for this reason have requested to leave here tonight, or else I should not be with my sister tomorrow; I shall make a short stay with her; but will write to you again while with her.

"I felt very lonesome on board the boat after you left me though I was surrounded by hundreds. The stage has come, and I must bid you goodbye, though very unwillingly; kiss all my dear children for me.

"I remain yours truly, and for the first time have the pleasure to subscribe myself,

Lucretia Esposimina"

The letter written, Lucretia handed it to the driver of a south-bound mail coach and stepped into her northbound coach. It was a crude conveyance, its body suspended on heavy leather straps and its interior reeking from the strong odor of the four horses the driver was whipping to their maximum pace—five miles an hour. She could hardly bear to breathe, and worse, the roads the coach was traversing were altogether miserable, mere twists of irregular-shaped logs. As the vehicle bumped along the logs' rough surface, she quickly became nauseated. So did her fellow passengers. A few said they couldn't possibly continue the trip and when the coach stopped at a roadside tavern to change horses, they descended to rest up and wait for later transportation. But Lucretia was determined not to coddle herself, not to give in to the motion sickness that was plaguing her. Had she not taken a long and difficult stage-coach ride before, when she had come from Massachusetts to Philadelphia? Of course, she'd been young then, stronger than she was now, less used to comfort. But she had done it, and she could do it again. If she remained in the coach, she should be in Syracuse in twenty-four hours.

She stayed put, sitting up all night and dozing off as best she could. In the morning she was awakened by ominous thunder. The driver put on a slick rubbery garment, a coat of a waterproof material that a Scottish chemist named Macintosh had recently invented, and Lucretia, her traveling dress rumpled and damp, peered out the window and saw that the sky was darkening again.

By afternoon torrents of rain were descending, the roads were thick with mud, and the horses were barely able to lift their hooves. Lucretia gazed forlornly at mile after creeping mile of dripping hemlock and pines.

The rain went on and on, and in the evening the coach was still a good fifty miles from Syracuse. He wouldn't reach the city that night after all, the driver informed her. He wouldn't reach it by morning, either. With luck, he'd get there by mid-afternoon.

She hadn't eaten since midday. A few hours earlier the driver had given her and the remaining few passengers a chance to get some supper, but she'd been too sick to her stomach to eat. Now she was hungry. But there would be no more stops till morning. Tired and in need of sustenance, she closed her eyes and tried to fall asleep despite the lurching coach and her rumbling stomach.

The mud-spattered vehicle finally arrived in Syracuse at about one o'clock the next afternoon, and Lucretia was deposited, just in time for the midday meal, at a large hotel called Comstock's, a grand four-story establishment with balustraded porches and a flag-bedecked cupola. The manager pointed out the inviting dining room, its windows shaded with colorful wallpaper remnants and its tables set with white linen, where waiters were laying out a buffet of oyster pies, smoked hams, roasted pheasants, and canvasback ducks. But although she was starved, instead of entering the dining room Lucretia sat down in the lobby and wrote another letter to Lino. "I have not lain down one minute either night or day, since I took leave of you in New York," she wrote, "nor have I taken but one meal a day...the bell is now ringing for dinner, and I am politely invited into the dining room; but I refuse to dine, or even call upon my sister, till I have taken the pleasure of writing a brief letter to my fond, to my very dear companion for life." Then, indulging in the fantasy of how much better shielded from hardship she would have been had Lino accompanied her on her trip, she assured him, "I very well know that if my dear Lino had been with me, he would not have permitted his Lucretia to have rode a second night, all night, without resting on her bed." His Lucretia. It pleased her to think of herself that way.

It pleased her, too, to think how soon she could be back home with him if she didn't dawdle, didn't take the time to eat a big meal.

Asking the manager to get her just a glass of lemonade and a few crackers, she requested that he post her letter with the driver of the next southbound coach, then set out at once to see her sister.

Lino was long back in Pennsylvania by the time Lucretia left Comstock's. His trip downriver to Philadelphia had taken him only about eight hours. He'd spent a couple of nights in town—the Cuestas had invited him to be their guest, he'd told Lucretia before they parted—and then, fresh and well-rested, he'd returned to the water, boarded another steamboat, and proceeded to Bucks County.

Descending from the boat and standing at the Andalusia wharf, that very wharf where just two months earlier he'd been thrown ashore tattered and virtually penniless, he felt pleased with himself. He was no longer shabby. He was wearing a brown suit, one of Watkinson's modish outfits. He'd been over to the tailor's during his stay in Philadelphia, been there to order a light-colored light-weight summer suit. But Watkinson had advised against the purchase, saying he might have to charge as much as forty dollars to make a suit from the fabric Lino wanted. Lino had told him scornfully that the price didn't worry him, that he'd often paid fifty for a suit in that fabric. But the snooty tailor had refused to make the garment. No matter. The brown suit was splendid enough.

Leaving the river, Lino strolled up the hill and headed toward the Chapman house. When he glimpsed it, that very mansion to which, with a snapping dog at his ankles, he'd come begging for a room, he felt a surge of pride. He was no longer a destitute suppli-cant. The house was his now. So was the land on which it sat. So, too, for that matter, was Lucretia's piano, her beds and sofas, her carpets, her horse and carriage, even her jewelry and clothes.

All these things were Lino's because in 1831 all that a married woman possessed—her earnings, her real estate, her inheritances, and her personal effects—belonged to her husband. Moreover, if she had been married previously and died without making a will, the children of her previous union could not inherit their father's property, for that, too, belonged to the man to whom she was wed at the time of her death. Early feminists like the charismatic lecturer Frances Wright were already denouncing such laws as encouraging robbery and possibly even murder. Lino, standing in the road and gazing at the physical manifestations of his good fortune, the graceful mansion, the tree-shaded lawn, the vast play yard that circled down to the road, was about to reap the benefits of those laws. Soon after traversing the play yard and entering the house, he made an inventory of all of Lucretia's household possessions. A day later he invited two men to the house, introduced them to the servants as the Spanish minister and his secretary, and gave them a large leather trunk to cart away. Inside it were many of William's expensive morocco-bound books, as well as Lucretia's ornate silver spoons.

Up in Syracuse, Lucretia was having trouble locating her sister, for Mercy and her family were no longer at the address she had for them. "They've moved from Syracuse," she was informed by friends of theirs, General and Mrs. Mann. "They've moved ten or fifteen miles into the country."

Lucretia was bitterly distressed.

"Spend the night with us," Mrs. Mann urged her.

But in her hurry to return to Lino's arms, Lucretia wouldn't hear of it. "I should not be able to sleep," she wailed.

Mrs. Mann heard the frenzy in her voice and directed her to the home of Mercy's eldest daughter, a young woman who had married a Syracuse man and was living in town with him.

Lucretia set out in the direction of her niece's house at once, walking rapidly despite her fatigue. When she reached her destination, she begged her niece for the indulgence due to an aunt and asked the young woman to drive her to her mother's place immediately. Mercy's daughter didn't own a carriage, but she borrowed one, and by late afternoon aunt and niece were sitting in it and heading for the farmlands outside the city.

Their progress was slow. The roads were still so muddy that it wasn't until ten o'clock at night that they finally arrived at Mercy's farmhouse, which was silent and dark by then. Astonished that she had the strength, for she had not been to bed for two nights, Lucretia pounded and pounded on the door until at last someone heard her. It was her night-capped brother-in-law, who dazedly lit her way in and awakened the entire family. Minutes later she was hugging and kissing her sister and a rash of little nieces and nephews she'd never seen, and Mercy was bustling around the kitchen setting out a midnight supper.

The whole family joined in the feast, and Lucretia told them about William's death. But she didn't mention her new husband. She wanted to talk to Mercy alone about that—that and the fact that she needed Mercy to come to Andalusia. She waited, patient now, till her brother-in-law and the children had eaten their fill and gone back to bed, and then she began telling her sister about Lino. She told Mercy how wonderful he was and how fortunate she felt to have found him. She told Mercy he was smart and rich and kind to her children. Then finally she asked Mercy to come back to Pennsylvania with her and look after her school and property while she and her wonderful new husband went to Mexico to obtain his fortune.

The child-burdened Mercy listened enviously to Lucretia's romantic tale, and when it was done she said yes, she'd go to

Andalusia. She'd take the littlest children with her, and be ready to leave in three days' time.

Planning, the two sisters stayed up until sunrise, when finally Lucretia excused herself and retired. But although it was now three nights since she'd last lain down in a bed and experienced the comfort of sheets and a plump quilt, she did not rest long. By eleven in the morning she was up and, with a manic energy, penning another letter to Lino. She wrote it as quickly as she could—Mercy had told her that if she got her letter ready swiftly, one of her nephews could take it into Syracuse and get it onto the afternoon mail coach. She called Lino "my pretty little husband." She told him she'd be with him in a week. She cautioned him to "be careful, my dear, and not spill and so lose our precious love" and, referring for the first time to her children as *his* children, too, asked him not to "let our children see the nonsense I have written." Then she paused. Outside, her nephew was already waiting with his horse hitched. He was snapping his whip impatiently. The way young men did when they were kept waiting. The way Lino did when he was kept waiting. It was time to stop writing. But she couldn't resist adding a few more endearments. "Goodbye, goodbye, dear Lino," she closed, "Goodbye. It seems a long time to wait till next Wednesday, before I meet the fond embrace of him who is so dear to me, as is my young General Esposimina."

The reunion between Lucretia and her young general the following week was not altogether blissful. At first Lucretia was ecstatic to be with him again. But her mood was somewhat dampened when she learned that Lino had given William's books to his friends from the Spanish ministry—"as a memento," he put it—and by the discovery that her silver spoons were missing.

"The black woman took them," Lino said, blaming the disappearance of the silverware on Ann, who was no longer employed at the house. "I followed her to Philadelphia and accused her," he went on. "She acknowledged the theft, paid me in part, and promised to pay the rest."

Lucretia accepted this explanation and in the next few days threw herself into preparing for her trip to Mexico. She sorted through her clothes, the flat, narrow shoes that pinched her toes but made her large feet look uncommonly graceful, the lace-up corsets she needed to wear under Esther's elaborate dresses if she was going to achieve the wasp-tiny waist the seamstress insisted on, the dresses themselves, so full-skirted and balloon-sleeved they looked like something that might be useful in a shipwreck. Would they be in style in Mexico? She supposed so. Dresses just like them were being shown in the latest issues of the new fashion magazine, *Godey's Lady's Book.* So were fanciful hats in shades of sea-green and lilac. She had her lilac-trimmed turban. She'd take that. And maybe her velvet cloak.

When she wasn't packing, she was giving last-minute instructions to Mercy about the school. There'd be two new girls this autumn—Mercy should treat them less sternly than the returning girls or they might get homesick and ask to be withdrawn. She shouldn't neglect the weekly exams, or forget to give the medals to those who scored highest—it was the best way to make the girls proud of their accomplishments. She should be sure to assign readings in all the subjects promised by the school's advertisements—Lucretia had shown Mercy all her preferred readings, hadn't she?

On the third day after her return, when she had gone over and over with Mercy the things she expected her to do, Lino announced that he ought to be attending to a chore that he and

Lucretia had agreed needed to be done: selling the horse and carriage to raise money for their honeymoon trip. He could do it that morning, he said. He'd drive into Philadelphia, and take little Lucretia along for company. If he got a good price for the horse and carriage, he'd sell them right on the spot, and if he sold them, he and the child would take the boat home.

Lucretia approved and helped her daughter get dressed for the excursion. Lino hitched up the horse, kissed her goodbye, and then, to her surprise, asked her to give him her watch.

"But you have William's already," she pointed out.

Lino said yes, but that he wanted something of hers to remind him of her while they were apart. In exchange, he would give *her* a memento—a pretty gold chain he'd received as a gift from one of his friends.

Lucretia, touched by his sentimentality, handed him her gold watch, and let him fasten his chain around her neck.

That evening little Lucretia came trudging up the hill from the steamboat wharf. She was alone, and in her hand she clutched a letter addressed to her mother. It was from Lino. He'd just learned, he wrote, from a note given to him by the Mexican consul, that his old friend Casanova, the man he and Lucretia had tried to see at Joseph Bonaparte's, had died suddenly in Maryland over the weekend and, before expiring, left him forty-five thousand dollars. The bequest was waiting for him in Baltimore, and he was going down there immediately to pick it up.

Aside from this untoward news, the letter was filled with extravagant expressions of love. Lino couldn't write English, but he'd located a bilingual scribe and dictated his sentiments to him. "My Beloved Wife," he'd dictated, "Consider my situation since my arrival in this city. The first news I get is the Death of my friend, then I am obliged to be separated from you. . . . But I pray that [the Lord] will sustain [me] in all my troubles and allow me to Return into those kind and endearing loving arms of thine. Oh! My Dear wife how is it possible that Lino could survive the loss of one so loving and so dear to his bosom should he meet with the misfortune of losing you. . . . I would first see the sun stop its Carrier through this wide world, and be plunged in the most green or blackest gulphs that demons could invent, than have it said that I should Repay you with ingratitude."

Lucretia, although startled by the letter, felt deeply sorry for her unfortunate husband. He'd lost his sister just a while ago. Now the poor man had lost his dear friend Casanova. She pored over his melancholy words, reading them again and again. She even read them aloud to Mercy, who declared Lino's letter to be an admirable piece of writing.

The following day Lucretia went to the Andalusia post office to see if there was any more mail from Lino. The postal clerk checked but could find no letter, and Lucretia returned home disappointed. However, increasingly addicted to self-deception, she refused to entertain the notion that her ardent new husband might be neglecting her, and instead began to worry that his delicate health might be adversely affected by his loss. After a few hours, she became so sure he was sick that she considered going down to Baltimore to look after him. But she was low on cash—she'd given Lino whatever money she'd had about the house before he left—and finally, deciding not to join him, she sat down and wrote to him again.

It was a loving letter, filled with mournful observations like "the whole house is dull without you; the doors themselves seem to move on their hinges with melancholy" and packed with domestic details—news of the servants, news of the children. Mary, the new laundress, had wept when she heard about the sad fate of Lino's friend. Little Lucretia had gotten over her disappointment at having had her excursion to Philadelphia cut short. Little John had asked his mother to send Lino a kiss from him. Little Abby Ann, usually so bashful about expressing her feelings, had asked her to send him twenty-seven kisses and say she loved him very much.

She addressed the letter to Lino in care of the general post office in Baltimore, and on the envelope she painstakingly printed a long row of asterisks, twenty-seven in all, with a note saying, "Those stars represent Abby Ann's kisses, sent to you, my dear, all given to me without stopping."

Lino had, in fact, written to Lucretia a day after telling her he was going to Baltimore. He'd sold the horse and carriage, receiving forty dollars for them, and used some of the money to book passage on a steamboat downriver. He'd boarded the boat, found a man willing to translate his words into English and write them down for him, and dictated a second letter to his bride, swearing that he'd be home soon and would never again absent himself from her. But either he or the scribe must have delayed in mailing the letter, for four days after the date on which it was composed, Lucretia still had not received it, and as those long days without word from Lino wore on, she became thoroughly convinced that nothing short of his being desperately sick could explain his not having written.

On the fourth night without word from him, in the sweltering darkness that kept her tossing and turning on her sweat-drenched mattress, Lucretia decided that, strapped for cash or no, she had best go down to Baltimore to look after her new husband. At three in the morning she climbed out of bed, borrowed money from Mercy, and, at the first signs of dawn, hurried out of the house to catch the early morning stagecoach into Philadelphia. She would pay a call on the Cuestas, she planned. Perhaps *they* had heard from Lino. If they hadn't, if there was no news of him at all, she would take the steamboat down to Baltimore.

The city was in the grip of a heat wave that morning, the thermometer already reading close to a hundred degrees. Tropical temperatures had arrived earlier in the week, but it had been uncomfortably hot all summer, and Philadelphians by the hundreds had been fleeing the torrid town. Many had flocked to the nearby New Jersey seaside resorts of Cape May and Long Branch, where both men and women could swim in the sparkling surf, albeit at separate hours, others had opted for more luxurious and distant retreats, traveling south to the little Allegheny town of Sweet Springs to cool themselves in mountain air or north to New York's Niagara Falls to enjoy its solemn rocks and mighty rush of waters.

The Cuestas had gone to see that spectacular waterfall. Lucretia didn't know this. She was sure she would find them at home—Lino had said that just a few days ago he'd received the news of his friend's death from Colonel Cuesta. Descending from the stagecoach, she proceeded on foot to Cuesta's house, regretting as she dodged bright stabs of sun that came slashing through the poplars that she'd let Lino take the horse and Dearborn. Without them, she'd not be arriving in the high style with which she'd first visited the consul. Indeed, she'd not be arriving in any style whatsoever, for her clothes were plastered to her body and the once-tight little curls of her upswept hair were hanging limp.

At the Cuestas' home she received the news of their absence. "They've gone to the Falls of Niagara," a servant told her.

Herself feeling the effects of the heat wave, she accepted that news without much surprise. But then the servant volunteered that the Cuestas had been gone for quite a while.

He must be mistaken, Lucretia said. Colonel Cuesta, she pointed out, had given Lino a letter at the beginning of the week.

The servant shook his head. "Señor Espos y Mina has not been here for a long time."

Then why had Lino said he'd been there? Lucretia wondered, and if the Cuestas had been gone for a month, where had Lino stayed when he went to Philadelphia after their wedding? At the LeBruns? At the United States Hotel? It was a favorite haunt of literary men and military officers and once, one gaudy clandestine night while William was still alive, Lino had taken her there. But if he'd stayed at the hotel, or anywhere else, why hadn't he mentioned that he *hadn't* stayed with the Cuestas? Her stomach began to churn as if she were still on the Syracuse mail coach.

A few moments later she took leave of the Cuestas' servant and set out to make inquiries about Lino at the LeBruns' and at the hotel. The merciless midsummer sun was fiercer than ever, and the streets almost deserted. She tried to cool herself, stirring the air with her fan as she strode, but she quickly became drenched with sweat, and when she passed the dark, welcoming entrance of Watkinson's tailor shop, she decided to go inside for a bit and refresh herself.

The tailor greeted her effusively, and before she could speak, surprised her by saying he'd driven out to Andalusia a few days ago to pay a call on her.

She told him she hadn't known, that she'd been up north visiting her sister, and she apologized for not having been available to receive him.

"I went to inform you that Mina was ordering too much clothing," the tailor said. "I thought it my duty to inform you of this."

His duty? Lucretia was puzzled by his words.

Then all too quickly the tailor was explaining them. He hadn't wanted to make Lino a summer suit he'd requested, he was saying, because he hadn't wanted her to feel obligated to pay for yet another suit. "It would be," he was saying, "like taking the bread out of your children's mouth."

Lucretia paled, but Watkinson didn't notice. "I think your Señor Lino is as great a scoundrel," he confided, "as ever lived."

Lucretia mustered whatever dignity she could and said, "I hope not, Mr. Watkinson." But within her, she could once again feel her stomach turning over and over.

"I sent to the consul's to inquire respecting him," Watkinson chattered on. "The consul said he knew nothing of him, and knew neither him nor his father. He said"—Watkinson hesitated for a moment and then plunged ahead—"he said that he believed Señor Lino to be an impostor."

Lucretia stared at him, and this time Watkinson noticed the effect his words were having on her. She looked, he would later recall, as if she had received an injury, as if his words had physically struck her. But she didn't acknowledge the hurt with *her* words. She thanked him, said merely, "You have acted perfectly right."

Then she stumbled out of the shop.

Once she was on the street again Consul Cuesta's assessment of Lino kept reverberating in Lucretia's ears. She tried not to credit it. Lino was incapable of insincerity, she told herself. Lino was incapable of inflicting on her the pain his being an impostor would produce. There must be some mistake. Still, some part of her must have known that what the consul had said might be true, for she abandoned her search for her missing husband and instead of proceeding to Baltimore went straight back to Andalusia.

When she reached home she began to go through Lino's belongings, searching his pockets, rifling through his bureau drawers, flipping through his mail. On the bedroom mantelpiece an unopened letter caught her eye. It was addressed to Lino in her care, and it bore the return address of the United States Hotel. She ripped open the envelope—her distressing day in Philadelphia had made her feel no qualms about reading Lino's mail—and found inside a bill directed to the attention of "Mr. Amalio." The bill said:

> July 8 to 9, 1831
> Board for self and 2 ladies $3.00
> Use of a private parlour $1.00
> TOTAL $4.00

July eighth. That was when she'd reached Syracuse after traveling, sleepless and starved, for thirty-six hours. July ninth. That was when she'd stayed up for yet another night, trying to prevail upon her sister to come to Andalusia—so that she could go to Mexico with her pretty little husband.

When she read the bill, Lucretia's eyes filled with tears. Lino, she would later say, had left the bill instead of a dagger to pierce her to the heart.

Lino continued to write to Lucretia. He wrote to her from Baltimore, telling her that a provision in American law was preventing him from claiming the money Casanova had left him, so he was going down to Washington to seek the assistance of "his excellency the President," who he was sure would receive him. He wrote to her from Washington, telling her that Jackson had indeed received him, not just once but several times, and that he'd visited him both alone and in the company of a friend, an English duke. On one of these visits, he said, the president "expressed great desire" to meet Lucretia, and he'd promised the great man he'd present her to him "speedily."

His letters were as flowery as usual. "I find your presence so necessary to my happiness that to be without you even for a short period is insupportable to me," he wrote in one. "As often as I remember your caresses my heart is afflicted," he wrote in another. "My blood is frozen with the most withering ice, and my eyes pour forth at every moment the most soul-shed tears." In a third he declared, "When I left Baltimore I really thought that I should lose my senses. My soul poured forth showers of tears. I looked upon the sky that stretched itself over Pennsylvania and I re-echoed in my heart the sweet name of Lucretia Esposimina. . . . Dear Lucrecia [*sic*], there is neither day nor night of pleasure for me when away from you. I neither eat, drink, or sleep. All is melancholy in my soul. I fear that I shall be hurried to the grave ere I see you and fold you in one long embrace." So effusive was he when composing this particular letter that the bilingual scribe to whom he was dictating his words appended his very own postscript. "The translator of the above," wrote the scribe, "cannot close his duties without expressing the hope of one day beholding a lady capable of inspiring such ardent affection as that betrayed by the foregoing letter—indeed he almost regrets having undertaken so dangerous a task [as] he fears that he has already received by contagion the passion expressed by the writer of this letter. He mentions this in hopes that the lady will find in it an excuse for the tremulous motion of his hand in writing the translation. He is the lady's slave."

Lucretia received *these* letters, and on a Sunday afternoon she spread them out on her desk and reread them. It was the first time in over a week that she'd sat at the desk. Shortly after finding the bill from the United States Hotel, she'd noticed that the flesh on her neck, where she still wore the chain Lino had given her, was turning a coppery green. She'd ripped off the chain, taken it to a Philadelphia jewelry appraiser, and learned that the chain wasn't gold at all, just a cheap fake. That news, combined with the hotel bill, had made her so depressed she'd taken to her bed, incapable of any activity. But today, the last day in July, she'd finally roused herself and decided to answer Lino's letters.

Picking up her pen, she wrote swiftly, furiously. She told Lino he'd perpetrated an "extensive robbery" on her and her innocent children. She said that it was true that before he went away, she'd given him many of her possessions, among them her "horse and carriage, gold and silver watches, breast-pins, finger-rings, medals, musical box, silver bells with whistle, cake basket," but that she'd done so with the understanding that he was going to sell them and return with the proceeds. And she said that now she had begun to suspect that he had no intention of returning and no intention of reimbursing her for her property. In which case he was a common thief.

Her words were bitter and stern. But despite all she had learned about Lino in the last ten days, she still seemed to believe his lies, among them that he had actually been entertained by Andrew Jackson. "You say in your last letter," she chided, "that as often as you remember me, you bathe yourself in floods of tears. . . . I cannot think you indulge in grief [when] you visit with the President frequently, and have the honour of walking with a Duke of England." And although she managed to demand that Lino never write to her again unless he paid her back, she still seemed to be in love with him, or at least she still felt possessive about him. Spinning out a painful fantasy in which she supposed Lino to have fallen for another woman, she charged him with having adorned that other woman's fingers with *her* rings, and jealously speculated that his new love was making *her* Lino "perfectly happy."

Then, in the midst of this dreaded scenario, she stopped herself, and in a sentence that would come back to haunt her, abruptly concluded her communiqué with, "But no, Lino, when I pause for a moment, I am constrained to acknowledge that I do not believe that God will permit either you or me to be happy this side of the grave."

When she was done, she signed the bottom "Lucretia"—she was no longer, as far as she was concerned, "Lucretia Espos y Mina"—and, taking the letter into Philadelphia, mailed it to Lino in care of the general post office in Washington.

Seven
❧

Departures
August – Mid-September 1831

*P*HILADELPHIA'S POLICE FORCE, WHICH numbered some
forty patrolmen and several junior officers and high constables, was one of the largest in the country. Among the high constables was sixty-two-year-old Willis H. Blayney, who as a young man
had never thought he'd rise so high. He'd been a printer then,
turning out books and broadsides, his fingers blistering in winter
from the touch of the icy type trays and his eyes aching, winter and
summer alike, from the dim light in the print shops where he and
his fellows slaved well into the night. But at last he'd given up that
difficult trade, entered the police force, and advanced rapidly from
patrolman to captain to his present exalted rank.

Along the way he'd garnered a reputation for being a sharp-
minded detective, and in the middle of August 1831, he got a chance to
test that reputation. He received word from the high constable of
Washington that in the course of investigating a local businessman's
claim to have been swindled by a fellow named Lino Amalia Espos y
Mina, his men had gone to the main post office, confiscated some
mail, and come across a mysterious letter indicating that the swindler
had already bilked a widow living in or around Philadelphia. The

letter might prove useless, Blayney's opposite number in Washington informed him, for it bore no last name, was signed merely "Lucretia"; he was, however, forwarding it up to Philadelphia on the off-chance the victim could be identified.

Blayney's investigative appetite was immediately aroused. But at first he got nowhere. One of his underlings, thinking the widow's letter insignificant because it was anonymous, had discarded it. Blayney railed against the man's incompetence, demanding that worktables and wastepaper receptacles be thoroughly searched, and in short order the document appeared on his desk—it had been tossed aside but not yet thrown out.

Fingering it carefully, Blayney saw at once that it was a mess, a peculiar web of underlined words, sentences that ended not just in exclamation points but sometimes in two such points, and phrases that scrawled sideways along the pages' narrow margins. The work of a very distraught person, the high constable concluded. But also of an educated person. The writer, accusing her correspondent of having made away with her silver and gold and horse and carriage, used bookish words—said the thief had a heart of "adamant" and that she was "thunderstruck" by his behavior—and her handwriting looked tutored and ornate.

The handwriting. He knew that handwriting, the high constable realized with a start. He'd seen it in the past, set type from words written in it. And then it dawned on him—the letter writer, this Lucretia-no-last-name, was none other than Lucretia Chapman. Mrs. William Chapman. He used to print broadsides for the couple's speech clinic. They'd moved away from the city, but once upon a time he'd known the pair well. Especially the missus. When she was single and teaching at the LeBruns' school, she'd lived in his mother's boardinghouse. When she'd started her own school, she'd hired his sister to teach dancing. She was a fine lady. Yes, there'd been some trouble about counterfeiters in a boardinghouse she and her husband ran for a while on Pine Street. But basically he'd never heard anything but good about Lucretia Chapman. Had someone gone and robbed that estimable woman?

Distressed, Blayney decided to show the letter to the mayor, Benjamin Richards. Then, remembering that Richards was on vacation, he took the document to the city's recorder, Magistrate Joseph McIlvaine.

The summer heat had baked Andalusia dry. The trees were thirsting, the grass was sere. Lucretia's eyes, too, were dry—she had at long last ceased her nightly weeping over Lino and made up her mind that she never wanted to see him again, without or even with the money he owed her. She was fanning herself on the porch and asserting this to Mercy, who'd stayed on in Andalusia to make sure she was all right, when they noticed a man making his way through the play yard. Lucretia blanched. She knew by the cocky familiar stride that it was Lino. She didn't want to see him, she told Mercy, and ran into the house. But it was too late. Lino was vaulting up the porch steps and, with Mercy close on his heels, strutting into the parlor.

"I've been to New Orleans," he announced, speaking to Lucretia as if nothing had changed between them, as if she still wanted to hear about his every exploit and adventure. "I went all the way on a railroad. Traveled night and day—at the rate of *thirty* miles an hour!"

"Leave me," she said with lofty disdain.

But Lino was acting as if he hadn't disappeared for a month, hadn't read her accusatory letter, didn't know she no longer considered herself his wife. Plunking himself down on the spindly, straight-backed sofa and tugging off his boots, he teased, "What's the matter? If an angel from heaven had come and told me a wife of mine would behave this way, I wouldn't have believed it."

Angered, Lucretia spurted, "The chain you gave me is not gold."

"If your affections are so slender as a chain," Lino shrugged off her accusation, "I can explain that to you. When I gave you the chain I told you a friend had given it to me—that friend might have deceived me, or might have been deceived himself."

Lucretia threw up to him his other deceptions, stormed that he had lied to her about where he'd stayed in Philadelphia, and with whom. He could explain those things, too, Lino insisted and, launching into a long tale, told her that because the Cuestas had been out of town, he'd taken a room at the United States Hotel and later gone to see a play at the Chestnut Street theater, only to get caught in a torrential rain. "I ran under the arcade for protection," he rattled on, "and while I was there, two ladies of distinction came and asked me if I had an umbrella." He didn't, but he was about to hail a carriage, and as the ladies were soaking wet, he'd chival-rously offered them a ride back to his hotel so that they could make themselves presentable before traveling home. "I was up all night with the servants of the hotel," he declared. "Drying their clothes in order that they might go home the next day."

Lucretia, fed up, wanted no part of his preposterous explana-tion. Neither did Mercy, who shot Lino an exasperated look.

Seeing it, Lucretia put on her sternest schoolmarmish expres-sion and, addressing her husband on her sister's behalf, said, "My sister is not at all satisfied with this conduct!"

"We had better be separated, then," Lino snapped. "I find I have more wives than one to please."

"The sooner, the better," she hurled at him.

He agreed, but, "Remember, Mrs. *Chapman*," he added, "before I go, I must tell you something."

"What is it?"

"I cannot tell you in the presence of your sister. If you will come in the other room, I will tell you."

Reluctantly, Lucretia followed him into the dining room. She stood there unyieldingly, and into her stony silence he said something that she would never reveal, not to Mercy, not to anyone, though she did admit to one friend that it was something darkly secret, "something between ourselves."

Shortly afterward, Lino left the Chapman house, never to return. But this time, too, he didn't leave empty-handed. Whatever he had said in private to Lucretia had caused her to agree to write a letter of introduction for him—a letter that, at his request, said nothing about their being married. It was addressed to her relatives on Cape Cod.

The Cape Cod Winslows were an affluent and powerful clan. They'd first taken up residence in the region back in the 1600s, purchasing and clearing large tracts of wilderness and turning their property into farms. But the Cape, and in particular the Barnstable County town of Brewster where Lucretia's relatives lived and to which Lino boarded a stagecoach after traveling by boat to Boston, had become a major center for New England's lucrative whaling and fishing industries. Some of Lucretia's relatives, like other members of the Cape's landed class, had branched out from agriculture to become sea captains or manufacturers of supplies for sailing vessels, and some had invested heavily in those vessels and reaped great profits. Their profits, and indeed New England's whaling and fishing industry itself, were soon to decline, but in 1831 many of Lucretia's kin were living high on the hog. Lino's coach was filled with young men eager to make their fortunes on the sea. But he had different ideas about how to make a living.

Promptly upon his arrival in Brewster, Lino brandished among Lucretia's people the letter of recommendation she'd written for him, which termed him "a very estimable young man." Then, embroidering as he went, he recited his usual tale.

He was a major in the Mexican army, he said, the son of that country's famous General Mina. He owned gold mines. Silver mines. Plantations. Just like his hero, Andrew Jackson. Mrs. Lucretia Chapman—he told no one that he was married to her—had been exceedingly kind to him, and because of that, and that alone, he'd given her ten thousand dollars in gold. But alas, he'd met with misfortune on his way up to the Cape. He'd lost most of his jewelry and a pocketbook containing five hundred dollars. The sum was inconsequential, for he had thousands and thousands of dollars and would make a draft on his Boston bank as soon as he got back to that city. But for now he was virtually out of cash.

Lucretia's relatives, among them her sister-in-law, Abigail, and a host of aunts, uncles, nephews, and nieces, proved highly gullible. They offered to put him up, and even to lend him money.

Lino couldn't have been more deferential and appreciative. When one of his new acquaintances asked if he knew the time, he pulled out his gold watch—it was William Chapman's watch, but he alone knew this—and not only announced the time but insisted on making a gift of the timepiece to the questioner. It was a calculated move. As Lino expected, his offer was refused, and he was able to slip the watch back into his pocket. But the tale of his impulsive generosity marched as swiftly as time itself through the small seaside community, and soon not just Lucretia's relatives but friends and neighbors of theirs began vying to have the distinguished foreigner stay at *their* homes.

One man who gave him hospitality was Elijah Cobb, a renowned ship's captain who was an old friend of Lucretia's. The author of a memoir about his seafaring days, Cobb had gone to sea at the tender age of six to help support his widowed mother and eventually sailed all over the world, visiting and trading in the West Indies, Africa, Russia, even France during the bloodiest days of the French Revolution. But exotic places, revolutions, wars didn't really interest him—"I saw Robertspeirs head taken off, by the [infernal] Machine," was Cobb's laconic observation about the demise of Robespierre, the mastermind of the Terror. Rather, he was interested in money, in making it through trading in palm oil, coffee, ivory, and gold, and by the time he met Lino he had made a great deal. Yet despite his wealth and worldliness, he was thoroughly taken in by "the Major," as the Cape Codders had begun referring to Lino.

Another man who believed Lino utterly was none other than the high sheriff of Barnstable County. To make his trumped-up tale seem credible, Lino had advertised his loss in a local newspaper— he'd done that in Washington with excellent results—and to bolster the claim, he'd reported the loss to the high sheriff. The officer, impressed by the newcomer's fine raiment and unfamiliar accent, took him at his word when he said he was a high-ranking foreign noble and treated him with exceptional courtesy.

Unfortunately for Lino, however, big city officials were not nearly so gullible. While he was being feted at the Cape, down in Philadelphia the swift-minded Blayney and McIlvaine had decided to investigate him.

Blayney looked into his activities in the capital. He learned that Lino had introduced himself to a number of wealthy men as General Mina's son, told them he'd lost a wallet containing hundreds of dollars, and begged them to lend him enough cash to get to Baltimore, where he had vast sums of money. Several people had fallen for this hard-luck tale, especially after reading about it in a newspaper, and lent Lino money, never to hear from him again.

McIlvaine interrogated Edwin Fanning, who'd requested an interview. The itinerant book salesman told the magistrate that he feared his deceased friend William Chapman had been poisoned to death by a man named Lino Espos y Mina.

Late in August Blayney and McIlvaine pooled their information and concluded that Lino ought to be brought in for questioning. But they didn't know where to find him. Then, reasoning that Mrs. Chapman might be able to help them out, they decided to pay a call on her.

They came on a Sunday, while Lucretia was at church, and waited uncomfortably on the hard-backed parlor sofa. When she returned home, accompanied by her sister and a chattering band of children, Blayney greeted her warmly, consoling her on William's death and giving her news of his mother and sister, but McIlvaine cut short the small talk and asked if they could speak to her in private. When she led them into an inner chamber, McIlvaine did all the talking. "I understand a person calling himself Mina spent some time in your house," he began abruptly, then inquired whether, when Mina left her house, he told her where he was going.

"He said he was going to the north," Lucretia replied.

McIlvaine wanted more. "I have in my possession very satisfactory evidence that the man is a swindler and impostor and it has become my duty to have him arrested. I also have reason to believe that you yourself suffered from his impositions."

Lucretia denied having been imposed upon by Lino. She didn't know that McIlvaine and Blayney had read her last letter to him. But when the magistrate pressed her, she admitted that Lino had made off with many of her possessions.

He wasn't surprised, McIlvaine offered, and informed her that

Lino had been in Washington for some time and had swindled several people there.

Washington? For some time? Lucretia was perplexed. "I'd supposed from his account that during his absence he'd been to New Orleans and back," she murmured. Then she added with awe, "He went all the way on a railroad and traveled night and day at the rate of thirty miles an hour."

McIlvaine snickered. "Madam, there *is* no railroad to New Orleans." A train to that city had long been under construction, but it was not due to start carrying passengers until the autumn.

Startled by the magistrate's information, Lucretia began to pale.

McIlvaine noticed the change in her complexion, but he was a businesslike man, one not to be swayed from his duties by any excessive reactions from the female sex. "From my knowledge of the character of this man," he intoned, "and of the lower classes of the nation to which he belongs, and from information I have received of the circumstances attending the death of Mr. Chapman, I have a very strong impression that Mr. Chapman died by poison, and that he administered it."

This time Lucretia's face turned ashen. There was no mistaking her distress. In all his years of interviewing witnesses and suspects, McIlvaine had never seen a face drain so completely and suddenly of color. Yet although clearly the woman had been affected by his statements, she didn't seem surprised by them. He'd hoped she would be, hoped she'd ask what reasons he had for making such a dire allegation about her boarder. But she said nothing, just put her face down on her arm.

He could no longer see her expression, but he pushed on. "Did anything occur," he said to her bowed head, "to make you suspect the same thing that I suspected?"

Lucretia took a long time before answering, so long that McIlvaine began to worry that she might have gone into shock. But after an interval she straightened up, her eyes focused firmly on his, and seemed to have mastered the feeling—what feeling it was, McIlvaine couldn't be sure—that had previously overcome her. "No," she said, her voice controlled, "No, I saw nothing of the kind. Lino was Mr. Chapman's kind nurse during his illness."

Afterward she went into detail about that illness. She went into detail, too, about why Lino had come to be in the house in the first place, and described at length his asking for charity, his revealing he was wealthy, and her and her husband's decision to let him live with them. McIlvaine heard her out with a certain amount of cynicism, thinking she was taking great pains to try to convince him that any attentions she'd paid to the man had been paid with her husband's full approbation. He made a mental note of this reaction of his, then once again urged her to give him any information she could about Lino's whereabouts. "He is a swindler," he pronounced, "and it is your duty to give me that information."

Lucretia denied having any information other than what she'd already provided. "I have no knowledge further than that he went to the north," she repeated dully.

Bidding her goodbye, McIlvaine swore, "If it is possible by any effort of the police, this man shall be taken and punished for his crimes," and once out of the house he directed Blayney to alert the police in Boston and New York to keep an eye out for Mina and arrest him at once if he turned up. But he was dissatisfied with how his talk with Lucretia had gone. It had left, he would say later, "a mystery upon my mind."

Up at the Cape, Lino had set his sights higher than on recouping false losses. He had made the acquaintance of an unmarried

Winslow woman, a niece of Lucretia's whose looks were modest but whose means were sizable, and decided to try to persuade her to marry him. If she consented, he would be able to obtain her property, just as he'd obtained Lucretia's.

He was staying at Cobb's, but he busied himself with Lucretia's niece, not the old sea captain. He took the young woman for walks down romantic country paths and along the water's pearlescent froth. He sang to her. He told her she was the prettiest woman he'd ever met. And one late summer's evening, when the air was tinged with a hint of autumn and the fading light foreshadowed the loneliness of winter, he asked her to marry him.

Lucretia's niece was flattered, and admitted she was drawn to him. But she anticipated, she cautioned him, that her family would oppose her marrying him, given that he was not just a stranger but a foreigner.

Lino told her not to worry about the family. He and she could simply elope and have a secret wedding in Boston.

His ardor was captivating. Lucretia's niece agreed to elope with him and accepted his suggestion that in order to escape detection, they travel separately to Boston, he setting out in a day or two, she coming down a few days later.

He had not communicated with Lucretia since he'd left Pennsylvania. But after her niece said she'd marry him, he decided, perhaps partly out of some unaccustomed twinge of guilt, to write to her again. He addressed her coolly, calling her "Dear Madam," and said nothing of his forthcoming marriage. But he told her he had opened an account with a Philadelphia banker named Juan Bitonia and suggested that if she needed any money, she ask Bitonia to give her some from his account. Additionally, he enclosed a bank draft for one thousand dollars and asked her to redeem it at Bitonia's and send him the cash in care of Elijah

Cobb's mercantile establishment in Boston. He would be leaving for Boston, he informed her, in two days.

The letter was intercepted by Blayney and McIlvaine.

Lino arrived in Boston sometime during the first week of September. Avoiding the Sun Tavern, from which he had so ignominiously fled two years earlier, he took a room at a fashionable hotel and at once began trying to make friends with the wealthy businessmen who frequented the hotel's public rooms. He was successful. In short order he met one such man, a prominent Boston merchant, and charmed him so thoroughly that when the merchant learned Lino was single, he invited him to a masquerade ball he was hosting on the weekend. His fete would be attended, he told Lino, by "nearly a hundred ladies of the first families."

Lucretia's niece had not yet come down from the Cape, and immediately Lino began to weigh the possibility of making an even grander match than the one with her had promised to be. Perhaps, he schemed, he could woo and wed not another provincial Winslow but a daughter of one of those first Boston families. The ballroom etiquette of the day required a host to see to it that every lady danced. Surely his host would press Lino into service. More, since etiquette also decreed that guests ought to assume that those introduced to them by respectable hosts were of a social standing equal to their own, surely his dance partners would view him as a fit suitor.

Exhilarated by his new possibilities, on the day of the ball Lino went shopping. He'd already spent most of the money that had been lent to him at the Cape. But he'd forged himself a few letters of credit and convinced a Boston bank of their authenticity. He'd even gotten the bank to give him a letter promising a cash advance the very next day, an advance of nine thousand dollars. Armed with the letter, he began looking for a proper outfit, something that would set him off handsomely as he swayed to waltz music and performed the intricate figures of the cotillions. What would look best? A military costume, he decided. It would suit the son of General Mina, and besides, he'd always fancied himself a military officer.

In a store that specialized in uniforms, he found just what he wanted—a Spanish officer's dress jacket; it had gold epaulets with fringes thick as mops. He bought the jacket on credit and then, spying a dashing hat bedecked with six velvety ostrich plumes, he bought that, too.

Back in his hotel room, he laid out his costume on the bed, bathed, and was about to get dressed when three Boston policemen burst into the room, pinioned his arms behind his back, and told him he was under arrest.

Lucretia didn't know yet that Lino was in jail, but on the day after he was arrested, she appeared in McIlvaine's office. She'd been to see a lawyer, John Campbell, a member of the Pennsylvania state legislature who'd handled a few matters for her and William in the past, and she'd told him that the police had been asking her about her erstwhile boarder. She'd also confessed to the lawyer that she was married to the man. With her consent, Campbell had passed this information on to McIlvaine, who'd demanded she come in for further questioning, and the politic lawyer had advised her to do so promptly. You have nothing to fear, he'd counseled, you're as much Mina's victim as any businessman he's said to have swindled.

Campbell wasn't with her on the day that, following his advice, she appeared at McIlvaine's. But taking her cue from what her attorney had said, she told the magistrate, "I have been deceived and injured by Lino Espos y Mina." Then she begged him to tell her how to protect herself and her character from any consequences she might face as a result of Lino's deceptions.

McIlvaine heard her out coldly. He'd been thinking ever since learning of her imprudent marriage that she was a trollop and her marriage the product of gross infatuation. "I cannot promise that any step you take will relieve you from the consequences of your rash conduct," he said to her stiffly. "But if you choose to be candid in your communications to me, if you show your sincerity by giving me all the means in your power to bring Mina to justice, I will do all I can, consistent with my duty, to rescue you from those consequences."

Lucretia nodded, and to show him she now no longer doubted what he'd told her about Lino's being a swindler, she handed him the letter Lino had sent her from Cape Cod. She had tried, she explained, to find Bitonia, the banker Lino mentioned in the letter. Tried and failed. "There is no man named Bitonia," she said bitterly.

McIlvaine had already seen the letter and its enclosed bank draft, seen it and afterward let it be delivered to the unsuspecting Lucretia. "Fictitious," he declared, glancing cursorily at the bank draft. Then, "Did Mina palm upon you any other documents or papers?"

Lucretia had come prepared. She showed him a will Lino had written two weeks after coming to stay at her house, a will promising her fifteen thousand dollars for having looked after him when he was sick, the money to be delivered to her in Mexico City in the event of his death. She also showed him a certificate from Don Tomas Montolla, the minister of Mexico in Washington, certifying that she and Lino were lawfully married.

McIlvaine knew why she'd brought him the will. Clearly she'd wanted him to understand why she and William Chapman had paid such extraordinary attention to their boarder. But the certificate from the Mexican minister? "For what purpose was this paper obtained?" he asked.

"Señor Mina's health is fragile," Lucretia said. "After we were married I repeatedly told him that in case of accident or death to him, I would have no means of claiming my rights to his properties."

McIlvaine studied the certificate and snorted, "It is in Lino's handwriting. And that seal on it is a forgery."

Lucretia had known all along that Lino had filled out the blanks on the certificate himself. He'd done so, he'd told her, because Montolla, being overly busy, had directed him to. But he'd also told her that the seal and the minister's signature were authentic. Now she knew that everything was false, the writing in the blanks, the loopy letters of the minister's signature, even the crested Mexican seal. And the promise of money from Bitonia's bank. And the bequest of fifteen thousand dollars. "I want to obtain a divorce from Mina," she said to McIlvaine.

"I can offer you no opinion on this," the magistrate replied in his chilly tone, and gesturing at the dubious certificate, said, "You must give me that paper. It will enable me to detain Mina on a charge of forgery committed in Pennsylvania."

Lucretia got up to go and deposited Montoya's certificate on McIlvaine's desk. Then she added the will, the letter, and the bank draft from Cape Cod. That done, she walked to the door of the magistrate's office. But at the door she turned, came back to the desk, and laid a gloved hand down on the papers. "Will these communications get me into trouble?" she asked.

"You have come to me voluntarily," McIlvaine said. "And I have pledged myself to you. I have nothing to add. It is for you to decide whether the papers should be left or not." He did not tell Lucretia that throughout their conversation he had purposely abstained, out of legal scruples, from asking her a single question about the death of William Chapman. Had he done so, McIlvaine thought, it might have been the end of their *voluntary* conversation.

Lucretia, her gloved fingers still on the documents, hesitated. She's agitated, McIlvaine surmised. But at last she left the papers on the desk and departed.

Two days later, as soon as McIlvaine received word from Boston that Mina was in custody, he sat down at his desk and wrote a letter to Lucretia, informing her of this fact. He also wrote to Thomas Ross, the deputy attorney general of Bucks County. He had a case to turn over to him, he wrote. A case of forgery. And possibly of murder.

On September 17, 1831, a week after Lucretia's visit to McIlvaine, the *Philadelphia National Gazette* printed an article that read, "We understand that a most consummate villain, who passes by the name of Lino Amalio Espos y Mina, has been arrested at Boston. . . . Since the arrest of Mina, circumstances have been developed which leave no doubt that he is a villain of no ordinary character. Mr. Blayney has been put in possession of facts which show that he married a respectable lady in the vicinity of Philadelphia, ten days after the decease of her husband, having induced her to believe that he was the son of the celebrated General Mina, and a foreigner of high distinction. He dispossessed the lady of all her valuable jewelry, plate, and personal property which it appears he converted into cash in Baltimore. There are circumstances almost amounting to positive evidence, which warrant the belief that the husband of the lady was poisoned. A forged draft for $1000, drawn by Mina on a merchant in Philadelphia, has been intercepted through the mail. . . . A demand having been made for

Mina by the Governor of Pennsylvania, he will of course be conveyed thither for trial."

Lucretia heard about the article before she saw it. She was expecting the imminent arrival of her two new students when her friend Sophia Hitchbourn knocked on the door and, fairly bursting with news of the story, cried, "I hear Lino's been arrested in Boston! On suspicion of poisoning William!"

"Is it possible?" Lucretia replied, sounding incredulous.

"I hear you married him!" Sophia exclaimed. "Ten days after William died. Did you have any idea he poisoned William?"

"Of course not," Lucretia said. Then, "Was my name in the paper?"

It wasn't, but Sophia, like most of Lucretia's neighbors, had met Lino, knew he styled himself the son of General Mina, and had easily figured out who the "respectable lady in the vicinity of Philadelphia" was. "Oh, Lucretia," Sophia demanded. "How could you have been so imprudent as to marry that man?"

She didn't answer, and Sophia said, "It must be a fact. Or they wouldn't dare to publish it."

"I thought he was very rich," Lucretia mumbled. "I thought it was best for me—and for the children."

As soon as she could, she got Sophia out of the house and ran to tell Mercy what had happened. Mercy collapsed. She fell on the floor, tears gushing down her cheeks, and Lucretia had to escort her to bed. Just then, the new students arrived, accompanied by their mother, who was planning to spend a few days at the school to see that the children settled in properly. Lucretia tried to collect herself and show the newcomers around. But her mind was aswirl. What would happen now? Would the police want to arrest her, too? She *had* to see that newspaper story—see it with her own eyes. She sent one of the new girls to fetch the newspaper from Sophia's house and then felt a terrible longing to talk to someone, to unburden herself. But to whom? Mercy was still sobbing away in her room. The mother of the new girls? Yes, she seemed a most sympathetic person. She'd talk to *her,* she decided, and asking the woman, a Mrs. Ann Smith, to step into her bedroom, she began chattering away like a demented person, her words pouring unstoppably out of her mouth.

She told Mrs. Smith how Lino had come to her house. She told her how she and her husband had thought he was rich. She told her how William had taken sick and died. She even told her how, just a handful of days later, she'd married the stranger.

Mrs. Smith listened to her with her mouth agape. "Mrs. Chapman, I shouldn't be surprised if this fellow had poisoned your husband!"

"Do you think so, my dear?" Lucretia sighed. "The police have intimated the same thing."

Mrs. Smith got thoroughly upset when she heard this final detail. Instead of comforting Lucretia, she told her she'd like to withdraw her girls from the school. Dismayed, Lucretia begged her to let them remain. "Hearsay is not proof," she reminded the woman.

Her axiom, and perhaps a refusal to refund tuition, proved persuasive. Mrs. Smith agreed to keep her girls at the school and to stay there with them for the weekend as planned. But Lucretia confided in her new acquaintance no more. It had dawned upon her that after hearing her story, most people, not just Mrs. Smith, would assume that Lino had poisoned William, and that many might assume she herself had played a role in the poisoning. That weekend she began pulling clothes out of her drawers—the clothes she had once hoped to wear in Mexico. She heaped them on her bed and bureaus, and on Monday morning, she directed the laundress to brush up her boots and braid-trimmed traveling dress.

She was putting on the traveling outfit when Mrs. Smith stopped by her bedroom. "Are you going somewhere?" she pried.

"On a short trip," Lucretia lied. "I'm going to town to sell some books."

Mrs. Smith didn't believe her. "Don't you think you are wrong to go off at a time like this?" she chided. "It looks like running off."

"I'm not running off," Lucretia insisted. "I'm just going a short way to sell some books and get some money. I'm badly off for money."

But it was not a short trip she had in mind. It was a long trip, a great long trip that would take her far from Pennsylvania, far from Constable Blayney and Magistrate McIlvaine. Mercy could handle the school, just as Lucretia had meant for her to do if she went to Mexico. Mercy could mother her children. At least until she figured out a plan. For now, she had none. For now, she wasn't even sure just where she'd go. Only that she'd best get away as soon as she could.

That afternoon she fled Andalusia. She was wearing her traveling dress, but in her bags she had secreted a man's frock coat, trousers, and a tall hat. She would don them, she had decided, if she went somewhere she was likely to be recognized.

Eight

✿

Friends and Foes

Late September – Early December 1831

✿

*H*ANDSOME, THIRTY-SIX-YEAR-OLD David Paul Brown, with his broad forehead, empathic eyes, and playful Cupid's bow lips, was one of the most famous men in Philadelphia—in his own opinion, *the* most famous. He was a lawyer and, as he would one day point out in an autobiographical work, not just a lawyer but an orator, a distinction he considered vital. "Hortensius," he wrote, "was a lawyer—Cicero an orator, the one is forgotten, the other immortalized." Brown had reason to be proud of his oratorical skills. In 1824 when the Marquis de Lafayette returned on a triumphal tour to the country he had helped free itself from British rule, Philadelphia had selected Brown to deliver the city's welcoming speech.

Brown had less reason to be proud of another skill of his—playwriting. But that didn't stop him from bragging about his play *Sertorius,* a tedious tragedy about a Roman patriot that was performed nine times by one of the greatest actors of the day, Junius Brutus Booth. The critics had loved *Sertorius,* he boasted; they'd said it was difficult to find a single jarring line in it, a reaction that, if you asked *him,* David Paul Brown, was quite odd, since he'd written the whole thing on horseback. He'd been trying a big case in Philadelphia at the time, but his wife and children had been vacationing thirty miles outside the city. Desiring to spend his nights in the company of his wife, he'd left the city at dusk each evening and trotted until midnight, and to make the journey seem swifter, occupied himself by creating his play while jogging along. Doing so had been no easy feat. "Composing upon all fours is sometimes expedient, but seldom very agreeable," he was wont to say, "or profitable."

Still, profit wasn't what motivated the multitalented David Paul Brown, or so he would always insist. He had been born rich, and later his legal work had made him even richer; by 1831, after fifteen years of law practice, his professional income exceeded one hundred thousand dollars—the equivalent of several million dollars today.

No matter. To hear him tell it, he spent money as fast as he earned it, spent it out of *principle* and not extravagance, spent it because if he had too much money around, he'd become indolent and lose in fame what he gained in wealth. And it was fame that, to steal a phrase from the man from whom he claimed to have learned everything, was *his* spur. When he was a child he'd been forbidden by his parents, kind-hearted Quakers though they were, to read the playwright. But he'd disobeyed those well-meaning parents, sought out the prohibited book, and by the age of ten, made himself master of all within.

Even so, his early days as a lawyer and orator were not enviable. He was admitted to the Philadelphia bar at the tender age of twenty-one but, to hear him tell it, weeks, months, finally a whole year rolled by without the tranquillity of his office being disturbed by a single client. Or, for that matter, by a single friend, for as he soon sadly observed, even the courteous shrank from and shunned the unfortunate. Then one day while he was walking near the courts, he noticed a crowd of people surrounding someone, he couldn't determine who it was, and shouting epithets about cruelty and barbarity. He pushed forward to see what the commotion was all about and came face-to-face with a little girl about eight or nine years old. She was wretchedly attired, her eyes were streaming with tears, and her limbs were covered with welts and dried blood.

No sooner had he seen the girl than someone in the crowd, surmising that he was in some way connected with the law, demanded that he point out the way to redress. Redress for what, he'd inquired, and an old woman had stepped forward and informed him that the child was one of a large family of German Redemptioners who, upon arriving in the country, had sold themselves as indentured servants to pay back their passage money. Mother and father, sisters and brothers, everyone in the family had been bought, each by a separate owner in a different, distant area of the state. And the little girl, the youngest of the brood, had fallen into the hands of a barbarous individual, a man who had starved her, beaten her, made her flesh raw.

He, David Paul Brown, was then not yet a parent, but as he was given to saying, nature ever prepares man for those affections which, when they arrive, are the most despotic and resistless in their sway. He took the girl by the hand, ushered her into the chief magistrate's office, and filed a complaint on her behalf.

On the day of the trial he came to court fearful that despite intense preparation, his supply of legal lore was so scanty that it would be insufficient to the task at hand. Opposite him were seated the haughty defendant and his counsel—two experienced and distinguished members of the profession, men accustomed to sway the scepter of the mind with kingly hand. They so intimidated him that when it was his turn to speak, he couldn't find his tongue, and his hands shook like aspen leaves in a storm. But his desire to vindicate the principles of humanity, to right the wrongs that had been done to the little girl, gave him courage, and suddenly all that he had ever known or read came flooding into his mind and his voice burst from his throat, roaring with rage and indignation. He was electrifying, if he did say so himself, so eloquent that the entire assemblage in the courtroom melted into tears, and he won the case handily, so handily that from that time forward his office was thronged with clients, all of them eager to unload their griefs and their pockets, and his life was thronged with friends, all of them eager to enjoy his erudition and his passion.

He had so *many* friends. Judges like Robert Porter, head of the Court of Common Pleas—he'd have been impeached if he, David Paul Brown, hadn't defended him. Journalists like Anne Royall—she'd made him famous all over the country, not just in Philadelphia, by saying in one of those books of hers that he was the very essence of the term "gentleman." Then there were the actors like Booth. The wits like Robert Waln, who went out on the town all the time but styled himself the hermit of Philadelphia. The scientists like William Chapman. Poor Chapman—people were saying he was the man alluded to in that article that had appeared in the *Gazette* over the weekend. The Bucks County man who'd been poisoned. How sad for Chapman's intelligent wife, Lucretia—she'd been *his*, David Paul Brown's, friend, too, back when the couple had their school in Philadelphia. Well, as he always said, all our days are anxious, all are made up of clouds and sunshine, and so continuous and unvaried is this truth that this uninterrupted variety actually becomes monotony, still running, as it were, in a circle, traveling over the same ground, and knowing no end.

Was there a doctor on board, High Constable Blayney called out to a boatload of gawking passengers on the afternoon of September

21, 1831. He and his deputy, Fred Fritz, had taken Lino into their custody in Boston early that morning, escorted him by stagecoach to Rhode Island, then hustled him aboard a Philadelphia-bound steamship where, despite his chains, Lino had eaten a hearty lunch. But just now, suddenly, he had started flailing around, his shackled arms and legs shaking, his head bobbing as if it might fly right off his body. Was it a real fit or just a ruse to create sympathy and get his limbs freed? Blayney couldn't be sure. He needed a doctor. Right away.

To his relief, soon after he shouted for one, a top-hatted man stepped forward and announced that he fit the bill. Pushing aside the nosy onlookers, Blayney helped the man to Lino's side. The doctor grabbed hold of the prisoner. He held him tightly and started talking to him. And that did it. The fit, or whatever it was, subsided.

Probably, Blayney reckoned, his prisoner *had* been faking sickness. Blayney wouldn't put it past him, because he was a wily fellow for sure. According to the Boston police, he'd talked some rich young woman from Cape Cod into marrying him; the poor thing, not realizing she'd just been spared by the police department's good offices from wedding an unscrupulous scoundrel, had come inquiring after her fiancé's whereabouts on the day after his arrest. He'd better not interact with such a scoundrel, Blayney decided. He'd best not even speak to him, because there was no telling what kind of trick the fellow might try to pull. Seating himself alongside his prisoner and keeping his mouth closed but his eyes wary, the high constable settled down to enjoy the boat trip as best he could.

It wasn't long, however, before Lino, who had already tried to strike up several conversations with the boat's passengers, interrupted the constable's effort to savor the voyage. "I wish," he said to Blayney, "to make some confidential communications to you."

"On what subject?"

"On the subject of Mr. and Mrs. Chapman."

"I don't wish to hear anything. Better keep it to yourself."

At this, Blayney changed his seat, putting more space between himself and his prisoner. But shortly after he moved, he saw that the unstoppable fellow was buttonholing his deputy and jabbering away at *him.*

What did the prisoner have to say, Blayney demanded of Fritz when the deputy succeeded in extricating himself from the troublemaker.

"That he and Mrs. Chapman were married," Fritz reported. "And that before they were married she used to come to his room very often."

Maybe, Blayney reconsidered, he *should* try to talk to the man. Maybe he could get something useful out of him, something more than the rubbish Fritz had gotten. A little while later, when Lino once again tried to start up a conversation with him, Blayney allowed him to talk.

He didn't learn much. "Mrs. Chapman came to me," Lino boasted. "We had connections a few days before Mr. Chapman's death." Blayney wasn't interested in the prisoner's sexual exploits. He wanted to know where he came from, whether he had a record, had ever been a pirate or a convict. But although the prisoner had kept saying he wanted to talk, he wouldn't answer questions, was reluctant to speak about himself, and was interested only in implying that Lucretia Chapman had been up to no good. Frustrated, Blayney resolved to try his luck with Lino another time and brushed him off again.

That night the fellow was seasick. Clearly no sailor, he. He threw up for hours, and there was no chance to talk to him. But in the morning he was better and still insisting he wanted to talk.

"So you've intimated two or three times," Blayney said to him coolly. Then, speaking firmly, he made his position clear. "If you'll answer two questions for me, I'll listen to you." When Lino still hesitated, he added, "Nothing you say to me will appear against you if you're indicted for the murder of Dr. William Chapman."

Reassured, Lino agreed to answer whatever he was asked, and Blayney proceeded to interrogate him. "Have you ever been in jail?" he asked.

"No," Lino said.

"Have you ever been a pirate?"

"No."

Blayney wasn't sure whether to believe him. He wasn't sure you could believe anything the fellow said. Especially the things that came spewing out of his mouth after he answered the two questions. Things like his saying that Lucretia Chapman had poisoned her husband. That she'd snuck some medicine out of the prisoner's private medicine chest and put it into her husband's soup. Or that he'd only married Lucretia because William Chapman, on the verge of dying, had begged him to marry her.

Blayney managed not to ask him how come, if he was married to Lucretia, he'd been about to marry again, up there in Boston.

While Blayney and Lino were making their way down to Philadelphia, two physicians arrived at the graveyard of All Saints Church in Andalusia to witness the disinterment of William Chapman. One was Dr. John Hopkinson, a surgeon and lecturer at the University of Pennsylvania Medical School. He'd been asked by Bucks County's deputy attorney general, who'd begun to suspect arsenic as the agent of Chapman's death, to perform an autopsy and remove any organs that might reveal that William had died unnaturally. The other physician was Dr. Reynell Coates, a general practitioner in the county whose flamboyant wife would one day scandalize his neighbors by being the first local woman to wear bloomers. Coates had come out of medical curiosity and offered to lend Hopkinson any assistance he required.

The two doctors, their heads protected from the warm September sun by tall beaver hats, watched as the sexton dug into the still soft soil over William's grave and began slowly raising the coffin. It was slightly indented, as if the weight of the earth had been too much for the casket, they noticed when the sexton set his burden on the ground, and the wood where the corpse's head would be lying looked damp. Some moisture might have seeped inside, the sexton warned them, then proceeded to pry open the lid.

As soon as it swung free, the physicians let out a gasp of amazement. It wasn't entirely because the face staring up at them was hideously black and putrid. No, the sexton had prepared them for that with his talk about moisture. What was amazing to them was the rest of the body. Despite its three months underground, it seemed hardly to have deteriorated at all. A sure sign of arsenic poisoning, both doctors thought, well aware of the use of arsenic in taxidermy.

In a few moments Hopkinson commenced, right there at the graveside, to cut through William's burial clothes. He exposed the abdomen and part of the chest, then made a surgical incision into the abdominal cavity. It was oddly firm and resistant, he observed as he cut. Odder still, it was dry, and gave off no offensive odor. Peering down, he stared into the arid cavity. The stomach didn't look right, he thought. It was unusually dark in color. Could the inside be inflamed? Deciding to check it more thoroughly, and to check the intestines as well, he asked Coates to help him with his examination of the internal organs.

They began with the small intestine. Hopkinson cut into the twisted tubes in many areas, and he and Coates studied the tissue closely. It, too, was dry, both doctors noticed with surprise. And although the small intestine was slightly distended, it was almost totally empty, except for two or three bits of fecal matter tinged with healthy bile. It was the same with the large intestine, which was also dry, and also virtually empty, containing nothing but a small quantity of bilious matter in the duodenum. Neither intestine showed signs of inflammation. Nor, for that matter, did the spleen, the liver, or the kidneys. As to the gall bladder, it had an unusually healthy appearance.

Hopkinson decided to leave all these organs intact and to remove only the stomach and duodenum. He tied them at each extremity, loosened them from the corpse, and put them into a clean wine-filled glass jar he had brought with him from Philadelphia. Finally, having noticed as he severed the stomach that a bit of the internal lining of the esophagus appeared inflamed, he removed and bottled the esophagus as well.

That done, he became tutorial. "Have I missed anything?" he inquired of his inexperienced assistant. "Should I cut further?" He and Coates debated the matter for a while, then agreed that everything that needed examination had been explored. Satisfied, Hopkinson returned William's body to its coffin, said a fond farewell to his young colleague, and transported the wine jar and its lugubrious contents back to Philadelphia, where he stored it in his home overnight.

The following morning he took the jar to Pennsylvania Hospital. The hospital, which had been founded by Benjamin Franklin in 1754, was a leading center for medical research, and Hopkinson had arranged to have Chapman's tissues studied at one of the already venerable institution's outstanding labs. The lab he had selected was that of Dr. John K. Mitchell, a renowned physician and chemist who had drafted two investigators to assist him:

Dr. Joseph Togno, a Philadelphia general practitioner, and Thomas G. Clemson, a young chemist who'd studied at the scientific mecca of the day, the Sorbonne. The three men showed Hopkinson around the big lab, with its many windows and high, flask-lined shelves, and after choosing a well-lit corner of the room, Hopkinson got out his surgical instruments, opened the wine jar, and cut into Chapman's stomach.

At once he was struck by a peculiar smell. He'd opened hundreds of bodies and never smelled anything like this before. "I'd compare it to pickled herring," he said.

"It more resembles," Mitchell commented, "the smell of a dried Scotch herring."

The others sniffed, too, then Hopkinson stepped back and Mitchell and his assistants went to work, poking at and fingering the exposed tissues. Mitchell was hoping they would be able to detect some solid bodies or particles clinging to the surfaces—if they could, he theorized, it would make it easier to detect the presence of arsenic. But neither he, Togno, nor Clemson encountered anything with any firmness whatsoever, and in the end they resigned themselves to scraping the internal walls of the stomach with smooth-edged bone spoons to collect the walls' viscid mucus.

Hopkinson watched them scrape for a time, then excused himself, for Mitchell and his staff would soon be starting their testing, a process that promised to be a lengthy one. They had indicated that they intended to test absolutely everything, solid pieces of the intestines and stomach as well as the mucosa they were so arduously harvesting.

The local newspapers were having a field day. The American public had long shown an avid interest in articles about robberies and killings and during the 1820s the country's press had begun capitalizing on this predilection, becoming increasingly sensationalistic. By 1831, according to one writer of the time, crime stories were making up "the *Domestic News*' of every journal. . . . . That which was once too shocking for recital, now forms a part of the intellectual regalia which the public appetite demands with a gusto." Murder was the favorite subject, and just as today, murders that took place within the privileged class excited the greatest interest. By mid-October the Chapman case, with its prominent upper-middle-class victim, was receiving intense coverage, and newspaper reporters, not content with the initial scandalous details, had begun dredging for more. On October 22, 1831, the *Philadelphia Saturday Bulletin,* which had been directing opprobrium chiefly against Lino, calling him "an accomplished scoundrel" and "a villain of no ordinary character," turned its attention to Lucretia, whom it had previously portrayed only as an object of compassion. She was a "woman of violent passions," the paper said; her disposition was "fierce and cruel"; the boardinghouse she and her husband had maintained in Philadelphia was a "suspicious" one that on at least one occasion had harbored counterfeiters. This malfeasance was hardly surprising, the *Bulletin* implied, for Lucretia Chapman "has a brother [Mark] now in the Massachusetts State Prison for forgery and counterfeiting."

From that moment forward Lucretia would be viewed by many of her contemporaries as a criminal, for the common psychological thinking of the time held that criminality was an inherited trait, and if one member of a family was a lawbreaker, chances were that the rest of the family was also felonious. In the 1840s this idea would become, in the hands of pseudo-scientists like Orson Squire Fowler, editor of the *American Phrenological Journal and Miscellany,* an argument for eugenics, the improvement of a population by genetic control. Fowler, who was convinced that "the disposition and mental powers of mankind are *innate*—are *born,* not created by education," believed that just about every human trait could be passed down from one generation to the next. People of African descent inherited their unique "mode of moving . . . tone of voice, manner of laughing, form of nose and mouth, color of eyes and teeth, and other peculiarities." People of Jewish descent inherited "intellectual superiority," but also such traits as "acquisitiveness" and "destructiveness." The English inherited "conscientiousness" and "benevolence." One day Fowler would use the fact that there were counterfeiters in Lucretia Chapman's family to advance his theory that criminality could be stemmed if people avoided marrying into tainted families like hers. In the meantime, Lucretia was throwing herself on the mercy of that family.

She was at the Cape, begging her relatives to help her find a way to avoid being located by the police. She didn't stay with any of her kin, assuming that to do so might be dangerous either for herself or for them. Instead, indifferent to comfort, she boarded in the rundown house of a stranger. And whenever she went out of doors she wore her disguise, the frock coat and trousers she had packed. With her long torso and tall legs the costume seemed to suit her. She was sure she would not be taken for a woman.

Upon their arrival in Philadelphia, Blayney delivered Lino to the jail in Doylestown, the governmental seat of Bucks County. It was here that the county's courts sat, here that the deputy attorney general had his office. The courthouse, a handsome cupola-crowned brick edifice, and the jail, which had high prison walls, an exercise yard, and two wings of double-tiered cells, had been erected in 1812 at the astronomical cost of thirty-eight thousand dollars. Both structures were, the *Bucks County Intelligencer* bragged, built with such fine materials that they were "unequalled by any County Court House and jail in the state." Nevertheless, jailbreaks had been a problem virtually from the start. Two prisoners had bolted in 1816, four in 1827, two more in 1830. Lino began thinking about how to escape as soon as Blayney handed him over to the warden.

At first it seemed impossible. He was loaded down with heavy iron chains. His wrists and ankles were shackled, and a chain went from the ankle shackles to the floor of his cell, allowing him to move only in a four-foot radius. The chain was so constricting that he could barely reach his low mattress, or its trunk of ragged bedding, or the rough wooden bench that sat alongside the hearth. He dragged himself to the bench from time to time and perfunctorily turned the pages of the Spanish Bible that lay upon it. But for the most part he prowled the cell, seeking its secrets and its hidden possibilities, and taking careful note of the barred windows, the hooked inner door, the padlocked outer door, and the fact that when he was brought food, it was already all cut up.

But the jail was smaller and cozier than the Philadelphia penitentiary. And the warden, Bucks County's High Sheriff Benjamin Morris, a plump, good-natured Episcopalian, was not a bad sort. Lino kept to his best behavior, and after a few days Morris unlocked his wrist chains so that he could keep himself clean, and even agreed to let him cut his own meat.

The next time Lino received his food, there was a blunt pocket-size knife alongside his tin plate. Lino eyed the knife excitedly. Might he be able to cause the warden to forget to remove it someday?

One evening he got sick on jail food. Morris sent for a doctor in the village, who agreed that he wasn't well, gave him some medicine, and suggested that a fellow prisoner be assigned to sleep in his cell and nurse him until he was better. That's how he came to meet William Brown, a thickset man with rippling imposing muscles, who'd been jailed for larceny.

Brown watched over him, and by the time Lino recovered from his food poisoning, he and Brown had compared notes on the layout of the jail. They'd also hatched a few escape plans and agreed that if one of them managed to get out of his cell first, he would free the other. The plans were rudimentary. They needed to be talked over some more. But when Lino tried to get Brown into his cell by once again complaining of sickness, the doctor said this time he was faking; there was nothing wrong with him.

So be it, Lino decided. He didn't require Brown for planning; he had imagination enough for the two of them. He required Brown for labor. All he really needed just now was to get possession of his dinner knife.

One afternoon he succeeded. Chatting and spinning stories with Sheriff Morris, he managed to so distract the man that when Morris removed his food tray, he didn't notice that the knife was no longer on it.

Lino concealed the knife in his mattress and that night, after scraping it into a tiny saw on the stone walls of his cell, forced his new tool into a rivet on his ankle shackle and sawed the chain open. To conceal what he'd done, he ripped strips of cloth from his bedding and wound them over and under the iron links.

In the morning, when Morris brought Lino his breakfast, he noticed the bandage. But Lino explained to him that he'd had to put a dressing on his ankle because the chain was tearing at his flesh.

Morris nodded understandingly. He knew that chains often did that.

Two nights later, after Morris had finished his ten o'clock cell check and retired to his house across the yard, Lino took a thin log from his hearth and with the tip of it burned a hole in his floor. That was one of the plans he and Brown had hatched: burn a hole in the cell floor and tunnel out. But although he held the end of the burning log to the oaken floor until it penetrated the thick boards, he discovered to his disappointment that underneath the oak was a second floor, this one made of stone. He tossed the log back in the fireplace and set his trunk over the hole he'd made.

A few nights after that frustrating first try, he tied a chip of wood to a piece of string, extricated another small brand from his hearth, burned a hole over the latch of his inner cell door with its glowing point, and passed the woodchip-weighted string through the hole. He dangled the string until he heard the chip hit the floor. Then slowly, patiently—he had never in his life been so patient— he worked the string along the far side of the door until he felt certain it was just below the latch and tried to jerk the wood up so forcefully that it would spring open the door hook. He tried many times. He was like a fisherman casting his line into an empty sea. But at last he gave one fierce jerk, and the hook flew open. He heard it give, and when he pushed on the door, the wooden portal swung wide.

There was, of course, still the outer door, the iron door, to get through. But he needed no contrivance for that. Just his hand. And the knife. He pulled on the bit of grating in the center of the metal, made a space wide enough for his fingers to go through and, using the handle of his knife, wrenched off the outer padlock. Then he ran to free Brown.

It took him just a few minutes to get his friend out of his cell, but longer to free him of his shackles. The handcuffs he was wearing came off readily enough, but his leg chains were stubborn. Lino's little knife made but slow and incomplete progress against the metal, and at last Lino told Brown they shouldn't waste precious time by trying any further. After all, he pointed out, Brown could move now, if somewhat slowly, and he'd be able to conceal the irons under his pants once they got away from the jail. *If* they got away. But how to accomplish that? Lino's first idea was that they make a breach in the floor in the day room, the chamber where prisoners, not kept the Philadelphia way and prevented from socialization, were sometimes permitted to gather and warm themselves in front of a big iron stove. He'd heard there was a cellar, not a stone floor, beneath that room. If they could get into the cellar, he told Brown, they could reach the yard, and if they reached the yard, they could scale the prison wall.

How? Brown asked.

He'd make a rope, Lino said.

They threw themselves into action. In the day room, Brown yanked some rods from the stove and began trying to pry up the floorboards. In his cell, Lino ripped up the bedclothes and twisted them into a sturdy rope. Then it occurred to him that he'd best make himself some kind of pack so that once he was over the walls he'd have a disguise, look like a peddler, not a prisoner. He flung the clothes from his trunk onto the floor, packed them into a bundle, cut armholes in the outer cloth so he could carry the bundle on his back, and stuffed his creation with mattress ticking to make it look fuller. Then he ran to the day room to assist Brown with the floorboards.

They were hours trying to lift them. But finally they succeeded. They made a breach, tumbled down into the cellar, and a moment later unlocked the cellar door and piled outside into the yard.

It was pitch-black out there. The night was like a princely cloak that swirled about them. The prison wall loomed like a ghastly monster. Lino threw his rope high over it and began to climb. But the rope hadn't caught well and he came tumbling down. Then Brown tried, but he, too, couldn't get over the wall. They took off their shoes and tried again. They tried again and then again. The blackness of the sky faded to gray. Birds began to twitter. Still, they were having no luck.

What was to be done? Lino wondered. In a short while the sun would be up. The warden would be rising from his bed. It wasn't fair. They'd done so much, worked so hard, and soon it would be all up with them. Or would it? In the shadows near the cellar door, he spotted an axe, and his heart leaped. Brown could break the great lock with which the yard door was fastened! It would make a terrible noise. It would awaken Sheriff Morris instantly. But it was their only chance. They would have to take it.

He shoved the axe at Brown, and his robust companion began swinging at the huge iron lock. With each blow his muscles bulged and the air reverberated with a thundering noise. At once, from behind the barred windows of the jail, prisoners roused from their sleep began cheering. Then there was another sound, a cry of command. Morris was racing across the yard and yelling at Brown and Lino to stand still. Brown swung again, with redoubled energy. The lock gave way and the door swung open a crack. It wasn't all the way open. There was another lock barring the door from the outside. But the crack was wide enough for Brown and Lino to squeeze through. Not wide enough for Morris, though. As Lino and his comrade skittered crazily into the fields beyond the wall, the portly warden got stuck in the crack. Lino abandoned his pack, shouted to Brown that they'd best separate, and, doubling his speed, began sprinting in the direction of what he hoped was Philadelphia.

A posse of public-minded citizens answered the warden's call for help and fanned out over the countryside, combing through every fall-fallow field and beneath every sparsely leafed tree. At around nine in the morning they found the chain-impeded Brown crouching in a pile of bark about a mile from town. Lino was farther away, but not as far as he'd hoped to be. The trouble was his feet. In his haste he'd left his shoes back in the prison yard, and now his feet were sore and bloody. He needed shoes. He needed them desperately, especially if he was going to make better progress.

At a quarry about seven miles out of Doylestown he spotted some workmen and, deciding to take a chance, came out from hiding and asked where he could buy an old pair of shoes. He said he was Chinese, figuring, he later explained, that this would account for his being barefoot. The few Chinese he'd seen in America were always dirt poor, too poor to own shoes.

The workmen seemed not to doubt his story. They asked him no questions and one of them even pointed to a nearby house and suggested that its occupants might be able to sell him some shoes. Lino, struggling forward on his ravaged soles, went into the house.

It was a mistake. He knew it as soon as he got inside. "You're Mina, aren't you?" someone said to him as soon as he stepped through the door. The inquirer looked athletic, and he was wearing the uniform of a major in the American army.

He's probably got a weapon, Lino reckoned. But maybe I can fool him. "No, I'm not Mina." He beamed a wide, sincere smile and, not knowing that handbills offering a reward for his capture had already been printed and distributed throughout the county, added, "If you don't believe me, you can take me right over to Doylestown, where you'll soon see you're mistaken."

A friend of the major's walked in just then, and the major smiled back and said he had in mind doing just that. Lino didn't try to run away. There were two of them now, to his shoeless one, plus the gang of workmen outside. He let the major and his friend tie his hands behind his back and put him into their wagon. He'd find some way, he figured, to trick his way free.

146

"Mina," he began as the wagon bumped along. "I'm not him. But I've met the man."

His captors looked interested. "That's not his real name, you know," Lino went on. "It's an assumed name."

The men wanted to know what else he knew of Mina. He threw them a few tidbits, said the newspapers had printed all sorts of falsehoods about the poor fellow, said Mina wasn't a bad sort at all.

The major and his friend seemed to believe he wasn't Mina. At least they said they believed him. But they refused to untie him and let him out of the wagon. "When we get into Doylestown," the major promised, "we'll stop at a tavern and see if we've made a mistake. If we have, we'll let you go."

Lino put his head down. He was out of ideas for once, exhausted from his long night's efforts and his foot-bloodying march that morning. "You may as well drive to the jail," he murmured in defeat. "I *am* Mina."

The major and his friend nodded and drove him right to the high-walled stone edifice. Scores of people were milling around it. They welcomed Lino, called out to him. Overnight, it appeared, he'd become famous, become someone everyone wanted to greet. It made him feel good. His mood lifted, and he laughed and talked with the crowd.

Then the warden took him inside and returned him to the same cell from which he'd fled just a few short hours ago. Only now both his bed and his bench had been removed, and when he was shackled to the floor again, the chain was so short he could no longer reach the paltry fire burning in his hearth.

Lucretia was in Greenfield, Pennsylvania, a small town in Erie County. With the help of her Cape Cod relatives, she'd obtained a position in Greenfield in the home of a well-to-do couple named

Newton. The Newtons had three children, and unaware of Lucretia's situation, they'd hired her as their governess.

She began her duties with trepidation, frightened at every moment that her whereabouts might be discovered, and on November 11, 1831, three weeks after she had come to live with the Newtons, her fears came true. She was in the schoolroom with the children when the sheriff of Erie County, accompanied by a postmaster, arrived at the Newtons' sprawling mansion and demanded to speak to her. She shooed the children away and asked the men what they wanted with her. But she knew, and she put up no struggle when the sheriff told her he had a warrant for her arrest. She simply gathered her belongings and let the men escort her to the Erie jail.

It was a dreary place, but she tried to keep her spirits up. She asked for books and spent time reading. She asked for pens and paper and wrote to her children, with whom she'd been out of contact since her flight from Andalusia. She also wrote to her friends. To Colonel Cuesta, the Mexican consul who had once been so kind to her, she wrote requesting that he please visit her lawyer Campbell and ask him if she should hire "an able Advocate . . . to aid him in pleading her cause." To Elijah Cobb, who had known her since girlhood and who had entertained Lino at the Cape because of her recommendation, she wrote, "Ah! From what a height have I fallen! But yesterday I had and enjoyed all that heart could wish; blest with competence, surrounded with a lovely family."

The letter to Cobb was lengthy. In it she romanticized William, saying he had been "the kindest and best of husbands," and she excoriated Lino, condemning him as a "demon" and "*cruel spoiler*," a term of opprobrium right out of *Charlotte Temple*, that poignant tale of seduction and betrayal she used to love. She also told Cobb that Lino was so mean that once, when her little son

John offended him, he said to the toddler that he would never again hug him because he never forgave injuries, and quite terrified the child by warning him that he "delighted in revenge."

Additionally, she assured Cobb that although she was guilty of having become infatuated with "a mysterious stranger—a base impostor" and guilty of having "precipitately married the cruel monster," she was innocent of William's murder and could explain why she had married so "imprudently." It was because she had been decoyed and duped. The impostor had tricked her into marriage. Why? "Ah! It was that he might better accomplish his diabolical designs to rob me and my children of our personal property."

She may have taken comfort in writing, in pouring out her side of the story. She may also have hoped that some of her words would be leaked to the press. Certainly the press got wind of them. Cobb, or someone to whom Cobb showed her letter, talked about it to a journalist, and on December 1, 1831, the *Boston Morning Post* published a brief, sympathetic article saying that the accused Mrs. Chapman was a "very wellbred and intelligent woman" who had conducted herself "imprudently"—her very own word. The *Post* also urged the public not to be too hasty in condemning her.

Several days later, when she had been in jail in Erie for three weeks, she was told to ready herself for a journey. She was to be taken under armed guard to Doylestown, five hundred miles away. There she would be put in a second jail, the same jail in which Lino was being held, to await trial on the unbailable charge of murder.

On the morning of December 10, 1831, David Paul Brown's renowned concentration was interrupted by a knock on his office door and the appearance at the threshold of a tall woman, accompanied by a warder. The woman's figure was striking, slender, and, he couldn't help but notice, well-proportioned. "What service can I render you,

Madam?" he asked, and offered his visitor a seat. She lowered herself into a chair and sat still, like a marble figure, nothing but the restlessness of her eyes showing any animation whatsoever. Then at last she spoke, in a groan that seemed to Brown to come not from her throat but from her innermost soul. "*Mrs. Chapman!*" she said, as if those two words alone would be sufficient to explain her entire lamentable story. Which in fact they were. He hadn't recognized her—she was haggard from her exhausting trip—but he knew all about her case, had even read in some unreliable public journal that he himself was going to defend her, though who could have put such an idea into the editor's head, *he,* David Paul Brown, had no idea. It wasn't true. The woman hadn't even written to him, let alone come to see him.

Now, however, at the recommendation of her family lawyer, she was here, under guard and en route to jail and indictment in Doylestown. Delicately, oh as delicately as possible, he proceeded to question her, asking her the precise nature of the accusation against her and what kind of defense she hoped could be mounted on her behalf.

The conversation was long and painful. She gave him a thousand details. Told him about the death of her husband, Chapman; about the impostor Mina; about her flight from the police; and about her five fatherless—and soon to be *motherless,* if the deputy attorney general had his way—children. He heard her out without rushing her, and thought about his own children and the advice he intended to give his sons should they one day follow in his footsteps and enter the practice of criminal law. It was that before they ventured to undertake a capital case they must be absolutely certain they were competent for the hazards of such a case. Remember, he intended to tell them, if you perform your task feebly, the blood of the defendant may be upon you. Do not, therefore, allow a feverish desire for notoriety blind you to the difficulties and dangers by which you will inevitably be surrounded, for the trumpet of fame cannot drown the small still voice of remorse.

Mrs. Chapman was coming to the end of her long tangled tale. She was begging him to represent her. It would cause him, Brown realized, no end of personal and professional inconvenience. The woman had waited until the eleventh hour to ask for his services. Her trial—it was to be a joint trial, with her and Mina standing together before the bench—was due to start in just a few short days. Worse, it was to be held not in Philadelphia, but out in Doylestown, where, if he agreed to handle the case, he would no doubt have to stay in some uncomfortable inn. He'd be deprived for who knew how long of the refinements of his pleasant home, that capacious Washington Square house which Mrs. Royall had called, in that book of hers, "a splendid mansion, in which wealth and taste are alike diffused." Still, he would take Mrs. Chapman on, Brown concluded. He would stand by her and see to it that she got a fair and impartial trial. Indeed, he would be like the commander of a ship in a storm. The cordage might snap, the masts go by the board, the bulwarks get carried away, the hull spring a leak, but he, the gallant commander, would stay by his helm to the last, determined either to steer his battered vessel into port, or to perish gloriously in the faithful discharge of his duty.

Soberly, he told the poor woman his decision, and before she was removed by her caretaker to finish her trip to the common jail in which the state had decided to consign her, he had the pleasure of seeing how happy he had made her. As to himself, he could not remember a more disagreeable sensation than that which he experienced upon bidding her goodbye. He had assumed, he told his friends, the responsibility of a cause upon whose outcome depended not only the life of an individual, but the hopes and happiness of all who belonged to her.

Nine

❧

Pennsylvania v. Lucretia Chapman,
Part One
Mid-December 1831–Mid-February 1832

*B*ROWN WAS IN A temper on December thirteenth, the day
before Lucretia's trial was scheduled to begin. On the short-
est of notice, he'd managed to hire an assistant, a talented young
lawyer named Peter McCall, and the two of them had taken a coach
out to Doylestown. But the county seat was jammed with gawkers
and journalists from all over the country, not to mention a horde of
prosecution witnesses. It was so crowded that even though the town
had six hotels and numerous smaller lodging places, Brown and
McCall weren't able to find accommodations. Were he and his new
assistant to be like Noah's dove, with no resting place for their feet?
he wondered as they traipsed from one inn to the next. Then finally,
quite late at night, they succeeded in finding quarters and were able
to set about preparing for the next day's work—work that promised,
Brown feared, to be a most awful and embarrassing business.
Because he had no witnesses lined up, or even any idea if his client
had witnesses. Not yet. The whole thing was happening too quickly.

In the morning, fighting a wintry wind that sent a chill through his bones, he and McCall hunched to the jail to confer with Lucretia. Brown was still edgy. His short stay in Doylestown had convinced him that not only did the prosecution have a veritable army of witnesses, but public prejudice was running high against his client. When he and his junior colleague passed through the prison's front door, the grated portal seemed almost to groan as it swung open, and the eerie sound gave him a momentary and uncharacteristic lapse of confidence. What could *he* do against so much prejudice and proof, he fretted. He needed helping hands.

Nevertheless, when he spoke to Lucretia, he tried to assume an optimistic air, for he didn't want her to know how worried he was. Who can help us? he asked in as cheerful a manner as he could muster. Who should we call to testify on your behalf?

She named all sorts of people. But many of them—like her first lawyer, Campbell, who'd gone off to sit with the legislature in Harrisburg, or her husband's speech student, John Bishop, who resided in Vermont, or her own student, Ben Ash, who lived in New York—were hundreds of miles away. Brown wasn't at all sure he'd be able to round up all the witnesses she was proposing, let alone these remote ones. Concerned, he said a hasty goodbye to Lucretia, and he and McCall hurried over to the courthouse next door, where they began furiously making out subpoenas. They wrote them with their own hands and hired court hangers-on to deliver them, paying the men right from their own purses. And as they dispatched the process servers they perversely hoped that if the trial actually began that day as docketed, the evidence against their client would take up a great deal of time; that way their servers would be able to locate and bring to Doylestown at least the nearest of Lucretia's witnesses. Then when it was *their* turn to present evidence, Brown and McCall vowed, they'd examine those first witnesses so lengthily that they'd give their emissaries time to search out and produce the more distant individuals. It was a forlorn hope, but it was almost all they had. Unless, of course, they could win a postponement.

That afternoon Lucretia and Lino were led into a courtroom in the cupola-crowned courthouse and placed, as was customary, not at a table alongside their lawyers but in an elevated dock in the front of the room. Lucretia, her face drawn, was dressed in her dusty traveling outfit, its sturdy cinnamon-colored fabric and even its trim of black braid showing faded patches. Lino was wearing the black frock coat Watkinson had long ago tailored for him, and he kept trying to improve his appearance by running his fingers through his cloud of curly hair. Neither eyed the other as the court's clerk began to read aloud the indictment against them that had been handed down two days earlier by a grand jury. "Lucretia Espos y Mina," the clerk boomed out, "and Lino Amalia Espos y Mina, not having the fear of God before their eyes, but being moved and seduced by the instigation of the devil, did mix and mingle certain deadly poison, called arsenic, in certain chicken soup, which had been prepared for the use of a certain William Chapman and by these means did feloniously, willfully and of their malice aforethought kill and murder him, contrary to the form of the Act of the General Assembly and against the peace and dignity of the Commonwealth of Pennsylvania."

One avid listener was the man who'd gotten the grand jury to indict, Deputy Attorney General Ross, a serious young lawyer whose long jaw, narrow nose, and purse of tight lips gave his face a stern and brooding expression. Ross had never before tried a case of this importance. Indeed, he had been admitted to the Bucks County bar only two years earlier. But within a year he'd been appointed the county's chief prosecutor. It had helped that he'd gone to Princeton, where he'd learned a bit about the law as part of his general curriculum; in the absence of law schools as such, attending college or apprenticing oneself to another lawyer was all that was required to enter the profession. It had helped even more that his father was John Ross, now sitting on the Supreme Court and for thirty years before that a circuit court judge with a great deal of political clout. Still, Judge Ross, for all his prestige, wasn't entirely popular in Bucks County. "Iago" and "old Judas," some newspapers called him. And when twenty-four-year-old Thomas took over as deputy attorney general, he'd had to put up with being dubbed "a stripling of old Judas." But Thomas admired his father and hoped to make him proud. This would be no easy task, for John Ross was a difficult man. Once, when Thomas had offered to assist him on one of his cases, his father had written him a note saying, "Dear Tom: When I require your advice it will be time enough to give it to me, and then, and not till then, will it be acceptable." But Thomas expected that if he could win a conviction in the Chapman case, his father would be pleased with him. So, too, his mother, an upstanding woman who had decided despite a fine education to devote her life to caring for his brain-damaged brother, John. His mother, Thomas may have reflected as he listened to the clerk read the indictment, was cut from a different cloth from the female defendant. *That* woman, he intended soon to tell a jury, was wanton, devoid of all moral scruples.

The clerk was addressing her now. "How do you plead?" he asked.

"Not guilty," she replied.

"How would you be tried?"

"By God and my country," she murmured, giving the ritual answer.

When the clerk finished questioning the woman, he directed

his attention to the male defendant. "How do you plead?" the clerk asked him.

"Not guilty," Mina said.

Like the woman, he, too, was being represented by two lawyers, the highly experienced Eleazar T. McDowell, and McDowell's apprentice, Samuel Rush. McDowell hadn't been hired by the defendant. The heavyset, doughy-faced lawyer, so sociable and witty that on the rare occasions when jurors voted against him they felt constrained to apologize, commanded high fees. But the first American Congress had made it possible for the courts to appoint attorneys to indigent defendants facing capital punishment, and McDowell had been assigned to handle Lino's defense. He wouldn't be receiving his customary fee, but he'd agreed to take the case on, no doubt because the trial promised other rewards, augured attention and publicity.

"How would you be tried?" Ross heard the clerk ask the male defendant.

"By God and my country."

But was it his country? Ross thought it was. But the man's own counselor, McDowell, seemed not altogether sure of this. He'd gone on record saying that in order to ensure his client a fair trial he might make the unorthodox request that at least half the jury be composed of foreigners. Ross wasn't certain that McDowell would actually proceed with the request, but he couldn't afford to worry about the matter. It was time for him to speak. Rising, he looked hard at the defendant. "Are you ready for trial?" he asked.

"Yes."

And was the woman ready for trial?

She didn't answer. Instead, Peter McCall jumped up, waved an affidavit in his hand, and asked for a postponement. His client, he declared, had witnesses who lived in New York; in northern New Jersey; in Vermont. They'd all been sent for, but it was doubtful they could be procured before the next court session in February. "To urge an immediate trial under such circumstances would be in the highest degree unjust," McCall called out, and requested that the case be put over until February.

Ross sat down and let his assistant, William B. Reed, handle this first argument. The two of them were the same age, but Reed was more experienced. He'd been admitted to the bar nearly six years ago, and since that time he'd not only practiced law in Philadelphia but done diplomatic work in Central America. Ross expected that Reed would skillfully present the prosecution's view that delaying the trial would cause their witnesses great inconvenience. And indeed Reed did. "We are ready to go to trial," he countered McCall. "Many of our witnesses have been brought to Doylestown from a distance, at a great sacrifice of convenience on their part and a considerable expense to the county. Many of them are females, unaccustomed to travel in an inclement season. Several are professional gentleman, whose time is valuable. I don't want to press harshly or unkindly upon the prisoners, but I think we should set an earlier trial date than February."

"January ninth?" the presiding judge, John Fox, suggested. As was customary in Pennsylvania at trials of capital crimes, he was one of a panel of three judges hearing the case. But he was the principal adjudicator, a solemn and aristocratic man who had himself once been the deputy attorney general of Bucks County. That had been years ago, before he got on the bench. Since then he had become an intimate of Andrew Jackson, had helped the president select his secretary of the treasury, had even served as Jackson's confidential adviser during his cabinet troubles. Since then he'd also become an enemy of Ross's father. But his animosity toward the father didn't seem to be affecting his treatment of the son. Rather, he was trying hard to go along with the state's desire to get the trial off to an early start. "January thirtieth?" Ross heard him offer when the defense attorneys declined the ninth.

But Brown and McCall were determined to get the matter put over until February, and in the end they prevailed. "Case continued," Judge Fox said, "until Monday, February thirteenth."

Lucretia's lawyers had won their first battle and during the next two months they devoted themselves to preparing for the trial. They spoke with potential witnesses, explored possible defense strategies, and decided that the most pressing requirement of the case was to get Lucretia's trial separated from Lino's, for the defense of one was likely to interfere with the rights of the other. To defend Lucretia, they would have to attack Lino; to defend Lino, *his* lawyers would have to attack Lucretia. It was a prospect that would put them all in an untenable situation. Well before February, Brown and McCall presented this view to Lino's team, persuaded them that severance was essential, and obtained their agreement to demand it as soon as the case was called.

Brown had been feeling out of sorts ever since the trip to Doylestown. But with the crucial issue of severance virtually resolved, he began to feel his health and stamina return, and along with them the confident feeling that "if life was to be lost, it would not be without a [valiant] struggle" on his part.

He had no idea that part of that struggle would be just getting back to Doylestown. Yet so it turned out. Early on the morning of February thirteenth, 1832, he and McCall left Philadelphia for Doylestown, expecting to get to the provincial courthouse in plenty of time for the start of the trial. But when they were still several miles from the town their carriage broke down.

The driver tried to repair the damage. He fiddled and fumbled with the broken vehicle while they stood at the side of the road.

Time passed, the sun grew high, the driver kept fiddling. Then at last he announced that it was hopeless. The carriage was totally disabled.

Brown and McCall had no choice but to heft their boxes of clothing and law books and proceed on foot to Doylestown. It was slow going, and they didn't reach town until late in the afternoon. Once they did, Brown realized there was no way they could start to try the case that day. Not in their soiled clothes, not with their dirt-streaked faces and aching feet. He sent word to McDowell to tell the judge of their mishap and implore him to postpone the trial's opening until the next morning, the fourteenth.

McDowell did as he was bid, and luckily for Brown and McCall, Judge Fox acquiesced.

Attending trials was a major form of entertainment in a society that lacked our modern diversions; on the morning of February fourteenth, when word spread that Lucretia's trial was at last actually going to commence, not hundreds but thousands of people gathered around the steps in front of Doylestown's courthouse. Enormous changes were brewing all over the country. In South Carolina planters were demanding that because of tariffs that protected northern manufacturing but neglected southern agriculture, their state should secede from the Union. In Virginia a legislator was speculating that the federal government had in mind outlawing slavery and thundering, "Mr. Speaker! Who can bear the thought of seeing a black speaker occupying that chair in which you are now seated." Everywhere, doctors were predicting that cholera, which had arrived in England and was spreading there like wildfire, might shortly decimate the United States. But to the crowd at the courthouse steps none of these harbingers of the momentous events that would soon alter both America's history and their own personal lives seemed to matter. They were focused on one thing and one thing only: getting into the courthouse. Jostling, shoving, trampling one another, they rushed the sheriffs and constables assigned to limit entry, crushing the ribs of one guard who barred the way, and poured into the small brick building. Some even pressed into the courtroom into which Sheriff Morris had just led Lucretia and Lino and, unable to obtain seats, massed themselves against the walls.

Lucretia, a journalist from the *Germantown Telegraph* noted, seemed determined to ignore the unruly spectators. She held her head straight and tried to adopt a firm and becoming expression. But she couldn't keep her lips and nostrils from twitching nervously.

She was once again wearing her traveling outfit, but this time Brown had made her hide her russet curls beneath a close-fitting cap and dark silk hood. In her fingers she clutched a fan, fluttering it back and forth despite the cool February weather, as if hoping that by busying herself with it she could stop the trembling of her hands.

Lino wasn't trembling or twitching at all. Sporting beneath his frock coat an embroidered shirt and a silk stock ornamented with a gleaming gold pin, he nodded and smiled at the crowd and seemed to be in high good humor.

As soon as the pair was ensconced in the dock, McDowell raised the issue of separate trials. "My application for separate trials is a mutual one," he addressed the court. "A juror who would be acceptable to one defendant might be challenged by the other, and in this way, injustice would be done if both were tried together."

Thomas Ross objected. "The mode and manner of trial is to be determined by the prosecution," he reminded the judge, "and if in their opinion the ends of public justice will be defeated by a severance, they have the right of insisting upon a joint trial. We so insist, and say the ends of public justice will be defeated if these defendants are granted separate trials."

Samuel Rush was on his feet at once. "If our application is refused, Your Honors, will the defendants have that which the law contemplates—a fair trial? May it please the Court, it is the defendants' purpose to make war upon each other! They strive, in effect, to cut each other's throats! But, say the gentlemen of the prosecution, 'We can't help that—nay, it is the very thing for us!' Shall human lives thus be lightly sported with? Lives that can never be given again, if taken in this affair? And is this to come within the discretion of the Attorney General! Sir, the powers of the Attorney General are well laid down and defined. They cannot be transcended. Let him show his right, based upon the incontrovertible law of the land. Until that is done, we protest against it; we desire, first and last, that it may not be granted."

Moved by Rush's eloquence, the judges adjourned the trial for a brief time so that they could consider the merits of each side's arguments. They left the courtroom and proceeded to their chambers.

While they were gone, the crowd outside the courthouse kept swelling. Suddenly it surged forward and, like a powerful wave, burst open the courthouse doors, flooding its way into already packed foyers, hallways, and stairwells. By the time the judges returned to the bench, more than six hundred people had fought their way inside, and the building seemed on the verge of collapsing.

"We can't proceed!" Judge Fox shouted, and directed police officers to eject the newcomers. They tried, pushing against the crowd with linked arms. But the crowd pushed back, and the struggle continued for over half an hour. Then finally, after enormous exertion, the police succeeded in expelling from the building everyone who did not have a seat in the courtroom.

In the restored tranquillity, Fox announced the court's decision. "The prosecution," he said, "has certified that if separate trials be granted, the ends of public justice will be defeated. To this opinion, we pay great respect. But we do not think it should prevent us from exercising our own discretion. And having been called upon hastily to decide the question, and considering the vast importance to the public interest that if conviction should take place all should be satisfied that the prisoners have had a full, fair and impartial trial, I throw the doubt on the side of the prisoners and direct that they be allowed to have separate trials."

At this, the disappointed Ross calculated quickly whose case he should proceed to try. Mina's? Or Mrs. Chapman's? He decided in favor of hers. "We would like," he said to the satisfaction of the remaining spectators, most of whom were far more interested in female than male transgression, "to take up the case of Lucretia Chapman first."

That afternoon prospective jurors were examined. They were all men—it would be many years before women would be permitted to sit on juries—and Ross and Brown were soon tangling over how to select them. Ross wanted to ask each candidate if he was opposed to capital punishment and if so, whether he was so opposed to it that his scruples would prevent him finding the defendant guilty of first-degree murder. Brown maintained that to ask such a question would be to subject a juror to "a sort of moral torture."

Ross stuck to his position staunchly, observing that if people who under no circumstances would find the defendant guilty were permitted to serve as jurors, "the doors of the prison might just as well be thrown open and the country saved the expense and the trouble of a trial." But once again Judge Fox came out against him. "It would be inquisitorial," he ruled, "to compel a juror to show that by reason of conscientious scruples he was disqualified from exercising the all important privilege of serving upon juries." Additionally, Fox rejected a further request from Ross to automatically exclude Quakers from the jury. Pennsylvania had been founded by the Quaker William Penn, and was heavily populated by members of the Society of Friends, as the Quakers called their denomination. Fox knew that many of the prospective jurors who would be called up today would be members of the Society. But he also was convinced that a man's being a Quaker didn't necessarily mean he was opposed to the death penalty. In the 1790s the Pennsylvania legislature, filled with Quakers, had abolished capital punishment for robbery, burglary, and sodomy, and for murders committed during the perpetration of these and other crimes, like rape and arson; nevertheless, it had retained the death penalty for murders that were premeditated. "Opposition to capital punishment," Fox pronounced, "is not a matter of conscience in the Society of Friends, as a society. Many of its members have such scruples, others have not."

That settled, he told Ross and Brown to continue interviewing jurors.

Obediently, the pair proceeded. They questioned nearly forty people and rejected more than half that number, some because they said they had already formed an opinion about the defendant's guilt and at least one because on his own and without being forced to provide the information, he told the court that he was opposed to capital punishment. After only a few short hours, the twelve-man panel was complete. The men who would pass judgment on Lucretia included the son of a delegate to the Constitutional Convention of 1790, the organizer of a society that promoted farming, and a prominent merchant of the increasingly popular new fuel, coal; the vast majority of them, including foreman John B. Balderson, were

Quakers, observant practitioners of their faith who asked to affirm rather than swear that they would execute their duties faithfully.

The dramatic structure of a criminal trial was much the same then as now. The prosecution opened the case, detailing the charges against the defendant and foreshadowing the evidence it would present in support of the charges. Next, witnesses for the prosecution were examined, and cross-examined by the defense, which then opened *its* case, questioned its own witnesses, and turned them over to the prosecution for cross-examination. Later, both sides had the opportunity to call rebuttal witnesses and to try to sway the jury in elaborate closing arguments.

Those closings and openings, however, were far more pompous in language and melodramatic in style than lawyers' speeches today. "Gentlemen of the jury," Ross began the Chapman case immediately after the jury was selected, "The crime of murder has occurred so frequently in this county within the last few years that it is calculated to awaken the fears of the community and to render it imperiously the duty of jurors to carry into execution the laws of the Commonwealth, without regard to the consequences that may follow a verdict of conviction. Scarcely has more than one year passed by since there was placed at this bar a *brother* charged with having imbrued his hands in the blood of a brother! Now, there is about to be placed upon her trial a *wife*. Charged with having been the destroyer and murderess of her own husband! The evidence which we shall lay before you will irresistibly lead you to the melancholy truth that the prisoner before the bar is guilty of the offense with which she stands indicted. The evidence will disclose such a scene of profligacy and immorality as has seldom been witnessed in this, or indeed in any other country."

As she listened to Ross, Lucretia's eyes filled with tears. So did the eyes of her children, who were all in the courtroom, sitting alongside their Aunt Mercy and a daughter and son-in-law of Mercy's. Ross ignored the tears and continued his blistering opening, promising to prove that William Chapman had been poisoned, and that although Lucretia's lover had been the one to purchase the poison, she herself had put it into her husband's soup and made sure it worked by neglecting him as he sickened. More, Ross pledged, "We shall lay before you a letter of Mrs. Chapman's, in which certain expressions are used, which will leave but little doubt upon your mind that they have reference to the crime of which she stands indicted. We shall show you very strong presumptive evidence of her guilt, such as treating her husband with so much cruelty and neglect during his illness that he was induced to complain that he believed his wife wished him gone. Such as flying from the county upon the first intimation that she was suspected. These circumstances will all be proved to you and will, I have no doubt, be sufficient to enable you to render a verdict of guilty."

He paused briefly after that, took a breath, and orated, "Blood, though it sleep a time, yet never dies."

Promptly the next morning, the prosecution began summoning its witnesses. Ross called first on Mary Palethorpe, who had been attending school at the Chapmans' the night Lino first arrived there. He directed her to tell the jurors in her own words what she had seen and heard that night, and when she had finished doing so, questioned her about her subsequent observations.

"They went up to Bonaparte's," Mary, twelve years old now, volunteered.

And was there anything different afterward? Ross asked.

"I saw Mina and Mrs. Chapman together often."

"Under what circumstances?"

"Mina used to have fits," Mary replied, speaking in a high-pitched, quavering voice. "He and Mrs. Chapman would go into a room together and shut the door—I don't know if they closed the windows."

Mary's mother had once advised Lucretia that it would be improper to walk beside Lino at William's burial. The girl, too, was interested in proper behavior. "I don't think Mrs. Chapman treated her husband right," she observed not long before Ross turned her over to the defense for questioning. "She called him a fool one Sunday, as we were going to church."

Cross-examining Mary, Brown was gentle. After all, he reasoned, she was just a slip of a girl. To be fierce with her might alienate the jury. But more importantly, she'd said nothing that could possibly hurt Lucretia. What wife hadn't called her husband a fool on occasion? And what kind of illicit activity could a woman be up to if she closed the door but not necessarily the shutters of the room in which she was supposedly disporting herself? Deciding that the child's testimony was unimportant, he asked her only a few innocuous questions: Was anyone else in the carriage with Lucretia and Lino when they drove to Bonaparte's? was one of them. Did Dr. Chapman or just Mrs. Chapman give Lino permission to stay at the house? was another.

The answer to both those questions was yes.

Ellen Shaw was the next witness. She hadn't wanted to come to what she would later call "this plaguey trial," and she had half a mind to tell the judge so. But she'd promised young Mr. Ross she'd testify, and he was counting on her. So she put her hand on the Bible and, lips pursed and back ramrod-stiff, shot a baleful look at her former employer and took the oath.

She told the jury that she hadn't liked the looks of Lino from the start. "His shirt wasn't worth anything," she explained. Besides, "He was a Spaniard, and a body didn't know what he might do." As to her employer, that benighted woman had deeply offended her sense of propriety. She and that butterfly of hers. "They used to kiss each other," Ellen grimaced. "They sang love songs to each other. They were often engaged in a private room by themselves."

Ross asked her to tell about some of the other shocking things she'd witnessed in that godforsaken household, and she said the worst ones she remembered. "Mrs. Chapman went up to Lino's room a good deal," she said. "I saw her come downstairs in the mornings. I saw her one evening sitting on his bed. He was in the bed at the time, so I don't know if he was dressed or not. She was wearing her nightdress!"

Might it be, Ross prompted her, that knowing the boarder was prone to fits, she'd gone up to his room to look after him?

"His spells," Ellen replied scornfully. "They didn't appear to affect his general health. He was soon over them."

The whole time she was up there she kept remembering poor Dr. Chapman. How he'd cried that time when Lino and his wife didn't come home from Philadelphia on time. How he'd once wanted to use the horse to break ground so he could plant potatoes, but Mrs. Chapman said *she* had to have the horse that day, and that she was mistress of her own house and could do as she pleased. Ellen told the jury about that, and about how Mrs. Chapman used to tell her husband to make his own bed and say that if he didn't get it done, he should have no breakfast. "She spoke pretty harsh sometimes," she said. "She used to tell him she was ashamed of him and she wished to God he was gone, for she was tired of him."

"Was that why you left the Chapmans' employ?" Ross asked.

"I left because there were things going on I did not like to see," Ellen shot out. "Also, my folks were against my staying there. They heard a great deal of talk about Mrs. Chapman and her boarder."

The woman's a human volcano, Brown thought, spewing flames, devastation, death. She's a female Iago. A modern Penthesilea, bent on total destruction. He was itching to get a chance to cross-examine her, and as soon as Ross finished the direct examination, he demanded to know if the witness had anything personal against Lucretia.

"I have had no difference with Mrs. Chapman," Ellen said. But Brown kept probing, and finally she admitted that when she quit, Mr. Chapman didn't pay her all the wages she was owed, and that she attributed his shortchanging her to his wife's influence. "Mrs. Chapman always had the chief management of the household," she sniped.

Satisfied that he'd suggested to the jury that the housekeeper harbored a grudge against his client, Brown proceeded to other areas of inquiry. "You say Mrs. Chapman and the boarder were often alone in a private room? What room was that?"

"The parlor," Ellen had to admit.

"You say she sang love songs to the boarder," Brown pressed her. "What songs were those?"

Ellen said she couldn't remember.

"Was this a religious household?"

"Religious service was performed during the chief of the time I was in the house," the witness answered. Then she added sarcastically, "And much good did it do!"

At this, even Judge Fox became annoyed with Ellen's opinionated testimony. "What did you mean by that last phrase?" he interrupted. "Do you know for a fact that the performance of religious service did no good?"

"No," Ellen subsided. "It just seems that way, seeing the way things turned out there."

The judge let the remark go and pursued a new tack, asking, "Was your employer in the habit of singing songs?"

"She was not in the habit of singing songs," Ellen answered. Then, as if realizing she wasn't being altogether truthful, she remarked that her employer did sing church songs. "She had a piano and played and sung hymn tunes."

"What hymns did she sing?"

"I can't tell the names of any of the songs," Ellen sulked.

She had been Ross's star witness, and she had done him as much harm as good.

That afternoon, wishing he'd been able to confer with his client during some of the testimony that had been presented against her, Brown decided to ask the court for permission to let Lucretia sit alongside him. He wanted to be able to whisper the occasional question to her, wanted to be able to have her clarify one thing or another. Besides, he didn't like the whole business of putting defendants in a dock. Penning them there. It was inhuman. Moreover, it made them look guilty, when by rights they were innocent until *proven* guilty.

He made his petition to Fox and the other two judges, hoping they'd see the value of his arguments. But they didn't. "This court has already refused an application of this kind in a former case," Fox summarily dismissed him, as if his petition had no merit whatsoever, and he and his client were left to listen to the next witness as if from opposite sides of the great glorious earth.

She was Esther Bache, Lucretia's friend and dressmaker. Esther told the jury about the time Lucretia had excused herself from a dress fitting, presumably to tend to an ailing Lino. She hadn't believed Lino was really ill, the dressmaker said; she'd heard him laughing up in the attic, and watched him eat heartily at the midday meal. She also said, as if revealing something markedly improper, that when he came to the table for that meal, he sat down at Lucretia's right—an observation that thoroughly irritated Brown.

Where else should the boarder have sat? he wondered. At the head? At the foot? If Lino had helped himself to one of *those* seats, then the dressmaker might have had something discreditable to complain about. Especially if he'd taken Chapman's seat. But as it was, the seamstress was trying to harvest forbidden fruit from nothing, nothing at all. No, she didn't worry Brown.

The next witness did, however. She was Ann Bantom, the pivot, Brown surmised, upon which the prosecution intended to rest its whole case. And indeed, the part-time cleaning woman told a story full of damning details. She said that on the Monday after Chapman first became sick, her employer informed her in the morning that he was feeling better, but that later that day, after eating soup and chicken made by his wife, he reported he was feeling worse. She hadn't seen her mistress put anything odd in the food, Ann admitted. Not in the kitchen, where Lucretia had sprinkled her concoction with a bit of pure salt, or in the parlor, where she'd carried it after it was cooked. But Lino had been there in the parlor, and the two of them had had a conversation. Not that she overheard it, Ann went on. She didn't know what they talked about, just that they talked. Then the food was sent up to the sickroom, and that was the last she saw of Mr. Chapman's meal until the leftovers were brought down to the kitchen, where she left them around for a while before throwing them out in the yard.

Brown knew what was coming. They'll have that farmer on the stand soon, he thought, that quack, that expert in quackery who's been claiming his ducks were poisoned by something in the Chapman yard. He had to show that if his client *had* poisoned her husband's food, she'd never have let her cleaning woman dispose of it, or even have let her leave it sitting around in a place where it could harm anyone or anything else.

"Who brought the soup and uneaten chicken back to the kitchen?" he asked Ann when he got his chance to cross-examine her.

"Mrs. Chapman put it on the table and left it there."

"Did Mrs. Chapman say anything about eating or not eating the leftover chicken?"

"I don't recollect that she said anything about eating the chicken."

"Was it thrown out right away?"

"No, the chicken stood on the table until teatime, and then I threw it out. I threw out the soup when I washed up the dishes."

"Was anyone else in the kitchen while the chicken and soup were sitting out?"

"The whole five of the children were in the habit of being in the kitchen every day," Ann complained.

Brown nodded his head sagely. Ann had given him the answer he'd been hoping to elicit.

He was going to press the point further, impress on the jury that at any time the leftovers could have been sipped or nibbled at by a hungry child, but before he could do so, Judge Fox interrupted with a question of his own. "Did Mrs. Chapman clean the pot?" he asked the unwary cleaning woman.

"I do not think she cleaned the pot."

"Did she tell you to throw away the leftover food?"

"Mrs. Chapman gave me no directions to throw the soup or the chicken away."

Brown folded the notes he'd made on Ann's testimony. The judge had done his work for him. He'd established that Lucretia had allowed the food—that presumably poisoned chalice!—to remain in the house for nearly half a day. That she'd allowed it to remain right where her servant—and her children; her children!—could have eaten it and turned deathly ill.

He had no further questions, Brown told the court, and as it was close to six in the evening, Fox adjourned the trial for the day.

Lucretia spent that night, as she had all the others since coming to Doylestown, praying and trying to keep warm in her chilly cell. But unknown to her, Lino, in his cell, was embarking on a new money-making scheme. It was a scheme that would make him one of the first in the long line of American criminals to profit from crime through publishing. Lino was composing a memoir.

Writing in Spanish and creating an aristocratic literary persona, he began the memoir with, "Carolino Estradas was born in the island of Cuba at the city of Trinidad and was the legitimate son of the Brigadier of Infantry Don Francisco Estradas de Arango and of Doña Rosa Maria de Mina, both formerly citizens of Spain. . . . he always displayed a love of what was proper, a warm and intrepid yet ductile spirit, was a foe to vanity and a stranger to pride, disinterested, generous, and liberal."

Then Lino described how his alter ego grew up surrounded by silver and gold, attended the University of Havana, and rescued from the clutches of pirates an exquisite, nobly born fifteen-year-old whom he married and with whom he had a child, only to lose both tragically and early, and, grief-stricken, to try to forget his sorrows by enlisting in the elite, danger-ridden service of the king of Spain.

Soon the autobiographer would get to his schoolmistress wife.

On Thursday, February sixteenth, when Lucretia's trial reconvened, the industrious Ross called six more witnesses. The book salesman Edwin Fanning testified that while William was sick, he complained that his wife was neglecting him. The tailor Richard Watkinson testified that Lino *and* Lucretia were in his shop on June sixteenth, picking up clothes for Lino. The brother of the clerk who worked at the druggist's across the way testified that later that day he encountered Lino, though not Lucretia, at the pharmacy. The clerk himself testified that Lino asked him for arsenic.

Elias Durand, corresponding secretary of the Philadelphia College of Pharmacy, was next. The handsome, long-nosed pharmacist, resplendent in a finely tailored Parisian suit, promised to be an impressive prosecution witness, but before he could get very far into his story, Brown and McCall tried to block his testimony. They asserted that Lino's having purchased arsenic had no bearing on Lucretia's case, that it was evidence against *him,* not her. The judges heard them out, but ruled that the fact that poison was purchased by any member of the defendant's household was admissible, for it established that poison was available in the house—though they warned Ross that he would have to connect Lucretia to that availability by producing evidence that she herself administered the poison. Then Durand was allowed to return to the stand, where in his lilting French accent he declared, "A quarter of a pound of arsenic was given to Señor Espos y Mina. I believe I weighed it and gave it to him myself."

Ross's final witness on Thursday was Dr. Phillips, who'd been awakened from his sleep to take a look at William when he first fell ill, and who'd attended to him faithfully during his final hours. The lanky, soft-spoken Phillips described William's deathbed agonies in vivid detail. But this aside, the doctor was hardly satisfactory as a prosecution witness. Not only did he not substantiate Fanning's assertion that Lucretia had neglected William during his illness, but under cross-examination he actually praised her care of her husband. "I saw no want of tenderness to William on her part," he said to the probing Brown. "There was nothing in her conduct that was unbecoming to a wife."

And there was more. When Brown was done with the witness, Judge Fox himself decided to question Phillips, for he was curious to know if, despite the doctor's once having thought that William had died of cholera morbus, he now believed he had been poisoned. "Might arsenic have accounted for Dr. Chapman's symptoms?" he asked.

Phillips was cooperative but cautious. "If arsenic had been administered, it would, I think, have accounted for some of the symptoms, and I am not prepared to say it would not account for all," he opined. "But neither am I prepared to say that natural causes and natural disease might not produce the same symptoms."

After Phillips's testimony was finished, the reporter for the *Germantown Telegraph* filed a story with his paper that said, "At present, the aspect of affairs is decidedly favorable to the prisoner. The intelligent gentlemen for the prosecution have shown a laudable and becoming zeal in sustaining the rights of the Commonwealth, but thus far they have not made out so strong a case as was expected."

When the trial resumed the next morning, there was a change in the spectators' attitude toward Lucretia. She had cried when Fanning and Phillips had described her husband's sufferings, a flood of tears coursing down her pale cheeks. This display of emotion, combined with Ross's disappointing performance, had made the crowd in the courtroom suddenly sympathetic to her.

But as Brown knew, the case against his client was still in its early stages. Ross had fifteen more names on his witness list. His first today was Dr. Knight, who was likely to prove a destructive witness for Lucretia because, unlike Dr. Phillips, he didn't think she had been sufficiently attentive to William during his agony. Indeed, "She absented herself," he said disparagingly, "more than I thought right."

Cross-examining him, Brown asked if Lucretia might have been forced to absent herself because she had no cook or housekeeper and thus many chores to perform—a point Dr. Phillips had made. But Knight remarked, "I do not remember her saying she had no servant." And although he'd testified on direct examination that both Lucretia and William had objected to the purgative calomel he'd prescribed, under Brown's needling he turned combative and, contradicting his previous testimony, blamed Lucretia alone. "I do not know," he said, "if Mr. Chapman had any reluctance to take the medicine."

Ross's next witness was Benjamin Boutcher, the poultry farmer, who described how his ducks, after pecking around in the Chapmans' yard on the day Ann Bantom threw out the chicken soup, had died suddenly and grotesquely. "There were between twenty and thirty that died that day and the next," he said.

Brown didn't cross-examine him. It was as if he hoped that by ignoring the man he could convey to the jury how beneath consideration he considered him. Later, however, when Boutcher asked to be recalled to the stand because he had omitted mentioning that the bones of the dead ducks had a strange appearance, Brown couldn't resist mocking him. "For him to describe these bones savors of quackery," he objected, stretching the bow of his lips into a mischievous grin. "Maybe the bones should be produced so they can speak for themselves! No doubt they'll speak with miraculous organs." Brown's objection was overruled and Boutcher told the jury that he'd seen little pieces of something white and glittery, like salts of arsenic, clinging to his poultry's bones.

Lucretia's confidantes—Sarah Palethorpe, who'd warned her it would be unseemly to walk with her boarder at William's funeral; Sophia Hitchbourn, who'd brought her the news that the papers were saying William had been poisoned; and Ann Smith, to whom she'd poured out the whole story of her abrupt second marriage— also took the stand that day, each of them testifying to Lucretia's infatuation with Lino. But the major event of the day was the reading of Lucretia's letters to Lino. Entering them as evidence was a risky business for Ross, since the letters clearly revealed that at least until she wrote the last one, Lucretia was ignorant of Lino's malevolent character. But Ross was banking on the fact that there was one line in her letters that might thoroughly incriminate her. It was the line in which, in her final letter, she declared to Lino that she didn't believe God would permit either of them to be happy on "this side of the grave." To the prosecution, the words were a clear reference to the pair's having committed murder.

Brown, of course, viewed the words differently. They were ambiguous, he thought, and could mean his client expected God's retribution because she and Lino had committed adultery, or even that she expected His punishment because they'd married too soon after William's death. In fact, he mused with a sophist's subtlety, that phrase of hers, that reference to "this side" of the grave, could be construed as indicating that she anticipated worldly suffering for worldly indiscretion, whereas if she'd committed murder, she'd have been anticipating the punishment that awaits the wicked *beyond* the grave. Yes, he decided, that was a good argument, one the jury might well appreciate.

"Several letters were put in evidence today," the journalist from the *Germantown Telegraph* reported to his editor that evening, letters that would one day surely be "sought after with great avidity." But he couldn't provide the paper with any quotes from the material. He and all the other journalists covering the trial had been enjoined from revealing the letters' contents, or indeed any of the evidence against Lucretia, not just until after her case was resolved, but until after Lino's case, too, had been heard.

There was one journalist in the courtroom who was determined not to wait so long before cashing in on the public's curiosity. He was William E. Du Bois, the son of a Doylestown clergyman. Du Bois had studied law, and although he had not yet passed his bar examination, he knew a great deal about legal matters. He also knew that books about sensational murder trials were newly the rage among book publishers.

The first such books—pamphlets, really—had begun appearing in America back in the early 1800s. But there had been precious few of them, and those there were had come packaged as morality tales, the crimes they dealt with fastidiously recounted and accompanied by sermons about the fate that awaited criminals once they met their Maker. By the early 1830s, however, the trickle had swelled to a great river, and the moralistic passages had disappeared. Readers were fascinated by the new crop of unsanitized murder trial books, and novelists and short story writers began capitalizing on the appeal of these works by using the books in their fiction. Hawthorne drew on one murder account for *The House of the Seven Gables,* Melville another for *Israel Potter,* and in time Poe would employ a third for "The Mystery of Marie Roget." What captivated these serious literary men about the new trial books, and indeed what captivated the American public, was that they omitted no detail, however perverse or grisly, in the process illuminating the darker side of human nature.

Du Bois wanted to create a book that would outdo all the others. He would make it a big book, a work, he anticipated, that would be longer and fuller than any similar book since the publication of the trial of Aaron Burr. He *owed* this to the public, he rationalized his sound commercial instinct, and told himself that in view of the excitement the Chapman case was stirring, it would be unfair of him to offer people anything less than a thorough account. One that included *all* the romantic and seamy details.

But could he get it out soon? Before the trial of Mina? And to whom could he turn for publication? Du Bois decided he'd propose the project to the nearby Germantown firm of G. W. Mentz & Son. Mentz made its money chiefly from wholesome works, from textbooks, songbooks, and Bibles. But Georg Mentz was a smart businessman. Du Bois was certain he'd see the wisdom in coming out with an account of the trial of Lucretia Chapman, especially once he heard about what was in those passionate letters that the deputy attorney general had just read aloud and that he, Du Bois, had spent the day laboriously trying to copy down.

On Saturday, February eighteenth, the prosecution began the most complex part of its presentation, the examination of expert witnesses. The experts were crucial, for in order to convict Lucretia of murder, the state needed to show that a murder had actually been committed. Ross, who during the past few months had meticulously boned up on the existing scientific knowledge about poison, was hoping that his experts would be able to establish beyond the shadow of a doubt that William had died of arsenic poisoning, and today, confident of his newly acquired learning, he commenced with Dr. Hopkinson.

The celebrated surgeon, responding to the deputy attorney general's careful questions, told the jury about his graveside autopsy of William. He described how foul-smelling and discolored the corpse's face had been, and yet how astonishingly odorless and well-preserved the body. He described the incisions he had made, and the organs he had removed. And he said that the two things that had most struck him were the absence of putrefaction in the abdomen, and the peculiar, pickled herring–like smell that had emanated from the stomach once it was opened. Both of these signs, he suggested, were indicative of arsenic poisoning, for arsenic was a preservative, a pickler so to speak, and could keep a body from putrefying.

Brown was quick to attack him on both those points. He'd learned from the Reverend Scheetz, whom he was planning to use as a defense witness, that the soil deep down in the graveyard of All Saints was unusually dry and sandy, and that William's coffin had been placed particularly far down. "Might the nature of the soil in which a body is buried affect the body's preservation?" he asked.

"Putrefaction might be retarded by dry soil," Hopkinson was forced to admit.

"And the smell?" Brown went on. "Is this smell typical of something treated with arsenic?"

Hopkinson backed off. "I never heard or read of the herring smell particularly belonging to arsenic," he said.

Brown had won those points, and soon he soldiered on. "What of cholera morbus?" he asked. "If a person died of cholera morbus, might his body have the same appearance as that which you describe?"

Hopkinson allowed that it might. "Though I have never," he insisted on adding, "known a case of cholera morbus to terminate fatally."

Hopkinson was on the stand for three and a half hours. When he was done, Ross's parade of medical experts continued, and Brown continued to try to poke little holes in their testimony. Dr. Coates, Hopkinson's assistant at the autopsy, testified that in his opinion, William had died from *some* corrosive poison, probably arsenic. Under cross-examination Brown got him to say, "No one can be certain that a man died by poison, unless the poison be found in the body." Dr. John Mitchell, the Pennsylvania Hospital chemist who had tried to find the poison, described boiling down bits of William's stomach and intestinal tissue, filtering the residue through paper, treating it with lime, nitric acid, powdered charcoal, and other substances, and comparing the results he obtained to those he'd gotten by performing the same tests on the tissues of a man who'd died a natural death at the poor house. But despite his meticulous research, he'd found no differences, and under Brown's questioning he admitted, "Chemical proofs of the presence of arsenic, though amounting to a strong presumption, were not conclusive of its presence." More, he even allowed that the meal William ate on the night his stomach first began to pain him might have caused his decline. "Smearcase and pork," he said, "eaten at night heartily, if the person be not accustomed to them, would be very sure to hurt him." But Brown had his greatest success with Thomas Clemson, Mitchell's Sorbonne-trained assistant, who testified that after one of their tests, there'd been a definite smell of arsenic in the lab. Under cross-examination, he reluctantly admitted that "Other substances can produce an odor so like that of arsenic that one may be deceived."

* * *

Call your next witness, Judge Fox ordered Thomas Ross the following morning. Then as now, part of a judge's function was to move courtroom proceedings along as snappily as he could, and Fox had been growing increasingly impatient with the prosecution's slow progress. Ross had put on what was for the time an extraordinary number of witnesses—twenty-five of them. Yet still he wasn't finished. He had one more witness, he'd informed the court, namely Willis Blayney, the high constable of Philadelphia. Fox urged him to examine the man as soon as possible.

He wasn't able to do so yet, Ross temporized. But Blayney was on his way. He was due on the next stagecoach from Philadelphia.

Fox was reluctant to wait. Most trials at the time were exceedingly short, many lasting only a few hours; this one had already dragged on for over a week. He warned Ross that he'd best produce Blayney as soon as his coach got to town, for he'd tolerate no further delays.

In his tin-roofed law office down the street from the courthouse, Thomas Ross waited fretfully for the arrival of the coach from Philadelphia, pacing the planked floor of the tiny building and taking frequent pinches from the gold snuff box in which he'd recently invested. But when the coach pulled into town, Blayney wasn't on it. Instead, the driver turned up at Ross's office and handed him a letter. The high constable had a sick child, the letter said. Plus he had official duties. *Urgent* official duties.

Lucretia's old friend Blayney had, it seemed, changed his mind about testifying against the woman he'd once so respected. Or at least he'd changed his mind about testifying against her voluntarily and decided not to come to court unless he was forced to take the stand. Very well, then, Ross resolved. He'd subpoena him. Fine him, too.

He marched back to the courtroom and explained to Judge Fox, "Your Honor, the stagecoach from Philadelphia has arrived. With Mr. Blayney's name on the waybill. But without his person." Then he pleaded for a short delay in the trial.

Fox was in no mood to be obliging. "No further delays!" he expostulated, and demanded that the prosecution close its case and the defense get under way immediately.

At this, Peter McCall stumbled hastily to his feet, for Brown had promised him the honor of opening their presentation. "May it please your Honors, and you Gentlemen of the jury," the untried McCall began humbly. "Personally a stranger to you all, with neither experience nor ability to entitle me to attention, I stand before you in defense of a ruined female, whose character and life and all that is sacred and precious to her, are staked upon the issue of your decision."

Ten

Pennsylvania v. Lucretia Chapman, Part Two

February 22–25, 1832

$\mathcal{B}$ROWN HAD GRANTED THE opening of the defense to his inexperienced junior man. But he himself had devised the defense strategy. His plan was to prove that William Chapman had not been murdered, and that not only had he died a natural death, but the allegedly tainted chicken soup he'd consumed hadn't even contained poison. To this end, Brown had up his sleeve a witness who would surprise and enthrall the courtroom—but he didn't produce her early on. Rather, an expert at timing and drama, he began the actual work of defending Lucretia with a decidedly unshowy offering, a written deposition from a medical expert who stated that it was almost impossible to distinguish death by arsenic poisoning from death by cholera morbus. He followed this with the testimony of another medical expert, one who iterated what Brown had already gotten the prosecution's chemists to say, albeit more reluctantly— namely, that Pennsylvania Hospital's attempts to find arsenic in William's body had been inconclusive. It was enough to put spectators to sleep and make the jury wonder if Philadelphia lawyers, who already had a reputation for shrewdness, were really that much better than their own homegrown attorneys.

But on the second day of the defense case, Brown introduced his surprise witness: Lucretia's middle daughter, ten-year-old little Lucretia. Like other witnesses, she had been sitting in the courtroom all along, which was apparently no bar to her being able to testify. Nor was her age. Children were allowed to give testimony provided they were first examined in the courtroom on their ability to tell the difference between truth and falsity.

When Ross demanded this privilege, Brown offered no objection, and the child, a reed of a girl, with sticklike arms and a chest as flat as a slate, took the stand gravely. She was composed, her big eyes fastened squarely on Ross's long-jawed face as he asked her sternly, "Do you know what you have come here for?"

Little Lucretia didn't answer right away. She thought about the question, then replied, "To swear to all I know."

"Do you know what will become of you if you do not tell the truth?"

This time the girl didn't hesitate. "I will be cast into hell fire forever," she murmured, her voice trembling but her gaze still steady.

Her grasp of the seriousness of the proceedings impressed the judges. They accepted her as a witness despite her youth, and Brown began taking her through the now familiar story of how Lino had arrived at the Chapmans' front door, and subsequently William had arrived at death's door. There was little new in her account, but it was filled with vivid tidbits, the kind of details that give a story the ring of truth. When Lino first appeared, little Lucretia said, "Pa was sitting in the rocking chair, nursing little John." When her father took sick, she was no longer allowed to sleep in the master bedroom in her familiar little "truckle bed."

When her father dined on smearcase and pork, she was in the dining room but no longer at the table; like many a child who finds protracted dinners boring, she'd gotten up and started reading a book.

By the time she came to her version of William's final days, she had fully persuaded the jury of the authenticity of her recollections. It was on the value of those recollections that Brown was counting. So he asked her to describe at length what had happened on the day William lunched on the presumably poisoned chicken soup.

"Mary brought the chicken and soup upstairs," little Lucretia said. "The soup was in a blue quart bowl. The chicken was on a plate, I think. It was whole. Pa cut it himself. Pa tasted the gizzard, but it was tough. He gave the rest to me and I ate it." Then she delivered her thunderbolt. "Pa ate only a few spoonsful of the soup, but he ate very heartily of the chicken. I ate some of the soup myself."

This was a stunning revelation. And although later the prosecution tried to suggest that little Lucretia was telling a story that had been concocted by her mother, the child insisted this was not so. "I have not talked to my mother about this," she averred. "I have told this story to my aunt and lawyer Brown—no one else."

Brown had no further feats of courtroom prestidigitation among his bag of tricks. As is common in criminal defense, he would have to win his case, if win he could, on the basis of cross rather than direct examination, for with the exception of little Lucretia, he had very little to offer other than character witnesses. That afternoon he called on several people who had known Lucretia over the years and examined them swiftly as to her exceptional probity. "Her character was more than moral," said the father of one of her pupils, and she and her family were "very religious." The Reverend George Scheetz supported this. Mrs. Chapman was a regular at his church, he said, and took communion from him frequently; moreover, since the rest of his communicants were prone to reporting to him the follies and foibles of their neighbors, "if anything had happened in the neighborhood calculated to impeach her character, I would have been informed of it."

Indeed, the prideful pastor was so firm a supporter of Lucretia's that when he was cross-examined, he went out of his way to say that he didn't find it at all surprising that spots had appeared on William's face. William, he'd happened to notice a while before the unfortunate man fell sick, had an infection "in the neighborhood of the ear."

The next day Brown cursorily questioned a few more character witnesses and two poulterers whose ducks had died suddenly, one farmer's after eating pickles, the other's after drinking water tainted with lime. Then abruptly, Brown declared the defense case finished. He had examined eighteen witnesses in a day and a half; Ross had taken six and a half days to examine twenty-four.

But now, it developed, Ross wasn't done. Telling the three judges on the bench that he wanted the prosecution case reopened, he announced that he had served a subpoena on Willis Blayney, that Blayney was here in Doylestown right now, and that it was absolutely necessary he be heard because he had evidence that had been alluded to during the prosecution's opening remarks.

The judges would not relent. The prosecution case could not be reopened, they told the deputy attorney general. But if Blayney's evidence contradicted something a defense witness had said, perhaps they would allow him to testify. Ross thanked the judges and offered Blayney as a witness who could rebut the defense's character witnesses.

The spectators grew excited. Philadelphia's high constable was something of a celebrity, a man whose exploits the press wrote about. They anticipated that such a man would provide them with a performance full of fireworks. But Blayney had come to Doylestown reluctantly and was in the courtroom only because he had been fined for his earlier failure to appear. Ignoring the air of expectation that pervaded the pews, he gave Ross what must have been the tersest testimony the prosecutor had ever elicited. "I believe I am acquainted with the general character of Mrs. Chapman," he said. "From 1818 to 1829 I always considered her character good. Since then I have considered it bad—gradually getting worse."

That was all he said, all that Ross could get him to say, other than that he had become a policeman in 1829. Hoping it was enough, Ross announced that he had no further questions.

Brown was stunned. No further questions? He himself had quite a few, and had been wondering if there was any way to turn Ross's cagey witness into a witness for the defense. When the high constable was handed over to him for cross-examination, he asked, "Isn't it true that within this past week you said to someone that you knew absolutely nothing bad about Mrs. Chapman?"

Blayney didn't deny it. "Not in those exact words," he replied. "I have said that if the prosecution expected me to give Mrs. Chapman a bad character, they would be mistaken. That is, to my personal knowledge, I have never seen anything but what was right."

So far, so good. But what *had* he seen, Brown wanted to know. In answer to the question, Blayney said, "She lived in my mother's house and behaved herself remarkably well. My sister taught music in her seminary for several years. I have visited at the home of Mr. and Mrs. Chapman. They lived very happily together—I never heard anything to the contrary."

"What then did you mean about her character being bad?" Brown asked him.

"I am speaking of a police report," Blayney said, and added with a touch of irony, "I can't say I ever heard a good police report."

Brown knew full well that police reports or "characters" of the kind Blayney was referring to were confidential. But he couldn't subdue the gambler's soul that inhabits every defense attorney, and he decided to take the chance of angering the court by asking the high constable to be specific in the matter of Lucretia's report. "By the way," he said, "what exactly did you learn about Mrs. Chapman from her police report?"

"Objection!" Ross called out at once, without explaining the reason for his objection.

"Sustained," Judge Fox ruled. "Though you can," he directed Blayney, "explain in general terms the kinds of things that might give a person a bad police report or 'character.' "

Blayney frowned, then said, "If I were to find stolen goods in a person's house, or if I knew that counterfeiters had been taken in that house, I would say that the owner of the house had a bad police character."

Brown was satisfied. To those inclined to consider Lucretia guilty, the constable's reply would add fuel to their fire by suggesting that she'd once harbored stolen property or counterfeiters in her Philadelphia boardinghouse. But to those who were inclined to be sympathetic, the implication of Blayney's remark might be altogether different. They might wonder why, if the police really had evidence of his client's having had a prior criminal history, the prosecution and not the defense had objected to revealing her police report. They might ask themselves if perhaps the report contained *no* evidence, if perhaps it cited her not as a wrongdoer but merely as the owner of a raided property. Maybe they'd even wonder if there was some secret police report on *them*.

The contents of the mysterious police report would never be revealed. But both prosecution and defense would refer to the high constable's testimony during their summations, and each side would treat the man's words as evidence that bolstered its own arguments.

It was three in the afternoon when those summations started. William Reed, who was to speak first for the prosecution, had been practicing his peroration for days beforehand, writing down phrases, crossing them out, and experimenting with a variety of postures and gestures while regarding himself in a mirror. But in a way, he had been practicing for years. Like most young men of his time, he had studied the art of public speaking back in grade school. Since an educated male was expected to know how to declaim, primers gave boys precise instructions in such things as how much to incline the body or lift the arm when emphasizing a point, and how best to compose the face when trying to convey a mood: to indicate melancholy, advised one textbook, "the lower jaw falls...the eyes are cast down, half-shut"; to indicate pride, "the eyes open, but with the eyebrows considerably drawn down, the mouth pouting out, mostly shut, and the lips pinched close."

Reed was a master of postures and facial expressions, but he was also a budding writer who would one day publish many books and articles on historical subjects. Employing the gestures and moues he had long ago learned, but augmenting his physical performance with writerly phrases, he began to speak, asking the jury "as husbands and fathers, knowing the loveliness of domestic love, appreciating the sanctity of domestic obligation" whether they could conceive of "a more unnatural, a more revolting crime than

that which blasts all these, and blurs the purity of woman's fame."
Then he suggested to them that if Lucretia's crime went unpun-
ished it might teach many other wives "in whose bosom the flame
of impure passion brightens, that there is a summary mode by
which she can remove the only check to licentious indulgence, and
suggest means and materials for the completion of the gloomy edifice of crime." In engineering the death of her husband, he went
on, the defendant had committed a heinous crime. But it was no
surprise, for Lucretia had already committed another heinous
crime. She had committed adultery, and if she was capable of that,
she was capable of murder, too. "In the moral law of God the first
great prohibition was, 'Thou shalt not kill,' the next, 'Thou shalt
not commit adultery'—and the interval between the two points on
the scale of human depravity is small, indeed."

The upright Reed was particularly hard on Lucretia for permit-
ting her children to attend the trial. Her doing so, he lashed out,
demonstrated how cruel and even barbaric she was. Indeed, such
abusive use of the young reminded him of how in famine-wracked
Egypt the starving, convinced that because they were sinful God
would be deaf to their prayers, drafted children to supplicate for
them, leading "little creatures from five to ten years of age" to the
dangerous tops of minarets "to lisp from their slender summits
entreaties for Divine mercy." Lucretia was every bit as manipulative
and cowardly. "The mercy this wretched woman does not dare to
ask, she has brought these innocent children to ask for her." But it
would do the defendant no good, he predicted. The sight of the
youngsters had simply reminded the jury that the children once had
another parent, a father whose death their mother had contrived.

Later, Reed also attacked Brown, accusing him of making sar-
castic faces about prosecution evidence and of intimidating prosecution witnesses with his withering frowns and the "thunder of

that voice, the lightning of *that* eye." But primarily what the prosecution's second seat did was marshal the evidence against Lucretia. Detail by detail, he went over the medical and chemical testimony, limning William's deathbed symptoms to show how closely they matched those known to accompany arsenic poisoning, and insisting that although it was true that the prosecution's chemists had failed to prove there was arsenic in William's tissues, they had established its presence by detecting a unique smell emanating from those tissues, a smell they believed was that of arsenic. He also read from Lucretia's letters—"filled as they are with disgusting effusions of passion"—using them, and the testimony of witnesses, to establish that she had had a twofold motive for killing her husband. She had killed him, Reed maintained, not only because of her licentious passion for Lino, but because she was avaricious and hoped by killing her husband to obtain "the wealth she supposed the seducer to possess...the rank and honors with which she believed him to be clothed."

Finally, Reed presented a scenario to explain why the presumably poisoned chicken soup had been left unattended in the kitchen all day. The entirety of the soup hadn't been poisoned, he contended, merely a portion of it, and it was that portion which little Lucretia had given to William. The child must have misremembered or lied when she said her sister Mary brought their father a quart bowl of the soup. Maybe Mary had brought two bowls—the quart bowl and a small, separate, *poisoned* bowl. Maybe the defense had feared this would come out. They'd put the ten-year-old on the stand. But they hadn't called Mary. "Why is Mary Chapman not produced?" Reed asked insinuatingly, and left the jury to ponder the meaning of his reproach.

It was seven in the evening when he finished speaking. He had talked without stopping for four hours.

* * *

David Paul Brown passed an uncomfortable night. He'd come down with a cold, and his famous throat felt painful and raw. Worse, he was afraid that Reed had made the jury believe in his preposterous two-bowls-of-soup proposition. But he was determined not to let either physical weakness or mental stress stand in the way of his fighting for Lucretia's acquittal. Was not one of the maxims he intended to pass along to his sons this: that although a judge and jury might take away the life of a defendant, they must not be allowed to take it away without reaching over a defense attorney's own body? His *prostrate* body, if need be. Yes, and he'd be damned if he was going to let anyone know how worried he was. That was another of the maxims he was going to pass on to his sons: a defense attorney must know no fear but that of failure, and even that he must hide from everyone. *Everyone.* In this case, that included young Peter McCall, with whom he was sharing quarters.

At dawn Brown dressed himself carefully, donning a costly silk waistcoat and sleek new boots—he'd never known a man to speak well in clumsy boots—awakened the still slumbering McCall, shared a hurried breakfast with him, then leaned on the younger man's arm and walked weakly to the courthouse. But there he straightened up, parted the horde that was milling noisily around the steps, and strode into the spartan courtroom as if he were the great Junius Brutus Booth himself, an actor stepping onto a grand and beautiful stage.

Inside, he let McCall speak first, and was gratified to hear his protégé effectively tackle the prosecution's witnesses and shred its ponderous medical and scientific evidence. The young fellow shows promise, Brown thought, and he's not without humor. As witness his bantering, "One thing that speaks volumes in the defendant's favor is that she managed to live more than twelve months under the same roof with Ellen Shaw!" More, the ambitious acolyte had a definite way with words. Telling the jury about one of the crucial defense positions—namely that Lucretia had not engaged in sexual activity with Mina before her marriage to him— he explained away that unfortunate marriage by coming out with, "Left upon the wide theater of the world, with a family of tender offspring looking to her maternal hand for protection and support, was she not bound by the most sacred ties of duty and affection to embrace every possible means of advancing their interest and promoting their happiness?" But McCall wasn't the orator Brown himself was. If Lucretia was going to be acquitted, it was going to be up to him, David Paul Brown, to find the words to make the jury let her off.

When his turn came, he started out mildly and told the panel he was feeling indisposed. But in a matter of moments his eyes were flashing and his voice was soaring through the austere chamber. Yes, he was sick, he was saying, "however, if fate should decree this speech to be my last, I do not know that my professional or earthly career can be more happily terminated than in the just defense of an oppressed fellow creature—a woman—hapless, helpless, friendless and forlorn."

He was off and running. Lucretia, he told the assembled throng, was a victim. She'd been assailed by "the storm, the tempest, the whirlwind of prejudice...the leprous distillment of pernicious rumor." But the jurors could rectify that wrong and refuse to permit "the sacred ermine of justice to be stained or polluted by the blood of the guiltless." If they didn't, he warned, they'd be condemning not just her but her children, and the time would come when their verdict, "should it affix crime to a mother's name, will enter deeply into the children's souls; the worm that never dies shall prey upon their hearts through life; and the curse that never spares shall stigmatize their memory when dead."

Soon he was telling the jury he had two major reasons for expecting an acquittal: first, because the prosecution had not shown that William had actually been poisoned, and second, because even if William *had* been poisoned, the prosecution had offered no evidence to indicate that Lucretia had any knowledge of the poisoning, let alone that she had participated in it. Dwelling on these arguments, he reminded his listeners of the many exculpatory admissions he had forced from the prosecution's scientists, and waved in the air one of the test tubes that had failed to reveal the presence of arsenic. It was, he said, his "dumb witness . . . small, it is true, but with a giant's strength."

His own strength seemed fully to have returned. He was Ciceronian, clear-headed, forceful. He slammed the prosecution's nonscientific witnesses, calling them vipers and liars. He presented his theory about the supposedly incriminating line in Lucretia's last letter to Lino, insisting that if she'd committed murder she wouldn't have written that she feared God's punishment on this side of the grave but that she feared it on the *other* side, in the world to come. He made light of Reed's two-bowls-of-soup proposition, pointing out that it stood upon no evidence, and mockingly asked why, if the prosecution believed only the soup consumed by Chapman had been poisoned, they had bothered introducing all that "quackery" about poisoned ducks. He justified his client's hiding her second marriage from the police, inquiring, "Was she to join in the general cry, was she to hunt down one to whom, bad as he was, she had plighted her faith? I openly rejoice that she did not, for fidelity is the brightest jewel that adorns the female character." And finally he accounted for Lucretia's flight from Andalusia by saying that any woman in her predicament would have fled. "She was the teacher of a large and highly respectable seminary," he cried out. "Her reputation was her stock in trade; exposure was but another word for death. That she should shrink from it, therefore, was natural—was excusable."

Had he demolished Reed? He hoped so. But in a last effort to get the jury to acquit, he *challenged* them to set her free. It would be an act of bravery, he told the sober-faced family men who faced him, for if they convicted Lucretia, each and every one of them would have to "return to your own domestic circle, to your own firesides, and surrounded by your partners and your offspring... tell them that the popular clamor was too loud and too general to be escaped, the popular prejudice too powerful to be resisted; tell them that under those influences you have consigned a mother to a timeless grave, and her children to endless ruin. And thereby give them to understand how frail and feeble is the tenure of human happiness—human character—and human life."

He was done. He had given one of his best performances. It wasn't just his own opinion. The press thought so, too. He'd been "powerful," a reporter from the *Philadelphia National Gazette* said; he'd fully justified his "fame for energy and eloquence," the man from the *Philadelphia Saturday Bulletin* said.

Thomas Ross's mother, Mary, a deeply religious Episcopalian, was a local heroine, at least among that portion of the Bucks County population that had supported Andrew Jackson for president. When he ran for office, Thomas's father had erected a large hickory pole, Jackson's symbol, in a corner of the family's property, but one night a posse of anti-Jackson men had tried to uproot it. Mrs. Ross had sprung from her bed and, without consulting her husband or sons, rushed out of doors, planted herself at the base of the shaft, thrown her arms around its rough-hewn surface, and told the vandals that if they wanted to remove the pole, they'd first have to remove her. The men had backed off. Opposed to Jackson as they were, they respected Mary Ross, with her passionate loyalties and scrupulous piety, and some had been direct beneficiaries of her kindhearted ways, including her habit of keeping a lamp burning in her window throughout the night to aid anyone who might feel lonely or frightened.

In the courtroom, despite the murmurs of admiration that greeted David Paul Brown when he finished speaking, Mary Ross smiled encouragingly at her son Thomas. She had no doubt he would be every bit as effective.

It was four in the afternoon, and some members of the jury were showing signs of weariness, their faces wan, their eyelids drooping. Thomas, mightily annoyed with Brown, cleared his throat. In his view the defense counselor had overstepped the bounds of courtroom propriety. He had taken a woman of base behavior and turned her into a victim of public prejudice and prosecutorial vengeance. He had turned the most grave and serious subjects, like the scientists' vials and poor Boutcher's dead ducks, into matters for gaiety and merriment. Determined to eschew such cheap tricks, the deputy attorney general glanced at his mother, opened the drawn purse of his lips, and solemnly reminded the panel that "the ground upon which you stand is holy; the moment you passed the threshold of this sanctuary of justice, an impartial administration of your duty required a sacrifice at its altar of every passion or feeling of excitement which you may have heretofore imbibed."

The heads of a few jurors seemed to nod in agreement, and Ross plunged ahead, presenting numerous arguments as to why the jury should deliver a verdict of guilty. Some of his arguments were analytic—like Reed, he dwelled on minuscule aspects of the medical testimony—and some were absurd, at least by modern standards. Among the latter were that Lucretia had been nasty to her husband, and that she had cuckolded him; "any woman who would compel [her husband] to make the bed in which he sleeps" must have, he asserted, "the feelings of a savage or a demon" and "the wife who can defile the marriage bed will have no hesitancy in taking the life of that husband."

He spoke inventively, providing jurors with little scenarios to help them see things as he did. They could discount little Lucretia's evidence, he suggested, because the child had either forgotten just what had happened when her father lay dying, or, already without one parent, she'd lied to protect the other so that she wouldn't be completely orphaned. They could accept the two-bowls-of-soup theory without believing, he assured them, that Boutcher's birds had been poisoned by Chapman's leftovers. No, Mina was so perverse that he could well have tried to amuse himself by tossing arsenic salt directly at the pecking ducks.

He also spoke passionately, implying that he detested the defendant with every fiber of his being. Lucretia Chapman has "gained a niche in the temple of infamy," he pronounced in language almost as flowery as Brown's. "She has inscribed her name upon the darkest page of guilt which the volume of man's crime unfolds. She has become not only the outcast of virtue, of peace, and of fame, but whatever may be your verdict, she will be the shame of her children, and her children's children, in each succeeding generation, until oblivion shall have wiped her name from the scroll of time."

When he was done, he committed the case to the hands of the jury, and begged them to find Lucretia guilty as charged.

His speech had been eloquent, and Mary Ross, listening

proudly to the only one of her eight sons to pursue the profession in which his father had made his mark, may have had at that moment an inkling of the brilliant trajectory that son's career would follow—how one day he would rival his father, the Supreme Court judge, by becoming a member of the United States Congress. But to the reporters in the courtroom, Ross seemed a pale second to Brown. He'd shown "persevering zeal," the man from the *Philadelphia Saturday Bulletin* decided; the man from the *Philadelphia National Gazette* thought he'd been merely "able."

What the jurors thought was not yet clear. They had been treated to two entirely different versions of Lucretia. In the prosecution's, she was not just a murderer but an adulterer, a souless woman whose acts threatened the very fabric of domestic life because they might inspire other lustful wives to emulate them. In the defense's, she was not only *not* a murderer, but not even an adulterer. They consistently maintained that she had not had sexual relations with Lino before their wedding, and that she had married him not to satisfy lust, but to safeguard her fatherless orphaned children.

At war in these two approaches was the very definition of womanhood in the third decade of the nineteenth century. The defense had opted to present Lucretia in the sentimental fashion in which women were generally viewed—as helpless, weak, and perhaps lacking in judgment, but essentially virtuous and asexual. The prosecution had attempted to suggest that female innocence was a myth, or at least that there were some women—women of "masculine intelligence and habits" like Lucretia—who possessed a sexual appetite to rival that of men.

Perhaps the jury was uncomfortable with the latter argument, which was, in its way, as troubling to their world view as Charles

Darwin's theory of evolution would be to their children's generation. Or perhaps they simply could not envision the frumpily
dressed figure they had daily been studying in the courtroom as
being capable of sexual appetite. She was, after all, over forty, a
middle-aged schoolmarm with a brood of children and a jaw that
was softening into jowls. Moreover, as her character witnesses had
testified, she was one of *them,* a churchgoing woman striving to
carve out for herself and her family a respectable living. And, as her
letters had revealed, she was a true American, daughter of a
Revolutionary War hero, an American who'd been bilked, as could
happen to any of *them,* by an outsider, a stranger to their homoge-
neous community. After listening with inscrutable faces to Judge
Fox's charges, they filed from the room, deliberated for just a little
over two hours, and announced they had reached a verdict.

At once the courthouse bell began ringing, its clangor piercing
the silence of the village night. It was nearly midnight. People raced
coatless from homes, taverns, and inns. The courthouse steps
became a perfect pandemonium. But inside the courtroom, where
the jurors were filing back into their seats, there was an ominous
silence.

Judge Fox regarded the jurors somberly and asked how they
found the defendant.

Foreman John Balderson arose, glanced sympathetically at a
shuddering Lucretia, and called out into the stillness, "Not guilty."

Leaving the courtroom that night on the arm of her champion,
David Paul Brown, Lucretia was surrounded by well-wishers. They
congratulated her, embraced her, clutched at the dun-colored skirt
of her traveling suit. She was baffled, for some of those who were
warmest to her had hissed and booed her at the beginning of the

trial. But she accepted their displays of affection and tried to forget the venom with which they had once looked at her.

Brown had arranged a room for her and the children at his inn, and unable to rest, she partied and petted and chattered with them for hours. Toward daybreak the youngsters collapsed into sleep, William Jr. and Mary in beds of their own, Abby Ann, John, and little Lucretia huddling together in hers. She lay down in their midst, little John's head nestling on her chest, the girls' scrawny arms tangling around her waist, and enjoyed the soundest rest she had known in months.

In the morning she took her leave of Brown, and with the children mounted a carriage for the journey home to Andalusia. As they started to move, a stranger's vehicle slipped behind their carriage. Then another's, and another's, until soon there were dozens of carriages following them, sulkies and shays, Abbotts and Dearborns, even market wagons, their horses whinnying, their drivers shouting their gees and giddyups, their passengers calling out Godspeeds and farewells. She sat tall beside the children and rode home at the head of a parade, a triumphal procession.

In his cell, Lino took up his pen. "The Creator who, in his infinite wisdom, foresaw that gold would be the cause of many evils to man," he wrote, "concealed that metal deep in the bowels of the earth, and having covered it with ground and rocks, he strewed upon the surface flowers and fruit, and all that was necessary to the comfort of the human family. But the insatiable avarice of man, impelled him to tear open the earth and snatch the hidden treasure from its deepest and most hidden caverns.

"It was the avarice of William Chapman that occasioned his ruin, as it is more than probable that it was the covetousness of his wife that drove her to murder him. Mrs. Chapman well knew that

Carolino had no mines in Mexico, because this fact had originated with herself... but she knew equally well that his parents were of princely opulence, and that by her arts she would inveigle him to marry her, and would thus enjoy his wealth... and at this stage of the case, we [will] see who was the prime mover of all the horrid circumstances which followed."

Eleven

❧

"Yesterday I Was a Wonder"

April–June 1832

*T*HE PRIME MOVER OF all the horrid circumstances. While
Lucretia tried to resume her former life in Andalusia, Lino,
still awaiting trial, continued his attempt to damage her reputation.
He'd already written a letter to Mary Chapman, with whom he'd
often flirted, begging the teenager to tell the authorities that her
mother had once confessed to him that she and she alone had murdered William. If Mary would do so, he promised the girl, "My
father, my parents, all will reward and favor you and take you away
from your mother and you will be in the bosom of my family as a
daughter." But he hadn't mailed the letter. Instead he'd begun con-
centrating on his memoirs, in the process presenting a Lucretia
who was not just a killer but a con artist every bit as talented and
devious as himself.

He'd known her *before* his visit to Andalusia, he wrote, met her
while traveling by steamboat from New York to Philadelphia.
She'd introduced herself to him under an alias. Miss Wilson, she'd
said her name was—and made a point of telling him she was
unmarried.

He hadn't been all that interested in her. His taste was for younger women. He'd recently seduced one, a beautiful girl from upstate New York, a "flower that would have bloomed in the genial rays of the morning sun of love," but whom he caused to "fall" to his "scorching" attentions. Still, Miss Wilson had found *him* attractive. And no wonder, for he'd been wearing a braid-trimmed coat and finely embroidered silk vest, and precious jewels had bedizened his fingers and chest. Where would he be staying in Philadelphia, Miss Wilson had asked him, and when he'd said he wasn't sure, she'd suggested he stay at the boardinghouse where she was going to lodge. He'd agreed, on the theory that though she was older than the kind of women he liked, he might nevertheless have some fun with her, might "succeed in overcoming her scruples of delicacy."

His theory proved right. "That very evening, Miss Wilson was sacrificed at the shrine of pleasure."

He paid her for her favors. Gave her twelve doubloons, took her out shopping for some new frocks, and, showing her his jewel-filled trunks, presented her with pearl earrings and an emerald-studded bracelet.

But Miss Wilson wasn't grateful for his largesse. After seeing his treasures, she played a cruel trick on him. She sent him, via one of her servants, a gold watch and musical snuff box, and demanded he purchase the items. He didn't want them, but Miss Wilson's servant was incredibly rude, and to get rid of her, he bought the lot for ten dollars, after which the ill-mannered servant promptly disappeared. As soon as she did, however, a corpulent police officer arrived, said the watch and snuff box were stolen goods, and dragged Carolino off to jail. Miss Wilson had clearly planned the whole thing, and while he was in prison, she gained access to his room and made off with his trunks.

He'd discovered this despicable act of his inamorata's when, freed from jail, he'd gone back to the boardinghouse to get his possessions. The previous landlady was gone, but the new proprietor told him who had taken his things. She was, said the proprietor, a woman named "not Miss Wilson, but Mrs. Lucretia Chapman" who lived "at a place called Andalusia about thirteen miles from Philadelphia." So he set out for that place, and find the thief he did. He spotted a house with a sign that said "Chapman," entered it, and discovered, seated in the dining room, "the very woman of whom he was in search."

This story provides a far more plausible explanation of why Lino turned up in Andalusia than does the one the prosecution presented at Lucretia's trial. But it is a difficult story to credit, since Lino told different versions of it on different occasions. When he sought release from the Eastern State Penitentiary, he told prison inspectors that the objects he was accused of stealing had been given to him by "another person of my own age" and made no mention of a mysterious woman's having planted them in his room. When he was apprehended for William's murder, he said nothing about Lucretia's having stolen anything from him, or even that he'd known her before coming to Andalusia; he also, at that time, claimed to have stopped in Andalusia purely by accident. While awaiting his murder trial, he told a journalist that he *had* known Lucretia before he was jailed for theft, that she'd been his sex partner and stolen his treasures, and that when he was released he'd set out to find her. But he also told the journalist that no one directed him to Andalusia, that he stopped there serendipitously, and that only once there did he recognize—to his great surprise— that the lady of a certain house had been his "*chère amie*" in Philadelphia."

It was as if he couldn't stop inventing and reinventing the story of his life.

* * *

On April twenty-fourth, a day on which a local newspaper reported the hanging of a Lancaster, Pennsylvania, man before fifteen thousand witnesses, Lino's case was at last brought to trial. He entered the courthouse nonchalantly that day, chatted confidently with his defense attorneys, and as soon as he was placed at the bar began picking his teeth, as if oblivious to his setting or its perils.

Once again Judge John Fox was presiding and Thomas Ross and William Reed were prosecuting. But this time something was different. When Reed led off the trial's preliminaries by inquiring whether the prosecution could ask prospective jurors if they had conscientious scruples against finding a verdict of guilt, Judge Fox unexpectedly said, "Yes. It is a proper question and I will allow it to be asked."

As soon as he'd spoken, young Samuel Rush, Eleazar McDowell's apprentice, called out, "Am I to understand your Honor to say that you have decided contrary to the opinion you gave in the former trial?"

"Yes, contrary to my own opinion." He had changed his mind, Judge Fox explained, after discussing his previous decision with several other judges and with the chief justice.

Rush and McDowell were dismayed. They hadn't, after all, asked for a jury of foreigners. But they'd been hoping for compassionate Americans, for the kind of jurors who, perhaps secretly harboring an antipathy toward taking the life of a fellow human being, might be counted upon to be automatic allies during deliberations. They tried to explain this to Lino, who with his limited English had been listening uncomprehendingly to the discussion. For a moment his face fell and he looked forlorn. But immediately afterward he recovered himself and glanced about him with an air of machismo.

The indictment was read. Jurors were selected—among them seven Quakers who did not abhor capital punishment. The prosecution delivered its opening remarks, promising to prove that "The death of Mr. Chapman was caused by a most deadly poison that the day before he was taken ill the individual at the bar purchased in Philadelphia." Yet still, Lino's nonchalance didn't fade— perhaps because he knew that at Lucretia's trial Ross had been unable to establish that poison was the cause of William's death. But Lino was in far more jeopardy than Lucretia had been. For one thing, the state's ability to tie him to the purchase of the deadly poison was potentially of greater significance to the jurors than was its inability to explain exactly how William had died. For another, unlike Lucretia, Lino was an outsider, an alien to the community.

Thomas Ross, who'd been bested by David Paul Brown despite all his hard work, his ambitions, and his dreams of glory, didn't intend to lose again. Not this time. He'd tightened his case, located witnesses who could add to the devastating evidence of Lino's having purchased arsenic by testifying to the fact that he'd lied in order to get it, that although he'd said he needed arsenic to preserve birds, he actually had no birds. Ross was ready with two such witnesses, acquaintances of Lino's, and with the whole cast that had testified at Lucretia's trial, including the medical men who had tended William while he was dying, those who had autopsied his body, and those who had searched for traces of arsenic in his tissues.

On the second day of the trial, he began producing his witnesses, and when he had examined them all, he capped his show with Willis Blayney. This time around he'd gotten Philadelphia's high constable to come to court voluntarily. And this time around Blayney was talkative. He described at length how he'd taken Lino into custody in Boston, how he'd escorted him by steamboat to

Philadelphia, and how he'd promised Lino that if he owned up to whether he'd ever been a pirate or a convict, Blayney wouldn't divulge in a court of law anything else he might reveal. But after saying all this, Blayney suddenly clammed up. He didn't want to break his word to the prisoner, he explained, and begged the court not to force him to report what Lino had said to him once he'd claimed never to have been a pirate or convict.

Judge Fox listened to him respectfully and said understandingly, "Any declaration a man makes that is drawn from him by the offer of favor or by threats cannot be given in evidence. But the question is, did you actually promise the defendant favor?"

Before Blayney could reply, all four attorneys rushed to give their opinions on the matter. Blayney *had* promised Lino favorable treatment in return for a confession, argued the defense counselors. "The defendant's confession cannot be given in evidence."

Blayney *hadn't* promised Lino favorable treatment, argued the prosecution lawyers, and in addition they made the point that what Lino had told their witness wasn't a confession. "It is a statement made by Mina with a view of shielding himself. There was no admission of his having participated in the murder."

After listening to the outbursts from both sides Fox asked Blayney to repeat exactly what he'd said to Lino. Blayney described once again how on the steamboat Lino had kept trying to talk to him and how finally in order to silence the prisoner he'd asked him to answer his two questions and promised that anything else he said would be kept private.

"That was not a promise of favorable treatment," Fox admonished Blayney. "You *must* tell us what he said."

The high constable accepted the judge's directive. He had no choice but to do so. "I asked Mina whether he had a medicine chest," he began. "He said he had, and had left it in the Boston jail.

I asked him whether he had arsenic in it. He said he had medicine or stuff in it that would kill people and kill rats. I asked him whether he gave any of the medicine to Chapman. He said no, he was innocent. He said Mrs. Chapman put the physic in the soup. He said, 'She take it from my bottles.' He said that afterwards, 'Mr. Chapman get very bad and die. Mrs. Chapman then come and kiss and hug me and say, 'Lino, I want you to marry me.' "

The story Blayney had managed to withhold at Lucretia's trial was now out—for whatever it was worth.

Lino's defense was a sorry affair. Rush was a very junior man—he had not yet even been admitted to the bar—and McDowell himself, court-appointed and not receiving his usual high fees, chose not to expend much energy on the case. The pair's cross-examination of prosecution witnesses was so perfunctory that the prosecution was able to get through all of its witnesses—there were twenty-three of them, almost as many as at Lucretia's trial—in a mere two days. Their presentation of their own case was even more swift. They produced no witnesses at all, contenting themselves with only two things: the verdict of acquittal in Lucretia's trial, and a deposition from a medical expert stating that it was difficult to differentiate death caused by cholera morbus from death caused by arsenic poisoning. Worse, despite his reputation for being a shrewd as well as likable attorney, McDowell did not deliver an effective closing argument. At least, whatever he said made little impression on the reporter from the *Saturday Bulletin,* who termed prosecutor Reed's summation "clear" and "powerful," but said nothing at all of McDowell's closing remarks except to note that he had made some.

Nor did McDowell's closing make much of an impression on William Du Bois, the law student turned true crime writer. He copied none of it down. But then Du Bois, who had been enjoined from publishing anything about the Chapman case until Lino's trial was over, seemed to have grown bored with the entire subject of William Chapman's murder. He didn't jot down *any* of the summations. Lucretia's trial had struck the writer as being of "exciting interest," and he had copied out virtually every word of it. But Lucretia was a woman of the same class as Du Bois and presumably of the same class as his readers. Lino was a lower-class foreigner. All that interested Du Bois about this second trial were the various legal arguments. And all he wanted, all that stood between him and financial fortune, was the verdict.

He got it soon enough. At nine o'clock on the evening of April twenty-seventh, only three days after the trial had begun, Judge Fox sent the jury out to deliberate, with instructions that they were to receive no dinner until they reached a verdict.

Despite their hunger, they stayed out a respectable period of time—nearly three hours. Then, at midnight, they pronounced Lino guilty of murder in the first degree.

"Take the prisoner back for the night," Judge Fox ordered the high sheriff. "Return him tomorrow for sentencing."

Lino was flippant. His neck was ready for the rope, he told reporters.

The next day, Saturday, April twenty-eighth, Fanny Trollope's *Domestic Manners of the Americans* was published. Among the many anecdotes recounted by the feisty Englishwoman, who had organized theatricals in Cincinnati before turning to writing, was one about two Pennsylvania criminals, one an American, the other an Irish immigrant. They'd jointly committed a robbery, and they'd each been sentenced to death, but, Trollope reported, "the Irishman was hanged and the American was not." Worse, she wrote, she'd heard but not yet been able to verify that such injustice was common in America, where ever since the Declaration of Independence nearly all the white men who'd been executed in the country were immigrants.

Whether Trollope's statistic was right or not, Lino was, on that Saturday, in grave danger of death by hanging—the requisite sentence for his crime—and to prevent that unfortunate outcome, his lawyers finally roused themselves to make a last-ditch effort on his behalf. There was as yet no legislation granting automatic judicial review to defendants convicted of capital crimes. But the common law allowed them to seek a new trial, provided it could be shown that at their original trial, improper evidence had been admitted. McDowell and Rush, convinced that Willis Blayney's evidence should not have been admitted, asked Judge Fox for permission to file an application for a new trial.

Fox gave them less than the customary four days. He'd expect their application, and their oral arguments, too, he said, at court's opening on Tuesday.

Over the weekend the two defense attorneys consulted the law books in McDowell's Doylestown office and began writing down precedents and salient points. In jail, Lino, who had lost faith in McDowell and Rush, also began writing. This time it wasn't another anecdote for his memoirs but a letter to the court asking for a few more months of life than the judges might be inclined to give him. "My name is Carolino," he wrote. "I was baptized in the Roman Catholic Church, and desire to die in its faith. I pray that a priest of that religion may be sent to me that I may prepare myself for death by confession and the blessed absolution, and by partaking of the holy communion according to the rites and ceremonies of that church.

"I have written to my father and brother, and expect they will come to this country to see me, and I have in the island of Cuba, a daughter four years old. It is necessary before I die, that I should execute some legal papers, in order to secure some property to my daughter. I therefore pray the Court to grant me at least a few months of existence, before I am ordered to be executed."

The letter was in English. He would ask to have it read to the judges, he decided, if McDowell and Rush proved themselves as inept at getting him a second trial as they'd been at handling his first.

"Is it necessary for the prisoner to be here as we present arguments as to why he should have a new trial?" Samuel Rush asked Judge Fox first thing on Tuesday morning.

"There is no such necessity," Fox replied, "if you are willing to argue the motion in his absence."

They were willing, Rush said, and began the petitioning. "The High Constable made a compact with the prisoner," he argued. "It *was* a promise of favor. It amounted to an offer of immunity from prosecution." To bolster his position, he cited two Pennsylvania cases in which judges had ruled differently from Fox about allowing similar police testimony.

At this, Thomas Ross demanded to be heard. But Judge Fox, gesturing him to silence, said it wasn't necessary for him to speak. "We have not changed our opinion since the trial," he declared. "We do not think that the statement or confession made by the prisoner to Blayney was obtained under any promise of favor whatever. It was at most a promise to keep secret a confession which Mina wished to make." A promise, he added, that had been made to the prisoner "upon the condition that his declaration that he was neither a convict nor a pirate should turn out to be true."

That said, Fox concluded imperiously, "We still think we were right, and therefore the motion for a new trial is refused."

Ross leaped to his feet. "I move the prisoner be brought up for sentencing!"

"Motion granted."

From the judge's tone it was clear that Lino's sentencing was inevitable, and in a matter of moments the prisoner was led into the courtroom. Briefly, he spoke to his lawyers, handed them the letter he had written, then took his place in the dock.

"Mr. Espos y Mina," Judge Fox demanded, casting a grim look at him, "do you have anything to say as to why the sentence of death should not be passed on you?" Lino was silent and from down in the well of the courtroom, McDowell answered for him. "The prisoner has drawn up a paper. We think it best if we read his words."

"Permission granted."

"My name is Carolino," McDowell began to read. "I was baptized in the Roman Catholic Church."

Fox leaned back, his expression inscrutable, and McDowell read on. "I have in the island of Cuba, a daughter four years old."

Judge Fox was a stern man, but he had no fondness for sending another man to his death, especially the father of a four-year-old. He started to look agitated.

"It is necessary before I die," McDowell continued, "that I should execute some legal papers, in order to secure some property to my daughter."

In the pews, spectators were weeping. Lino, with his taut words, had become for them not the embodiment of evil but a man. A parent. It was a shift in attitude that would soon have serious repercussions for Lucretia.

"I pray the Court to grant me at least a few months of existence," McDowell finished, "a few months before I am ordered to be executed."

When the lawyer sat down, Fox was silent for a moment. Then he began to speak, but his usually ready words came out slowly and with a difficulty that was noticed throughout the courtroom. "These matters will be laid," he said. "Before the Governor. Who will no doubt. Grant the request which you make."

Lino tipped his head in acknowledgment.

Fox was still visibly distressed. But he managed to continue speaking, to say as boldly as he could what it was now required of him to say: "Lino Amalia Espos y Mina, the sentence which the law imposes upon you is that you be taken hence to the prison of Bucks County, from whence you came, and from thence to the place of execution, and that you there be hanged by the neck until you are dead. And may God have mercy upon your soul."

"Back out! Back out at once," a voice from within Lucretia's house shouted at a peddler making his way up to the porch a few weeks after Lino was sentenced. The peddler was carrying copies of Du Bois's book, *The Trial of Lucretia Chapman,* which had just been published. The book, some copies of which included a brief supplement on Lino's trial, had become an instant success. Philadelphia's bookstores were selling scores of the volume each day, and vendors were lugging it door-to-door all over Bucks County. This peddler, however, had come to the wrong door. Within moments unseen assailants—they were probably Lucretia's children—began hissing and hooting at him, and he was forced to scamper away as quickly as the weight of his heavy sack allowed.

The effrontery of the peddler was only one of the humiliations Lucretia began to endure once Lino was sentenced. In part her difficulties arose from the very fact of that sentencing: now that Lino was facing death, people were feeling sorry for him, speaking up for him. In part her difficulties arose from the public's gullibility.

Du Bois's book had given wide circulation to Blayney's report that Lino had claimed to him that Lucretia, not he, had poisoned William's soup. Since making that claim, Lino had told variations of it to journalists who sought him out. The journalists hadn't printed his stories; they'd been under judges' orders not to write about the case until it was resolved. Now, however, they'd begun publishing information they'd gotten from Lino, including one story in which he had Lucretia poisoning not William's soup but his dinner wine. She did it, he asserted, by first humiliating her husband, directing him to touch her lover's curly head and feel how soft his hair was, and only then, when William's attention was diverted by this small bit of wifely cruelty, delivering the coup de grâce and slipping arsenic into his glass.

One might have expected people to read such accounts with a certain skepticism. Lino's history of fabricating stories—his lies to the Chapmans, his lies in Washington, his lies in New England— had emerged at both of the trials. But print has an almost magical effect on credulity, a phenomenon that was well known to Lino, who had used print to remarkable effect when setting up scams. Now, as his new accusations against Lucretia began to be printed, many who had championed her after her acquittal began turning against her. Neighbors stopped inviting her to social events. Local children declined to play with her children. Parents refused to send their offspring to her school. And one bright spring morning she found that she could not even travel at will anymore.

She'd wanted to take her children into Philadelphia for the day, and she'd waited with them on the turnpike for the stagecoach to Philadelphia. But when the coach arrived and they began to clamber aboard, the driver shot her an ugly look. Then he told her and the children to step down. He would not, he said, allow the likes of them onto his vehicle.

Hurriedly she hustled the children over to the steamboat dock. But there, too, they were turned away.

We'll hitchhike, she decided, and she and the children set off on foot toward Philadelphia. But although several times she signaled to passing vehicles that she needed a ride, and several times drivers began reining to a stop, when they pulled up and recognized her they whipped their horses and sped rapidly ahead.

She and the children, fatigued after a few miles, returned home to Andalusia.

In Doylestown, Lino was basking in celebrity. An artist from Philadelphia came to sketch his portrait for an engraving and a marble bust. Reporters interviewed him constantly. They described his cell, noting that it was airy and comfortable and contained a writing table on which a letter to a man the prisoner claimed was his father, one Bridgadier General Esposimina in Cuba, was prominently displayed. They also filed numerous and erroneous stories about Lino's origins: "He is a native of Cuba, where his connections are respectable," said the *Philadelphia Saturday Courier;* "He is the *illegitimate* son of a very rich gentleman of Cuba," said the *Philadelphia Saturday Bulletin.*

Lino was indignant about the *Saturday Bulletin*'s story. He had been slandered, he complained to a reporter from the *Germantown Telegraph;* he was many things, but he was not illegitimate, not, he said, an "unnatural" child. Still, all in all, he was pleased by the attention he was receiving, particularly when a distinguished publisher expressed interest in obtaining his memoirs.

The publisher was Robert DeSilver, who had started a bookbinding and bookselling company back during the War of 1812. Since then he'd gone from merely binding and selling the books of other publishers to acquiring and publishing titles of his own. In

1818 he'd acquired the rights to Captain James Cook's exciting narrative of his voyage to the Pacific. In 1819 he'd bought the memoirs of the Revolutionary War general Nathaniel Greene. In 1824 and 1831 he'd brought out profitable Philadelphia city directories.

DeSilver told Lino that the fact that his manuscript was written in Spanish presented no problem for him. He would see to it that the work was rendered into English by a skillful translator.

Lino gave him the rights to his manuscript, and eventually DeSilver would indeed get it translated—and would publish it, under the title *The Life and Confession of Carolino Estradas de Mina,* along with a translator's note explaining that useless tautology and repetitions had been expunged and numerous indecent passages eliminated in order to make the narrative inoffensive to "the most delicate ear, to make it more more acceptable to the female portion of the community." In the meantime, Lino kept working. Months before when Lucretia's youngest son had offended him, he'd frightened the boy by telling him that he *never* forgave injuries and that he delighted in revenge. Now it was Lucretia, walking free while he awaited hanging, upon whom he hoped to wreak vengeance.

In pursuit of that goal he added to his portrait of her as a con artist details that limned her as so unsavory and cruel that after she inveigled him into marriage he decided to punish her by acting "as freely as it pleased him in her presence, and when her punishment would be sufficient to abandon her and return to Cuba."

Part of the punishment he devised was to seduce her daughter Mary. He and the girl kept their relationship hidden, but eventually Lucretia caught wind of it and in his absence beat Mary barbarously. "Her body [was] lacerated and torn over its whole surface by the blows of her mother." That a mother could so abuse her child caused Carolino, upon his return, to be "suddenly struck

by the thought that Mrs. Chapman had murdered her husband."
So he pointed a knife at her throat and demanded she confess,
which she did, in the process telling him just how she'd gone
about the murder: she had "purchased [a] phial of poison from a
doctor in the vicinity and had given him one hundred dollars for it,
and a promise of secrecy on his part as to his having sold it."

DeSilver didn't bring out Lino's memoir until after its author
died. But prior to his death Lino showed parts of his manuscript to
the *Germantown Telegraph*'s reporter, who had taken to visiting
him frequently, and on June sixth the *Telegraph* printed a story saying the paper had learned from an "official" source that "Mrs.
Chapman called upon a physician in the city a short time previous
to the illness of her husband and desired his advice as to the effect
of arsenic. She wished to know the quantity which was administered in cases of sickness and the smallest quantity which could
possibly produce death. She enquired fully and particularly as to
the general properties of arsenic; and, as we understand, gave the
Physician a fee for the information which she obtained."

The story went on to imply that the attorney general's office
might soon be charging the unnamed physician with having been
an accessory before the fact.

No such charges were ever leveled. But this didn't prevent
Lucretia's neighbors from believing what they'd read, and by mid-
June she'd realized that it might be wise for her and the children to
leave Andalusia.

Virtually penniless now that she no longer had students, she
thought first of going back to her ancestral home. Her father, the
old Revolutionary War colonel, had died, but her mother was still
alive, and although strapped for money, she had offered to take in
Lucretia and the children, provided they could pay their own way
up to Massachusetts. In pursuit of an inexpensive way of getting

there, Lucretia asked one of the few neighbors who still had some pity for her to drive her into Philadelphia and once there solicited help from the captain of a packet boat that sailed to New England frequently.

"My children and I have suffered unparalleled affliction," she told the captain. "If you would convey us on more moderate terms than the usual ones, it would be an act of holy charity."

The man seemed sympathic at first. "What's your name?" he asked.

"Lucretia Chapman."

"*Mrs.* Chapman?" Suddenly the captain's expression turned ugly, and, throwing up his hands as if to make her keep her distance, he told her to clear out. "All the wealth in the world would not induce me to take you aboard!" he said. Then, as if she didn't know, he added, "The way of the transgressor is hard."

Execution followed hard on the heels of conviction in the 1830s, and despite Lino's plea for a few extra months of life, George Wolf, the governor of Pennsylvania, had not granted a delay but issued a warrant for prompt execution. Benjamin Morris gave Lino the disappointing news, and showed him the ornate calligraphed document that specified he be hanged on June twenty-first.

Lino took the news calmly. "The governor writes a very good hand," he said indifferently.

He wasn't always so calm, Morris had noticed. Indeed, often when night came, Lino talked to himself in Spanish for hours on end, sometimes whispering in a supplicating tone, sometimes shouting manically. One night he'd asked Morris to come into his cell and see the Devil. Morris had gone in to investigate, but spotted nothing out of the ordinary. "In what shape," he'd humored Lino, "does the Evil One appear?"

"In the shape of that cricket," Lino replied, pointing to a cricket hovering in a corner of the cell. The cricket was the Devil, he asserted, the Devil himself.

A moment later he began talking to the cricket. He told it to sing, he ordered it to keep still, he cursed it, he praised it, and finally, when the insect started to leap away, he said, "Be sure to call and see me again." He said this so courteously that it seemed to Morris that he truly believed the poor creature was some higher order of being.

Another time he asked Morris to send for his lawyer because he had something of the greatest importance to convey to the man. Morris dispatched a messenger to McDowell's office, the lawyer hurried over to the jail, and Morris took him into Lino's cell. Then suddenly Lino flung a piece of paper at McDowell and demanded that Morris lock up the lawyer. It was an arrest warrant, Morris discovered when he'd safely gotten McDowell out of the cell. Lino had somehow managed to get his hands on a blank copy of the embossed court document, and he'd forged a judge's signature on it.

The man's always up to something, Morris told the reporter from the *Germantown Telegraph* after the incident. He's especially fond of taunting clergymen. Men of the cloth come to give him solace regularly. They aren't all Catholics like he is. Some are Baptists, some Episcopalians. Lino listens to them politely when they're in his cell, but as soon as they leave he makes obscene gestures behind their backs.

"My dear Thomas," the kindly Mary Ross wrote to her son one day while Lino was awaiting his execution. "I saw the death warrant . . . you have performed a duty, I think with honor to yourself. No doubt you feel satisfaction in acquitting yourself so well, and very justly, and every man ought to feel pleased when he can reflect that he has done with credit what was entrusted to his care. That past, how much more agreeable would it be to relieve suffering humanity. That pleasure will remain when many others have vanished." Then she begged Thomas, for the good of his own soul, to go to see Lino, "a stranger in a strange land, not a friend to sympathize, pity or console him." If Thomas obeyed, if he went to the prisoner and showed him some compassion, "It might happily give him more consolation than others [could], and you would be forgiven, and if you should give one ray of comfort to so miserable a stranger who must soon meet his horrid, dreadful, awful doom, believe me it will not only be lasting but stronger than any other pleasure."

On June sixteenth, five days before the date on which Lino was scheduled to be executed, Ross decided to honor his mother's wishes and demonstrate compassion for the condemned man by paying him a call. He greeted Lino, who was still secured by the two-foot-long chain he had had to wear ever since his jailbreak, and politely but stiffly said he was sorry that he would soon be facing death, but that it was the law of the land that murderers be executed.

"But I am entirely innocent of Mr. Chapman's murder," Lino interrupted. "I am innocent of everything except a love of mischief."

He sounded so sincere that Ross was taken aback. Had he in fact convicted an innocent man?

"I am not even really married to Mrs. Chapman," Lino went on. "I just pretended to marry her. I tricked her. In order to get her money."

Ross studied the candid expression on the face of the man whose death would be on his hands, no matter who pulled the rope at the hanging, and suddenly it seemed possible to him that the prisoner was telling the truth. Possible, too, that unless he investigated his story, he, too, might be a condemned man, sentenced to a lifetime of doubt and an afterlife of anguish. He told Lino that he was inclined to believe him, or at least that he believed him enough to ask the governor to suspend the execution while he looked into his allegation.

Lino thanked the deputy attorney general effusively, and Ross left his cell feeling almost as pleased as the prisoner. He had, just as his mother had advised, offered the unhappy man a ray of comfort, and that ray had curiously comforted him as well.

He went immediately to the slant-topped desk in his little law office and penned a letter to Governor Wolf, requesting a stay of execution. Then he leafed through the papers he had put into evidence in the trials of Lino and Lucretia. His letters to her. Her letters to him. Their marriage license. Picking up the license, he began to examine it more closely. "I hereby certify," he read, "that on this fifth day of July, in the year of our Lord one thousand eight hundred and thirty-one, Lino Amalia Esposimina and Lucretia Chapman were by me united in holy matrimony agreeably to the form prescribed by the Protestant Episcopal Church of the United States of America." The words seemed authentic enough. So did the signature at the bottom: "Benjamin Onderdonk, Bishop of the Protestant Episcopal Church in the State of New York." But perhaps the document was a forgery. Perhaps, as Lino had just said, he hadn't actually married Lucretia. If he hadn't, then perhaps he'd even been telling the truth when he said he wasn't guilty of Chapman's murder. Ross wanted to know. Needed to know. For the good of his soul.

Abruptly, he placed the license in a carrying case, hitched up his carriage, and set off for Philadelphia. He knew of a man named Onderdonk, a brother of the New York bishop, who was living there. He'd pay a call on Mr. Onderdonk and see if the fellow could identify the handwriting.

When he reached the city, Ross pulled up first at the office of the recorder, Judge McIlvaine, having realized it would be wise to have the judge along when he questioned Onderdonk. He explained his mission to McIlvaine, helped him into his carriage, and knowing that if Lino was to be reprieved, he had precious little time, drove hastily to Onderdonk's home.

Once there, the two officials introduced themselves breathlessly and spoke almost simultaneously, directing Onderdonk to look at the marriage certificate they had brought with them and tell them if he recognized the handwriting.

Onderdonk studied the license. Then, without hesitation, he said that the handwriting on the document was his brother's.

Was he sure, the two men asked him.

Onderdonk nodded. "The signature is genuine."

Ross and McIlvaine talked to him a few more minutes, long enough to find out that his brother had told him that he had officiated at the marriage of Lino and Lucretia. "He mentioned it to me several times," Onderdonk said.

Ross's misgivings were satisfied. He put the certificate back in his case, dropped McIlvaine back at his office, and in the evening dusk headed straight for Doylestown. He no longer felt the least bit troubled. Indeed, he felt foolish, as if Lino had conned him, tricked him just the way he'd tricked the people who'd lent him money in Washington, the sheriff who'd vouched for him up on Cape Cod, the Brewster woman who'd followed him to Boston expecting to be his bride. As soon as he was back in his office he fired off another letter to the governor, this time retracting his first note and saying he no longer wanted Lino's execution postponed.

That done, he walked the few yards that separated his office from the jail and once again asked to be let into Lino's cell.

Sheriff Morris complied, deferentially unlocking the heavy door. It was dim in the cell now. A tiny window framed a sliver of ebony sky, and a small oil lamp cast more shadows than light. Ross faced Lino angrily, determined to tell him he was a liar. But before he could speak Lino asked Ross—demanded of him, Morris would later tell the reporter from the *Germantown Telegraph*— "Have you done anything for me?"

"No," Ross answered coldly.

Lino flew off the handle. "You are a contemptible miscreant!" he shouted. Then, scurrying forward to the full extent of his chain, he thrust out an arm and socked the deputy attorney general. Slammed his first right into the prosecutor's long square jaw.

Ross, rubbing his face, stumbled out of the cell, his jaw aching but his conscience no longer paining him at all.

Lino spent the next few days writing poetry. He had finished his memoirs, but the creative spirit that had fueled them was still coursing through his brain. He composed a melancholy ballad about his oncoming death—"Flowers! Learn from me," he wrote, "What happens between yesterday and today. Yesterday I was a wonder. And today am not the shadow of myself." The world would miss him, he went on. Dumb creatures like the fish in the sea, the birds in the trees, even "the sorrowful whale...in the bottomless waves" would be saddened, while America's youth, its "nobility," and "the ladies of Pennsylvania" would weep.

The grandiosity of his sentiments was stirred by the commotion taking place outside the jail. The ordinarily quiet streets of

Doylestown were resounding with martial music, the tooting of fifers, the pounding of drummers. Lino could hear them practicing for the execution. For *his* execution.

He wrote a sonnet, a farewell to love. He was, he wrote, like the great god Jupiter who'd been willing to don human form to woo his beloved, like the hero Orpheus who'd been willing to descend to the underworld in pursuit of his. Like them, he longed to demonstrate his "sincere love."

The object of his testimonial was a woman in Baltimore. Just as Lucretia had long ago suspected, he *had* fallen in love there. He'd had an affair with the woman, an attractive young widow, and promised to marry her, then gone off on his travels. Now he was sorry, he wrote, for he had truly cared for her and yet "robbed her of the inmost jewel of her soul." But she would come to know that his last thoughts had been of her. He would ask DeSilver to include with his memoirs his "*Soneto*," composed "for the young lady at Baltimore."

Lino's moods swung drastically in his final hours. The day before the execution he twice attempted to kill himself. The first time he smashed his ink bottle, pounded the glass until it was powdery, then sprinkled the finely ground shards over his food. The second time he extricated a nail from a piece of his cell's wooden furnishings, sharpened it on the irregular stone walls, and plunged the point into a vein in his arm. Neither attempt proved fatal, however, and by nighttime, with a jailer stationed right in his cell so that he couldn't cheat the state of Pennsylvania out of doing away with him, he was claiming that he had not actually intended to commit suicide but simply to weaken himself in the hopes that this would make hanging easier to endure.

Doylestown was aswarm with military men, foot soldiers and

cavalrymen decked out in their blue tunics and stiff-brimmed varnished hats. Lino had gossiped that he was such an important citizen in his home country that his government would be sending an armed force to rescue him. The rumor had spread widely and wildly, and Governor Wolf had ordered up for execution day the largest body of uniformed men Bucks County had seen since the Revolution.

The town was also overrun by ordinary citizens. Lino's hanging was to be the county's first since 1693, and all day the prurient, as well as peddlers, promoters, and pickpockets, had been flooding into the county seat. They'd filled the six hotels, jammed the inns and boardinghouses, imposed on friends and distant relatives, and even persuaded reluctant farmers to rent them sleeping space in their sheds and barns. Nevertheless, there weren't enough quarters to go around, and visitors who'd been unable to find any sort of indoor accommodations were camped out on the winding streets, so many of them that the little town resembled, said the *Germantown Telegraph*'s reporter, Philadelphia on the Fourth of July.

The reporter had, like everyone else, come to town to witness the execution. But he was hoping to get an interview with Lino on this inauspicious night. By ten o'clock he had succeeded in arranging one, and Sheriff Morris let him into Lino's cell.

The prisoner looked unusually pale, the reporter thought when he saw Lino. But aside from his pallor, he seemed well enough, seemed, in fact, quite cheerful and animated. He asked the reporter how *he* was feeling, and talked gaily and even proudly about the troops and military bands that were turning the town into a veritable battlefield, with him as the sole enemy.

"I myself used to be a soldier," he bragged. "And I gloried in the profession. I was in active service for five months in succession, fought almost every day, received several severe bullet wounds! One in particular nearly proved fatal."

The *Telegraph*'s man spent an hour with Lino, then went to his inn and wrote, "My own reflections after the interview were by no means pleasant or agreeable. [The prisoner's] total unconcern about his end, now so near at hand, seems more than extraordinary, and his levity in speaking of his death not less. A similar instance, I believe, can scarcely be found on record."

Lino stayed up the whole night, nibbling on cakes and candy, and in the morning ate a big breakfast. Then he put on his still-chic frock coat and a pair of striped pants and spoke at length with a bilingual Catholic priest named Father Tuljeaux, who had come to hear his confession.

"I am innocent of murder," he told Tuljeaux. "But I am penitent and ready to die."

When the priest finished hearing his confession, Sheriff Morris added to Lino's smart appearance the accessory that was deemed essential to a condemned man's final excursion—a rope—and positioned it loosely around his neck.

Not wanting to look disheveled, Lino smoothed down his shirt collar where the rope had rumpled it. "It's cruel of you to hang me up like a dog," he said to Morris. "But I'm determined to die without flinching, like a soldier."

At nine-thirty, Morris placed him, with the rope dangling from his neck, in an open carriage and, accompanied by a troop of cavalrymen, escorted him a couple of miles out of Doylestown to a grassy field alongside the Neshaminy Creek. Morris had chosen the site by default. He'd hoped to find a spot close to the jail, one that wouldn't require him to drive the prisoner a long distance and thus prolong his anticipation of hanging, but none of the owners of nearby fields had wanted the crowds and chaos of an execution, not in their backyards. So Morris had had to settle for the field near the Neshaminy. It wasn't private property the way the farmers' fields were; it was town property, part of the land allotted to the almshouse.

Throughout most of the drive through the early summer morning, Lino was silent, and Morris hoped he was making his peace with God. But as the carriage neared the site and they saw the thousands of soldiers and civilians gathered there—ten thousand people, according to the newspapers—Lino reverted to his usual bravado. The military men, he told Morris, were lacking in spit and polish.

A few moments later Lino spotted the gallows. It was on a small rise in the center of the field, and it was surrounded by another detachment of cavalry and a phalanx of infantrymen. He let Morris hand him down from the carriage, and walked resolutely to the scaffold.

From up there, Lino could see the river, a thin band of silver that glistened in the boisterous golden sunlight. He could also see faces. Unsmiling faces. Mostly men, though here and there he spotted a female face looking up at him with curiosity. He could see the tops of trees, too, trees bursting with June leaves and swaying in a breeze that was like a whisper from on high.

Sheriff Morris was whispering, too. He was saying that it would be he himself who would be pulling the rope. Then Morris read out his death warrant and asked if he had anything to say.

"I do," Lino answered, and directed Father Tuljeaux to translate what he had to say. "*Americanos!*" he yelled. "*Mira una víctima inocente!*"

"People of America," Tuljeaux echoed him in English. "Behold an innocent victim!"

Lino went on speaking in Spanish and Tuljeaux went on translating. "You thirst for my blood," he heard the priest say after he had shouted out the phrase in his native tongue. "And you shall have it. But you chastise a poor innocent. To whom have I done wrong? If I have done wrong, let all pardon me. If I ever did wrong to any, let him forgive me, because I forgive myself to all my enemies, in order that God may pardon me, and grant me everlasting life in heaven. I do not fear death. I am not a feeble, but a courageous man. I am able to show that I am strong and not feeble."

His own words, sailing back to him in the language he understood but had never fully mastered, made him feel every bit as brave as he had just declared himself in Spanish to be. He was a strong man. A hero not a scoundrel. There must be people in the crowd who recognized this, people who might like to touch him, to take him by the hand before he died. He thrust out his fingers and asked if anybody wanted to ascend the scaffold and shake his hand to bid him farewell.

Several men rushed forward and climbed the stairs. He clasped their hands gratefully, clasped them firmly. He didn't tremble. Then he knelt on the scaffold, bowed his head, and prayed.

When Morris fixed the rope over the beam and drew a cap over his head, Lino turned in the direction he thought the crowd had been thickest, bowed twice, and, his voice muffled now, called out in English, "Farewell, my friends. Farewell, poor Mina, poor Mina. He die innocent. He die innocent."

It was the end. The trap was knocked away and he swung up into the sky.

Lino was the penultimate prisoner to be publicly executed on state charges in Pennsylvania. By 1834 the legislature had passed a law forbidding such execution. But in June 1832, not only was hanging considered a fit and proper sight for the public to view, but all its grisly details were considered a fit and proper subject for newspapermen to dwell on. They described in full how Lino's body had convulsed in the breeze, his chest heaving and his limbs flailing, and how the convulsions had lasted a good ten minutes because the amount of rope used had turned out to be insufficient to break his neck at once. They described, too, how dry-eyed the crowd had been, and how after being exhibited for a full half hour, the body had finally been cut down and handed over to a group of Philadelphia physicians.

The physicians had come to conduct an experiment on Lino's dead body—common practice in those days, when medical students routinely dissected the organs of executed prisoners and doctors tutorially displayed their skeletons in their offices. The experimenters had with them a large battery. They intended to use it to deliver an electric shock to the dead man, to see if he could be revived. They attached their device to the corpse and pressed down on the lever. But nothing happened. The battery had malfunctioned, the doctors concluded. Either that or they'd been made to wait too long after the strangulation to try out their device. Next time, they assured the public, the experiment of raising the dead with electricity would most likely work.

Lucretia, hiding away in the big stone house in Andalusia, read about Lino's demise with eyes as dry as those of any who had witnessed the hanging. Lino's death was like something that had already happened to her. He had died, for her, months ago, back when she had first realized that he intended to abandon her.

Since then she had felt empty and diminished, she who had once dreamed of uncommon love and untold wealth. Since then she had become not just a pariah but a nobody, no longer the proprietress of a prosperous school, no longer the wife of an acclaimed scientist let alone of a rich grandee, no longer even so much as a schoolteacher. Nor likely ever to be one again, she suspected, for who would entrust their children to her care?

The house was silent, the play yard no longer ringing with the cries of students, the big classroom empty not just of pupils but of the grammars and globes and slates she had long ago so enthusiastically purchased. She had sold them to make ends meet. She had sold, too, her cherished piano, the extra beds with which she had furnished the slate-roofed mansion's many bedrooms, and whatever had remained, after Lino's predations, of William's valuable scientific tomes. She was subsisting, she and her children, on handouts from the few local people who still felt some Christian charity toward her.

But there must be a way out, she reasoned, a better way out than living on alms or even of returning to Massachusetts and burdening her aged mother. After all, she was an educated woman, good at reading and recitation. Surely such a woman didn't need to take charity or live off a parent; surely such a woman didn't even need to be a schoolteacher. Perhaps she could find other work, go into the theater the way other educated women were doing, women like Fanny Trollope, who launched dramatic productions; women like Frances Wright, who got up on the stage and gave lectures.

The idea revived Lucretia. She began picturing herself on a stage and imagining herself applauded and appreciated, a breadwinner for her children and a woman of substance once again.

Soon after Lino's death, she closed up her house in Bucks County and, with her children in tow, lit out for the West and there embarked on a second career as an actress.

Epilogue

*L*UCRETIA'S THEATRICAL CAREER WAS only partially a success. She joined a troupe of strolling players and toured in
various parts of the country, but from time to time theatergoers
realized who she was and shunned her performances. In Cincinnati, in November 1834, she was hissed and booed off a stage.
"How she has fallen!" a Philadelphia man wrote to one of his
brothers after reading of the incident, and went on to marvel at the
fact that "degraded as her present occupation is, even [out West]
the finger of scorn is pointed at her and she is greeted with hisses
and general disaffection."

Did she deserve such scorn? Was she as lacking in guilt as her
acquittal had implied, or was she in fact a woman upon whose lips
an enigmatic smile sometimes played as she slipped into her cos-
tumes or fashioned her hair, the smile of a woman who has gotten
away with murder? Her neighbors thought this might be the case,
so did many of her former friends, and in time in Bucks County
she came to be viewed as having been every bit as evil as the well-
known poisoner whose Christian name she shared, the infamous
Lucretia Borgia.

I myself see her differently, see her as a woman maligned by
Lino and consequently by history, for Lino has had the last word
till now.

I don't think she participated in William's murder. But I do suspect she was an accomplice after the fact. It's my belief that the secret things Lino told her the last time he set foot in Andalusia were that he had killed William, that if he was apprehended he would blame the murder on her, and that if she knew what was good for her she'd get him out of her way by recommending him to her relatives at the Cape and keeping her mouth shut about both his revelations and where he was going. As we know, she recommended him to her relatives and kept silent about that last conversation.

I could find no solid clues to what became of Lucretia after her abortive performance in Cincinnati in 1834, although one 1909 commentator on the case said she worked for a time as a silhouettist, drawing and cutting out the black profiles that were so popular in her day. But he also said she died in 1841 in Florida, and Florida's archives contain no record of the death in that year of either a Lucretia Chapman or a Lucretia Winslow.

Perhaps she changed her name to hide her identity. "Quite likely," said a Tallahassee archivist who helped me in my search. "Probably a lot of the people who came to Florida in the early 1840s were trying to hide something. Otherwise why come here? The state was mostly a mosquito-infested swamp."

Whether or not she changed her name, and wherever it was that she died, Lucretia did die in 1841. She was fifty-three years old. After her death, her remaining property was sold at auction, and each of the children received a one-fifth share of the proceeds. They were all still minors, except for Mary. Little is known about what became of the children except that William Jr., who apparently inherited his father's scientific bent, attended college, graduated, and became a dentist and that Mary went to live in Massachusetts with her Winslow relatives.

The Chapman house itself, situated as it was just off the turnpike, struck its first buyer as an ideal spot for a tavern. He turned it into one, the Old Union, and it remained a tavern until being bought in 1861 by a Reverend Doctor Horatio Thomas Wells, who turned it back into a school, first a school for boys seeking "moral, religious and intellectual training," then a college he founded and named Andalusia College. Today none of the original house remains, and a Catholic church, the Church of St. Charles Borromeo, occupies the corner of Lucretia's land that faced the turnpike, which still exists, albeit jammed now with automobiles. But across the way from the church there's a dilapidated old brick-and-stucco structure. "That building was standing at the time of the murder you're writing about," said an expert on the early architecture of Bucks County who was helping me locate sites mentioned in my research.

I imagine it might have been the Boutchers' farmhouse.

As to William, he was as unfortunate in the manner in which his name lived on after his death as he was in the manner of that death itself. His scientific work faded into oblivion. And the inscription on his tombstone seems to have done so, too. According to the records of All Saints Episcopal Church in Hulmeville, where he was buried, William is still interred in the church's graveyard. But although when I visited the graveyard I saw in the oldest part of the yard the tombstones of quite a few Chapmans who were buried there in the first years of the nineteenth century, I saw no stone for William—at least no stone with his name. Most of the tombstones in this antiquated section of the graveyard are sturdy gray slabs with clearly legible inscriptions. But one stone is different from all the others. It is so bubbly and disintegrated that it looks as if it is made of melted sugar, and whatever inscription it may once have borne is totally indecipherable.

I suspect it's William's, and that Lucretia, out of bitterness or distraction, never put up a proper tablet.

After the Chapman case was over, some of the people who had played roles in the affair lived lives bright with achievement.

The pharmacist Elias Durand became the second vice president of the Philadelphia College of Pharmacy, where his portrait still hangs.

David Paul Brown became even more famous than he was at the time of Lucretia's trial and wrote a fascinating book about his career, *The Forum, or Forty Years of Practice at the Philadelphia Bar.*

Thomas Ross not only got elected to Congress but gained a national reputation by making a speech welcoming California into the Union.

The two men participated in another important trial besides that of Lucretia Chapman, but this time they were allies, not adversaries. In 1838 they were hired by a black abolitionist to help prevent an escaped slave named Basil Dorsey from being reclaimed by his Maryland owner. Brown did the talking for his and Ross's side, arguing that the slave owner from whom Dorsey had fled had offered no evidence to show that under the laws of Maryland he was entitled to own a fellow man.

His client didn't have to introduce such evidence, said his lawyer. "Everybody knows that Maryland is a Slave State."

Brown thundered, "Everybody is nobody! Common report does not pass before a court of justice." Then, arguing that he couldn't believe Maryland's laws would allow such an egregious offense as slave owning, he demanded that a copy of the laws be produced, but insisted it be a *certified* copy.

The slave owner's counsel didn't have a certified copy of Maryland's laws with him, and asked for time to get one.

Brown and Ross maintained that until such time as he produced the document, the case ought to be dismissed.

It *was* dismissed, at least temporarily, and while the court was in recess, Dorsey was hurriedly spirited off to New England. The judge who dismissed the case was John Fox—"a man," said the abolitionist who'd hired Brown and Ross, "with human feelings [even] if he was a judge."

Some of the other figures in the book had more troubled, checkered, or even tragic lives.

Sheriff Morris had so many nightmares about having pulled the rope that ended Lino's life that he quit law enforcement and became a tavernkeeper.

William Du Bois became a department head at the U.S. Mint, where he falsified numismatic facts and earned a reputation as a crook.

High Constable Blayney's twenty-five-year-old son was murdered in a street brawl.

And what of Lino? Only this, that a year after his execution he was blamed for a terrible natural disaster. The waters of the Neshaminy, the creek alongside which he'd been hanged, roiled and rose and swept away all the bridges that crossed the creek. It was the dead man's vengeance, said the locals, and they named the catastrophe the "Mina Flood."

Endnotes

Years ago, when I first began writing about legal and criminal matters, an attorney friend who wanted to encourage my new interest gave me as a gift a rare copy of William E. Du Bois's *Trial of Lucretia Chapman,* with its supplement on the trial of Lino Amalia Espos y Mina. "Read this," my friend said. "Maybe you could write something comparing how murder trials were conducted in the early nineteenth century with how they're conducted now. Besides, it's a great read. A scandal, plus a murder by chicken soup!" But I was busy, preoccupied with scandals and murders of the moment, and I put aside the decaying volume with its crumbling pages and minuscule print. Twenty years rolled by and the book languished on my shelf. Then one day in a moment of leisure, I picked it up, and when I did I was immediately enthralled. After finishing the book I immersed myself in the Chapman case, delving into old newspapers, memoirs, and biographies, and discovering in the process that the murder of William Chapman, although altogether forgotten now, had been one of the major crime stories of the nineteenth century. I understood why, for I was hooked by the tale, and eventually I began writing this book.

For anyone who wants to know more about the case, the three best resources are the Du Bois work, the newspapers of the period, and David Paul Brown's *The Forum, or Forty Years Full Practice at the Philadelphia Bar.*

Du Bois produced what was, in effect, the equivalent of a modern-day trial transcript, recording almost every word of the witnesses' testimony; the lawyers' opening statements, legal arguments, and florid summations; and the rulings made by the judges. His account does not, however, read the way a contemporary court transcript does. For example, Du Bois often didn't write down the lawyers' questions, merely the witnesses' answers, so I have at times had to surmise the questions from the answers.

The newspapers covered Lucretia and Lino's trials in great detail and with increasing prominence. Indeed one paper, the *Barnstable Patriot,* after running several pieces about the case in its inner pages, moved the story to the front page, apologizing for this unprecedented placement of a murder story by explaining, "We supposed it would be as interesting to many... as the President's Message," a standard front-page item.

Brown's book is interesting on the subject of himself—he was a man of vast ego—as well as on his various cases and what it was like to be a criminal defense attorney in mid-nineteenth-century America. Alas, his account of Lucretia's trial is short. Still, he does explain his strategy and talk about some of his personal experiences during the trial.

In addition to these three resources, a fourth that is of considerable interest is a collection of documents concerning the trial and its principals that was donated to the Bucks County Historical Society by the late George B. Ross, a descendant of prosecutor Thomas Ross. The collection, the Mina-Chapman Murder Case Papers, includes originals of the letters exchanged between Lucretia and Lino, as well as Mary Ross's letter urging her son to visit Lino before his execution, William Chapman's alien registration and citizenship papers, Dr. Hopkinson's autopsy report, some of Lucretia's tuition bills, and many other fascinating tidbits.

I would also recommend looking at Lucretia and William's book on their United States Institution for the Treatment of Defective Utterance, and Lino's *The Life and Confession of Carolino Estradas de Mina*. The latter, filled with miraculous events and lush descriptions of tropical scenes, reads in places like a tale by Gabriel García Márquez.

These were my principal research tools. I also used many additional sources, including books, newspaper articles, government documents, and information provided by the individuals cited in my acknowledgments.

In reconstructing events and providing dialogue, I have adhered to the historical record. Regarding the dialogue, while it was occasionally necessary to render as direct quotation remarks that appeared in the source material as indirect discourse, the remarks all come from the court testimony recorded by Du Bois or the accounts written by Brown and various contemporary journalists. Only rarely have I made alterations in these remarks, other than to clarify a speaker's meaning with small grammatical changes, and wherever I deemed it requisite to make an alteration, I have provided the original words and an explanation for my change in the chapter notes that follow.

ABBREVIATIONS

DPB Brown, David Paul, *The Forum, or Forty Years Full Practice at the Philadelphia Bar,* 2 volumes, Philadelphia, 1856.

WC Chapman, Mr. and Mrs. William, *United States Institution for the Treatment of Cases of Defective Utterance Such as Partial Speechlessness, Stuttering, Stammering, Hesitancy, Weakness of Voice, Mis-Enunciation, Lisping, Etc., Etc.,* Philadelphia, 1826.

TLC Du Bois, William E., *The Trial of Lucretia Chapman,* Philadelphia, 1832.

STMC Du Bois, William E., *Supplement to the Trial of Mrs. Chapman: The Trial of Lino Amalia Espos y Mina,* Philadelphia, 1832.

CEM Mina, Carolino Estradas, *The Life and Confession of Carolino Estradas de Mina,* Philadelphia, 1832.

M-CMCP Mina-Chapman Murder Case Papers, Spruance Library, Bucks County Historical Society, Doylestown, Pa.

CHAPTER NOTES

CHAPTER 1 BUCKS COUNTY, PENNSYLVANIA

1 Dr. John Phillips's eminence, his willingness to see patients, and his attitude toward doctors who had not been trained at the University of Pennsylvania Medical School: Green, *A History of Bristol Borough,* pp. 181–82.

1 Lino's appearance: *Germantown Telegraph,* Feb. 22, 1832.

1 Phillips's height: Green, *A History of Bristol Borough,* p. 181.

2 My description of Dr. Phillips's visits to the dying William Chapman is drawn from his testimony as well as from testimony given by Dr. Knight, Ann Bantom, and little Lucretia Chapman; see TLC, pp. 24, 32–33, 69, and 89–91.

3 Lucretia's appearance: *Germantown Telegraph,* Feb. 22, 1832; see also DPB, vol. 2, p. 419.

3 "A beefsteak would do me more good than anything else": TLC, p. 33.

4 "Not much" and "He may eat plenty of that": TLC, p. 90.

4 Calomel drops: Calomel drops were considered effective against even Asiatic cholera. I came across a yellowed newspaper clipping from *Hall's Journal of Health,* pinned inside an 1849 cookbook, *Mrs. Putnam's Receipt Book and Young Housekeeper's Assistant,* that stated

that "a pill made up of ten grains of calomel with a little gum-water" could arrest cholera "unless it is in the very last stages . . . in nine cases out of ten."

5 "I'm drowsy from waiting on Mr. Chapman" and "Call me if I'm wanted": TLC, p. 34.

CHAPTER 2 CAPE COD AND PHILADELPHIA

7 Cape Cod: I am indebted to Thoreau for my description of the Cape: see Thoreau, *Cape Cod*, p. 14.

7 Mark Holman: The story of Lucretia's girlhood romance with Holman was told to me by Al Clark of the Barre Historical Society. Clark wasn't sure whether the young couple's indiscretion occurred in Barre or at the Cape, and I have set the incident at the Cape because it seemed to me for a variety of reasons more likely to have happened there.

8 Lucretia's grandfather and great-grandfather: Holton, *Winslow Memorial*, pp. 71–89, 130–131, and 403.

8 Zenas Winslow's history: Holton, *Winslow Memorial*, p. 403, see also Josiah Paine, *A History of Harwich, Barnstable County, Massachusetts, 1620–1800*, Rutland, Vt., 1937, p. 340.

8 Disgraced girl written about by Lucretia's neighbor: See Vicery, *Emily Hamilton, a Novel, Founded on Incidents in Real Life,* published in Worcester, Massachusetts.

8 An age well past that at which most of the girls she knew were not just already married but already mothers: See Wright, *Views of Society and Manners in America*, p. 33.

9 Lucretia goes to Philadelphia: In a letter to a friend, reprinted in the *Germantown Telegraph* on February 15, 1832, Lucretia remarks that she left the Cape and went to Philadelphia in 1813. She does not say just when in 1813 she went there. I discovered the month of her arrival serendipitously, while leafing through 1813 advertisements in Philadelphia newspapers: see *Germantown Telegraph*, Feb. 15, 1832.

9 Endured such a rattling and shaking . . . skulls would be crushed: My description of Lucretia's harrowing stagecoach ride was inspired by Charles Dickens's description of a stagecoach ride *he* took several years later; see his *American Notes*, p. 254.

10 Heavily accented English: Bergerac's accent is an assumption on my part, based on the fact that he was already in his thirties when he emigrated from France. See Naturalization Records, 1789–1880.

10 Location of Bergerac's academy: See the *Philadelphia Aurora General Advertiser,* Sept. 7, 1813.

10 Somewhere en route, all her possessions had disappeared: See the *Philadelphia Aurora General Advertiser,* Sept. 7, 1813.

12 Lucretia's sallies around Philadelphia: In constructing a likely itinerary for Lucretia, I drew upon numerous sources, among them *Relf's Philadelphia Gazette* and *Philadelphia Poulson's American Daily Advertiser* for the months of September to November 1813, an article by Frederic Trautman that excerpted the diary of the early nineteenth century traveler Ludwig Gall, an album of watercolor illustrations of old Philadelphia houses painted by G. Albert Lewis (now in the possession of the Library Company of Philadelphia), and the books of Merritt Ierley, Ellis Paxson Oberholtzer, John F. Watson, and Edwin Wolf. The books portray, for the most part, a Philadelphia that was orderly and sparklingly clean. But Gall, who was there in 1819, noted that the streets were muddy and the houses draped with drying laundry. The odd information that dentists of the time transplanted human teeth is something I came across in both Watson and Oberholtzer. Watson, writing in 1830, says, "It may surprise some of the present generation to learn that some of the aged persons who they may now meet have teeth which were originally in the heads of others" (*Annals of Philadelphia,* p. 167). Oberholtzer cites an Eighth Street dentist's 1818 advertisement suggesting that patients "who have objections to the use of . . . human teeth can be supplied with natural teeth which are not human, to answer all the valuable purposes of the grafted human teeth" (*Philadelphia,* p. 119). Such teeth were apparently taken from the jaws of horses, hippopotami, and other animals (*Philadelphia,* p. 118).

12 ablaze with a . . . fiery light: The illumination of Philadelphia occurred on September 24, 1813. See *Relf's Philadelphia Gazette,* Sept. 25, 1813.

12 The office would specialize, he announced . . . collecting overdue debts: See *Philadelphia Aurora General Advertiser,* Sept. 24, 1813.

13 William's emigration from England on the *Roebuck:* see Passenger and Immigration Lists, Philadelphia, 1800–1850.

13 Information about the *Roebuck* and about the hardships experienced by passengers at the start of the nineteenth century: Interview with Norman Brewer of the South Street Seaport Museum in New York, and Diane Snyder Ptak, *A Passage in Time: The Ships That Brought Our Ancestors, 1620–1940* (Albany, N.Y., 1992).

13 William's sparse possessions: See Baggage Entries, 1799–1856, Records of the Port of Philadelphia.

13 Schoolteacher: See "Visa of William Chapman," M-CMCP.

14 When he spoke . . . fearsome grimaces: See WC, pp. 2 and 4.

14 "A stammering tongue signifies a weak understanding, and a wavering mind": *Aristotle's Master-Piece Completed* (New York, 1798), p. 101.

14 "Painful commiseration" WC, p. 2.

14 "the most respectable references": *Philadelphia Aurora General Advertiser,* Sept. 24, 1813

14 He had also applied to become a citizen of America: See Naturalization Records, Philadelphia, 1789–1880.

14 Interviewing prospective citizens in local taverns: See the *Philadelphia Aurora General Advertiser,* Sept. 22, 1813.

14 Officially an alien, and as such, forced to register: "Registration as Alien of William Chapman" and "Visa of William Chapman," M-CMCP.

15 William promptly signed up: It is certain that William, who according to *Kite's Philadelphia Directory for 1814* was the only William Chapman residing in Philadelphia that year, volunteered to serve his new country. Pennsylvania's archives contain several references to a militia volunteer named William Chapman, one to a William Chapman serving under a Captain Tucker, the others to a William Chapman serving under a Captain whose name is given variously as McMillen, McMillin and McMullen. It is less clear whether these references are to one man or two, and consequently I have simply placed William in the militia, without specifying in which company he served. See Pennsylvania Archives, 6th Series, vol. 7, pp. 80, 347, and 351, and vol. 8, p. 15.

15 Called to an onerous duty: According to Oberholtzer, "*all* [italics added] the old companies [of volunteers] and several new ones were formed into one body" to protect the approaches to the city. See Oberholtzer, *Philadelphia,* p. 18.

15 "Not a stitch of dry clothing in the camp. Never rained harder since the flood": Thackara, *Diary of William Wood Thackara,* p. 305.

16 "Three cheers for Cadwalader": Thackara, *Diary of William Wood Thackara,* p. 308.

17 For the rest of his life he would revere that year, mark it as a turning point: See WC, p. 2.

17 The edict of Philadelphia's administrators and the exodus from Philadelphia: Oberholtzer, *Philadelphia,* p. 17.

18 "The damned British have been defeated and their general killed": Oberholtzer, *Philadelphia*, p. 20.

18 The investigation of Mark and Edward Winslow: *Commonwealth v. Edward Winslow*, 1814–1818.

19 LeBrun's method: see Charles LeBrun, *Le Directeur des Enfants Depuis l'Age de Cinq Ans Jusqu'à Douze*, Philadelphia, 1811.

19 A bee who so surfeited himself on nectar that he could no longer fly: The bee story appears in N. Picket, *The Juvenile Expositor, or Sequel to the Common Spelling-Book* (New York, 1810), pp. 28–29.

19 The good little boy who broke his family's best mirror but confessed: The mirror story, one of many such stories about children who couldn't tell lies—most notably George Washington—appears in Picket, *The Juvenile Expositor*, p. 24.

19 "Without frugality, none can be rich": Picket, *The Juvenile Expositor*, p. 33.

19 "Diligence, industry, and proper improvement of time are material duties of the young": Picket, *The Juvenile Expositor*, p. 35.

20 An expensive instrument cost as much as a small house, while even an inexpensive one . . . a half-year's wages: Larkin, *The Reshaping of Everyday Life, 1790–1840*, pp. 249–250.

20 "To beautify the room by so superb an ornament" and "the only thing that distinguishes 'decent people' from the lower and less distinguished": Larkin, *Reshaping of Everyday Life*, p. 143.

20 "masculine": *Germantown Telegraph*, February 22, 1832.

21 Girls . . . being educated would benefit the country: See Appleby, *Inheriting the Revolution*, p. 106.

21 "A new race" and "any nation on earth": Wright, *Views of Society and Manners in America*, p. 35.

21 "Miss Winslow most respectfully informs her friends and the public . . . useful and ornamental branches of a polite education": *Relf's Philadelphia Gazette*, Sept. 27, 1817.

22 "rely on the most scrupulous attention being paid to . . . morals and improvement": *Relf's Philadelphia Gazette*, Sept. 27, 1817.

22 "Have you rose early enough for the duties of the morning. . . . Have you combed your hair with a fine tooth comb, and cleaned your teeth every morning": from "Rules for the School and Academy," written in 1814 by Eliza Ann Mulford, a student at Miss Sarah Pierce's Female

Seminary in Litchfield, Connecticut, and printed in Emily Noyes
Vanderpoel, compiler, *Chronicles of a Pioneer School from 1792 to 1838,
Being the History of Miss Sarah Pierce and Her Litchfield School*
(Cambridge, Mass., 1903), p. 147.

23 "Show" meat: Oberholtzer, *Philadelphia,* pp. 82–85.

23 Waxwork displays, balloon ascensions, inhalation of nitrous oxide gas:
Oberholtzer, *Philadelphia,* pp. 46–47.

24 "crowds upon crowds of buyers, sellers, and gazers": Oberholtzer,
p. 103.

CHAPTER 3 MARRIAGE

27 Methods of correcting stammering: see Alfred Appelt, *Stammering and
Its Permanent Cure: A Treatise on Individual Psychological Lines*
(London, 1929), pp. 31–38, and Benson Bobrick, *Knotted Tongues:
Stuttering in History and the Quest for a Cure* (New York, 1995), pp.
85–94.

28 "tell, reveal . . . Rules thereunto belonging": Agreement, M-CMCP.

28 "the" cure: *Germantown Telegraph,* August 3, 1831.

28 Sign language schools: Wilson, *Picture of Philadelphia,* pp. 85–86 and
91–92; see also Oberholtzer, *Philadelphia,* p. 128.

28 Lino's birthplace and family: Davis, *History of Bucks County,
Pennsylvania,* 1876, p. 858–59.

29 Lino's father's employment: Davis, *History of Bucks County,
Pennsylvania,* 1905, p. 357.

29 Lino as a daydreamer and tale-teller: See CEM.

29 The idealization of mothers and the appearance of the first child-
rearing manuals: Larkin, *The Reshaping of Everyday Life,* pp. 52–53
and 70.

30 "tender" and "seemed to enjoy an uninterrupted happiness in each
other's society": TLC, p. 95.

31 "The bills are true except for the signature of the bank's president": See
testimony of Nathaniel Crocker, *Commonwealth v. Edward Winslow,*
1814–1818. Crocker's exact words were: "the Bills were true except the
signing of the President's name."

31 "Here I stood to make some money, but there must always be some
damn fool in the way": See testimony of Nathaniel Crocker,
Commonwealth v. Edward Winslow, 1814–1818. Crocker's exact words

were that Winslow "stated there had been a great chance for him to make some money but there must always be some damn fool in the [illegible word]."

31 "in the land of the living . . . this world of trouble and anxiety": Zenas and Abigail Winslow letter, in Documents Pertaining to the Incarceration and Pardon of Edward Winslow, 1820–1823.

31 Edward's reformation: A document signed by Seth Lee, Eleazar James, and others, included in the collection cited above, asserts that by 1823 Edward was "humble" and had "become a sincere penitent."

31 Mark's persistence as a counterfeiter: Mark was arrested in 1826, and died in prison in 1832. I was told by Barre local historian Clark that according to one account he'd read but was unable to locate, the citizens of the town were so afraid of Mark, against whom some of them had testified, that when his coffin was brought to Barre for burial, they implored a doctor to open the casket and make certain that it was his body and not a wax effigy that was laid out within.

32 "the vulgar term *drunk* [to] give place to *inflated*": Hamilton, *Men and Manners in America*, p. 221.

32 Tilghman and Hopkinson's membership in the Wistar Society: Oberholtzer, *Philadelphia*, p. 32.

32 "there is no country in which scandal . . . is so rare as in the United States": Grund, *The Americans in Their Moral, Social and Political Relations*, p. 37. Grund goes on to write that a French gentleman, remarking to him that he found American society dull because "it precluded the very idea of a *liaison*," termed the United States " '*le paradis des maris!* ' "

33 The visitor from Scotland: He is Thomas Hamilton, who wrote that Philadelphia "is Quaker all over. All things, animate and inanimate, seem influenced by a spirit of quietism as pervading as the atmosphere"; see his *Men and Manners in America*, p. 196.

33 "The collar of my coat appeared to stiffen . . . my hands folded themselves upon my breast of their own calm accord": Dickens, *American Notes*, p. 139.

34 Lino's predations on the Cuban country folk: see Davis, History of Bucks County, 1876, pp. 858–859.

34 "discovery": *Philadelphia Gazette*, Sept. 16, 1826, cited in WC, p. 25.

35 "We are perfectly satisfied that no other person in the country possesses the *effectual* cure for stammering . . . have spent their time and money

fruitlessly with such pretenders": Leigh, *Facts in Relation to Mrs. Leigh's System of Curing Stammering,* p. 2.

35 "Mr. and Mrs. Chapman respectfully inform the people of the United States that they have conducted an Institution for upwards of NINE YEARS": WC, p. 2.

35 "is the first institution of the kind that has been established in the United States": WC, p. 3.

35 "the inventor": WC, p. 3.

35 "Original Discoverer," "secret," and "an all-wise Providence": WC, p. 2.

36 "irksome": WC, p. 6.

36 "violent contortions": WC, p. 4.

36 "That numerous instances of cures have been effected by Mr. Chapman cannot longer be questioned": WC, p. 30.

36 "If a great and important discovery demands a tribute of admiration . . . the superlative benefits of which shall continue to be felt through the rounds of time": WC, p. 31.

37 Andalusia's exotic name: Wainwright, "Andalusia," p. 7.

37 Andalusia in the 1790s: McNealy, "Andalusia," p. 91.

37 Tenant farmers: Conversation with Terry A. McNealy in August 2002.

37 Boutcher: Davis, *History of Bucks County Pennsylvania,* pp. 858–59.

38 Bristol's market: McNealy, "Andalusia," p. 50.

39 Lucretia's advertisement for her school: A copy can be found in M-CMCP.

40 Exceptionally well versed in the catechism: See the Reverend Scheetz's testimony, TLC, p. 92.

41 Lucretia's criticisms of William: TLC, pp. 66–67.

CHAPTER 4 LINO

43 The raid on the royal treasury in Havana: *Germantown Telegraph,* June 20, 1832.

43 He was insane: *Barnstable Patriot,* June 27, 1832.

44 Lino's affection for his daughter: In his final days, Lino demonstrated his strong feelings about the girl by attempting to bequeath property to her: see STMC, p. 9.

44 Lino's arrival in Boston: *Barnstable Patriot,* June 27, 1832.

44 The Sun Tavern: See ads for the tavern in the *Boston Morning Post,* Feb. 20, 1832, and Feb. 26, 1832.

45 The meteor on December 31, 1829: Lichtenwalner, *Bensalem,* p. 311.

45 A. Bronson Alcott's school in Germantown: Madelon Bedell, *The Alcotts: Biography of a Family,* New York, 1980, p. 55–67; see also *Germantown Telegraph,* Feb. 22, 1832.

45 The use of globes: James McIntire, *A New Treatise on the Use of Globes* (Baltimore, 1826), pp. 63–64.

46 The teaching of botanical nomenclature and classification: See Mrs. Lincoln Phelps, *Familiar Lectures on Botany* (Hartford, Conn., 1829).

46 "My friends are on the other side of the Atlantic": TLC, p. 69.

46 Sophia's proximity to the Chapmans: see Bensalem Township Census, 1830.

47 Bonaparte's grounds: Clarence Edward Macartney and Gordon Dorrance, *The Bonapartes in America* (Philadelphia, 1939), p. 87.

47 Bonaparte's art collection: Owen Connelly, *The Gentle Bonaparte: A Biography of Joseph Bonaparte* (New York, 1968), p. 250.

47 Some visitors grew faint at the sight: Connelly, *The Gentle Bonaparte,* pp. 252–53.

48 Confidence men: The term "confidence man" is believed to have been coined in 1849 by the New York press while covering the trial of a swindler named William Thompson; Halttunen, *Confidence Men and Painted Women,* p. 6.

48 Advice manuals: Halttunen, *Confidence Men and Painted Women,* pp. 1–32.

48 Lino's scams while at the Sun Tavern: *Philadelphia Saturday Bulletin,* October 22, 1831.

49 Celestino Almentero: This name was used by Lino until he left prison. The keeper of the prison Anglicized the name and called him Celestine Almentarius. See STMC, p. 11 and TLC, p. 66.

49 Lino's appearance: See eyewitness descriptions of Lino in *Philadelphia Saturday Courier,* May 26, 1832 and *Germantown Telegraph,* June 20, 1832; see also the lithograph portrait of him in the Prints and Photographs Division of the Library of Congress.

50 Philadelphia's Eastern Penitentiary: The prison, which is now known as Eastern State Penitentiary, is still standing and is open for tours April through November.

50 "I am persuaded that those who devised this system of Prison Discipline ... which slumbering humanity is not roused up to stay": Dickens, *American Notes,* p. 131.

51 Lino's cell and his work in prison: The Eastern Penitentiary was a

must-see destination for most foreign travelers to the United States. I used several eyewitness accounts to describe the cell, among them Dickens's *American Notes* and Hamilton's *Men and Manners in America*. I also used information provided to me by Brett Bertolino, program coordinator of the Eastern State Penitentiary. Lino's prison job is mentioned in the testimony of the keeper of the prison, Israel Deacon, TLC, p. 66.

52 Lino's letter to the prison inspectors: STMC, pp. 10–11.

52 Only four dollars . . . departing prisoners: Conversation with Bertolino.

53 Lino's behavior on the morning of his release: *Philadelphia Saturday Bulletin*, Oct. 22, 1831.

53 The steamboat's luxurious furnishings and elaborate breakfast buffet: see Oberholtzer, *Philadelphia*, pp. 70–71.

53 Lino's refusal to buy a ticket and his being thrown off the boat: *Philadelphia Saturday Bulletin*, Oct. 22, 1831.

54 First stop for northbound steamboats: MacReynolds, *Place Names in Bucks County, Pennsylvania*, p. 7.

54 "I need victuals and lodgings for the night": TLC, p. 20.

54 His shirt was a disgrace. Not worth anything, she thought: See Ellen Shaw's testimony, "His shirt was not worth anything," TLC, p. 22.

54 Lino asked if he could see the master or mistress of the house: TLC, pp. 19–20.

55 "I need a night's lodging"; "They refused me"; "There's a tavern *up* the hill [italics added]"; and the story Lino tells upon arriving at the Chapmans': TLC, p. 20.

55 Carolino Amalia Espos y Mina: Lino's last name appears variously in the documents of his day. Sometimes it is spelled Espos y Mina, sometimes Esposimina, sometimes Esposymina. (Lino himself signed his name as both Esposimina and Esposymina, but never Espos y Mina.) Similarly, his second name appears variously as Amalio and Amalia. I have chosen to use Carolino Amalia Espos y Mina, the spelling William Du Bois chose for *The Trial of Lucretia Chapman*.

55 "My father's a Mexican general. The governor of Upper California" and "My dear, if you think so": TLC, p. 37.

56 Jackson's dismissal of Sam Ingham: Yerkes, "John Ross and the Ross Family," p. 373.

56 Joanna Clue: *Philadelphia Saturday Bulletin*, April 30, 1830.

56 The story Lino tells at supper: TLC, p. 27; see also Kenderdine, "The Chapman-Mina Tragedy," p. 455.

58 "What am I to do for shirts if this Lino has them all": TLC, p. 22.

58 "Suppose you go with this gentleman and get someone to drive you": TLC, p. 57.

58 Bonaparte's generosity and his reputation as an easy mark: Wright, *Views of Society and Manners in America*, pp. 141–42.

59 Bonaparte's sculpture: Wright, *Views*, p. 137.

59 "Count Bonaparte has company. He cannot be seen for two or three hours" and "I have to return to my school tonight": TLC, p. 37.

60 Lucretia's evening prayer: see "Evening Prayer" in *Prayers for Female Schools* (New York, 1825).

60 "You'd best let him alone. He's a Spaniard. A body don't know what he might do" and "He's a fine young man . . . one of my own sons": TLC, p. 20.

61 "Sir, I have the pleasure of addressing you . . . acquiring such an addition to his English education as the time may admit of" and "four hundred and eleven [such] pupils of both sexes . . . great distances in the United States"; "Lino, you know I do not understand your language. If you will write the letter, I will sign it"; and "I have done for you . . . for I have signed what I do not understand": TLC, p. 38.

62 "Dear Madam" and "I am happy to inform you . . . at the table"; TLC, p. 38.

63 The high style of Chestnut Street tailors: Wright, *Views of Society and Manners in America*, p. 128.

63 "He has no money . . . hasn't a suit fit to visit in"; "Make the clothes and charge them to me"; and "Could hardly hold them up": TLC, p. 26.

64 "My name is Carolino . . . I beg you to hear my misfortunes,": TLC, p. 81.

64 General Mina in Philadelphia: Connelly, *The Gentle Bonaparte*, p. 255.

65 Strange fellow. . . . Looks more like a beggar than the son of a Mexican nobleman: Cuesta mentions in his testimony that Lino was "so dirty that he looked like a beggar." See TLC, p. 81.

65 "Your manners, your way of speaking. These do not show you to be such a man as you would have me believe": I've adapted this quotation slightly; Cuesta's exact words were that "I observed that his manners, and his bad language, did not show him to be such a man as he would have me believe": TLC, p. 82.

65 "It's true" and "I am an ignorant man. . . . to improve my manners":
TLC, p. 82, although I have added the phrase "by whom I was raised"
because Lino gave Cuesta this information earlier in his monologue.

65 "I did not know there was any governor by the name of Mina in
Mexico"; "I only heard it from my grandfather"; "He is in some high
employment, and I thought it was governor"; and "Where in Mexico
did you reside": TLC, p. 82.

66 "You're lying to me" and "You've never been in Mexico": Adapted
from Cuestas's statement "I knew from his answer that he had never
been in Mexico, and told him so": TLC, p. 82.

66 "All I've stated is true. But I have been suffering so much . . . that I am
almost out of my senses"; TLC, p. 82.

66 "Give me some proof that you're Mexican"; "What proof"; "Your
passport"; "I have none"; "Your certificate of baptism, then"; and
"Lost": TLC, p. 82.

66 The man has an answer for everything . . . brought him here in it: These
thoughts are expressed by Cuesta in TLC, p. 82.

66 "I have some business in town. I'll come back for him in an hour"; "I'm
ashamed to write in front of you because my handwriting is very bad";
"I'm busy. Write to your mother yourself—particularly as it's rather her
fault that you write badly, isn't it"; "It is a custom in my
country . . . merely as an act of politeness"; and "We are just beginning
to eat . . . honored if you would": TLC, p. 82.

67 "Would they like a sweet? And you? Would you care for a drink":
Adapted from a more wordy statement of Cuesta's about how he offered
Lucretia and her children sweets and a drink: TLC, p. 83.

67 "Cold lemonade": TLC, p. 83.

68 "Romania speaks a little English. She can keep you company while you
wait for Señor Mina": Adapted from Cuesta's statement, "I went
upstairs to ask my elder sister, who could speak a little English, to be
company for her till Mina was done": TLC, p. 82.

68 "In his own country he's very rich": Lucretia Chapman, letter to
Cuesta, TLC, p. 86.

68 "You must come and see me at *my* house" and "And you must come
and see me here again": adapted from Cuesta's statement, "She told my
sister she would be glad to see us at her house; my sister reciprocated
her politeness by the same offer," TLC, p. 83.

68 Altogether dispelled: TLC, p. 107.

70 She asked William to help Mary... kick with her foot: TLC, pp. 19, 21, and 67.

70 Esther Bache's visit: This scene is drawn from Esther's testimony, TLC, p. 23.

71 "We fear for his life" and "Mr. Chapman hardly understands anything": TLC, p. 23.

72 The next morning... they'd be back in the evening: See TLC, pp. 21–23.

73 "Who wants to be troubled with a butterfly like you": TLC, p. 22. At the time, according to the *Oxford English Dictionary,* the term butterfly meant "a light-headed inconstant person" or "giddy trifler."

74 "Maybe they've run off to Mexico"; "I wouldn't be surprised. The way they've been going on"; and "I wish the ship that brought Mina from Mexico had sunk": TLC, p. 67.

74 The thoughts attributed to William in this scene are drawn from the testimony of Edwin Fanning, TLC, p. 68.

75 "A rogue" and "I'd rather be poor than have my peace disturbed the way it's been since this fellow came here": TLC, p. 68.

75 "In all probability their object is to tarry until the family has retired and perhaps then to engage in improper conduct": Abbreviated from Fanning's report that William said to him, "In all probability their object is to tarry until the family has retired, and I would like to know whether they would be guilty of improper conduct after they do return." See TLC, p. 68.

75 "If I know of their going together... by God I'll kill him" and "You stay up, and if they come home and go to that rogue's room, you let me know": TLC, p. 68.

76 William's sympathetic treatment of Lino: This scene, too, is drawn from the testimony of Edwin Fanning, TLC, p. 69, as well as from that of little Lucretia Chapman, TLC, p. 89.

76 William's letter to Watkinson: TLC, p. 174; see also TLC, p. 38.

77 Durand's pharmacy: England, *The First Century of the Philadelphia College of Pharmacy, 1821–1921,* pp. 101–02, and 357–59.

77 "We haven't. But we might prepare it" and "If you have plain arsenic powder, that would answer": TLC, p. 30.

78 Arsenic was a principal ingredient in taxidermy: An eighteenth-century French apothecary named Becoeur was the first to use a paste

containing arsenic to preserve animal skins. He was reluctant to publish his recipe, but in 1820, taxidermist Louis Dufresne did so, and by 1831, when Lino made his request, arsenic had become the chief ingredient in preservative formulas. It remained in widespread use throughout the nineteenth century, and continued to be used by some taxidermists until the 1930s. See *WAAC Newsletter* (a publication of the Western Association for Art Conservation) 18, no. 1, Jan. 1996.

78 My description of Durand is based on the portrait of him in England, *The First Century of the Philadelphia College of Pharmacy.*

78 William's first uncomfortable night: See TLC, p. 90.

79 "The doctor will only give me medicine. I have drops for stomachache in the house. I'll take those": TLC, p. 90.

79 "You've had a mild attack of cholera morbus": TLC, p. 32.

79 "A beefsteak would do me more good than anything else": TLC, p. 33.

79 She decided on rice gruel . . . helping out in the kitchen: TLC, p. 90.

80 Little Lucretia was keeping William company. . . . He was vomiting again: TLC, p. 90–91.

81 "Not so well as in the morning. I have a misery at my stomach. It feels very much like fire": TLC, p. 24.

81 "Tarry with me through the night": TLC, p. 31.

82 "When Don Lino is sick all attention must be paid to him. But now that I am sick, I am deserted. I am left.": TLC, p. 68.

82 "Then give him some salt and water . . . heard it recommended": TLC, p. 31.

82 "I cannot live so": TLC, p. 32.

84 "Bury them"; "Fish water can kill ducks"; and "They've been poisoned": TLC, p. 35.

85 "Fifty-five beats in the minute" and "Now it's forty-five": TLC, p. 34.

86 "I studied medicine for two years": TLC, p. 35.

86 The Marsh test and the history of arsenic: Dr. Anil Aggrawal, "The Poison Sleuths: Arsenic—The King of Poisons," *Science Reporter,* February, 1997.

88 "Why would Don Lino not do," "Because he's a stranger. A stranger, and undersized," and "Yes. I see no impropriety in that": TLC, p. 35.

88 Scheetz had scolded the sexton . . . Dug right through the loamy clay to the sandy soil beneath: TLC, p. 92.

89 Putting straw on coffin lids: According to Nathaniel Hawthorne, this

New England custom came about because "the clods on the coffin-lid have an ugly sound." See Larkin, *The Reshaping of Everyday Life,* p. 101.

89 Covering the mirrors with white cloth: I'd always thought this a Jewish custom, but Larkin cites it as a New England one as well. See his *Reshaping of Everyday Life,* p. 100.

CHAPTER 6 BETRAYAL

91 Lucretia's remark that even the sun looked gloomy to her: TLC, p. 37.

92 According to Lucretia, it was Lino who proposed: TLC, p. 53; see also TLC, p. 75.

92 "Lino never forgets a favor. If you will marry me . . . shall share a part of them"; "Would it not be more proper for you to marry my daughter Mary"; "No, it is you . . . not knowing who I was"; and "It would be thought nothing of in Mexico": TLC, p. 39.

92 "Lino, I want you to marry me," "Not till I ask my father," and "I love you so much": STMC, p. 3.

93 "My Dear Lino . . . Lucretia Esposimina": July 5, 1831, letter, Lucretia Chapman (Albany, N.Y.) to Mina, M-CMCP.

93 It was a crude conveyance . . . mere twists of irregular-shaped logs: See Hand, *From a Forest to a City, Personal Reminiscences of Syracuse,* Syracuse, NY, 1889, p. 36; see also Franklin H. Chase, *Syracuse and Its Environs,* Lewis Historical Publishing Co., Inc., New York, vol. 1, p. 306.

94 My description of Lucretia's ride from Albany to Syracuse is drawn from the July 7, 1831, letter, Lucretia Chapman (Syracuse, N.Y.) to Mina, M-CMCP.

95 Comstock's Hotel: see *Syracuse Courier,* Syracuse, N.Y., March 15, 1880.

95 "I have not lain down one minute . . . dear companion for life" and "I very well know . . . without resting on her bed": July 7, 1831, letter, Lucretia Chapman (Syracuse, N.Y.) to Mina, M-CMCP.

96 Lucretia's ascetic lunch: It was probably just as well that she didn't take the time to eat a big meal. Charles Dickens, who dined at Comstock's some years later, complained, "I have tried all the wines in the house and there are only two wines, for which you pay six shillings a bottle, or fifteen, according as you feel disposed to change the name of the thing you asked for. (The article never changes.) The bill of fare is in French,

and the principal article . . . is 'Paettie de shay.' I asked the Irish waiter what this dish was and he said: 'It was the name the steward giv' to oyster patties — the Frinch name. These are the drinks you are to wash it down with: 'Monseuz,' 'Abasinth,' 'Curacco,' 'Marschine,' 'Anise,' and 'Margeaux.' " See "Dickens' Correspondence," *Syracuse Journal*, Dec. 8, 1879.

97 The property of married women: In 1831 all that a married woman possessed belonged to her current husband; New York, the first state to pass an act protecting the property of married women, did so in 1860. See "The Married Women's Property Act," in Miriam Schneir, *Feminism: The Essential Historical Writings* (New York, 1972), p. 122.

97 Early feminists . . . were already denouncing such laws: Frances Wright called the laws governing married women's property "absolute spoilation" which permitted "robbery, and all but murder, against the unhappy female who swears away, at one and the same moment, her person and her property." Cited in Tyler, *Freedom's Ferment*, p. 428.

97 "They've moved ten or fifteen miles into the country," "Spend the night with us" and "I should not be able to sleep": July 7, 1831, letter, Lucretia Chapman (Syracuse, N.Y.) to Mina, M-CMCP.

99 "My pretty little husband," "be careful, my dear, and not spill and so lose our precious love," "let our children see the nonsense I have written," and "Goodbye, goodbye, dear Lino . . . as is my young General Esposimina": July 8, 1831 letter from Clay, N.Y., included with July 7, 1831, letter, Lucretia Chapman (Syracuse, N.Y.) to Mina, M-CMCP.

99 "As a memento," "the black woman took them," and "I followed her . . . pay the rest": TLC, p. 39.

100 Lucretia's clothes: see "London Female Fashions for May," *Godey's Lady's Book*, Philadelphia, June 1831, and "Philadelphia Fashions for the Month of July 1831," *Godey's Lady's Book*, July 1831.

100 Two new girls: TLC, p. 37.

101 "But you have William's already": TLC, p. 39.

101 "My Beloved Wife . . . Repay you with ingratitude": July 18, 1831, letter, Mina (Philadelphia) to Lucretia Chapman, M-CMCP.

102 "The whole house is dull . . . with melancholy": TLC, p. 44.

103 "Those stars . . . given to me without stopping": TLC, p. 44.

103 Receiving forty dollars for them: Receipt, Lino to Samuel Miles, n.d., M-CMCP.

104 Heat wave: *Philadelphia Poulson's American Daily Advertiser*, July 22, 1831.

104 The resorts of Cape May and Long Branch: Oberholtzer, *Philadelphia*, pp. 50–51.

104 The resorts of Sweet Springs and Niagara Falls: *Philadelphia Poulson's American Daily Advertiser,* Friday, July 22, 1831.

104 "They've gone to the Falls of Niagara": July 31, 1831, letter, Lucretia Chapman (Andalusia) to Mina (Washington), M-CMCP.

105 Gone for quite a while: Cuesta left the city long before Lucretia's visit. He departed on June 20, 1831, TLC, p. 84.

105 "Señor Espos y Mina has not been here for a long time": July 31, 1831, letter, Lucretia Chapman (Andalusia) to Mina (Washington), M-CMCP.

105 The United States Hotel: see Hamilton, *Men and Manners in America*, p. 215.

105 "I went to inform you . . . duty to inform you of this," "I think your Señor Lino is as great a scoundrel as ever lived," "I hope not, Mr. Watkinson," "I sent to the consul's to inquire . . . to be an impostor," and "You have acted perfectly right": TLC, pp. 26–27.

107 The bill directed to the attention of "Mr. Amalio": Lucretia included this bill in the letter she sent to Lino on July 31, 1831.

107 Lino had left the bill instead of a dagger to pierce her to the heart: TLC, p. 48.

107 "His excellency the President": July 28, 1831, letter, Mina (Baltimore) to Lucretia Chapman, M-CMCP.

108 "expressed great desire" and "speedily": July 26, 1831, letter, Mina (Washington) to Lucretia Chapman, M-CMCP.

108 "I find your presence so necessary . . . insupportable to me": TLC, p. 44.

108 "As often as I remember your caresses . . . most soul-shed tears": July 26, 1831, letter, Mina (Washington) to Lucretia Chapman, M-CMCP.

108 "When I left Baltimore . . . one long embrace": July 25, 1831, letter, Mina (Washington) to Lucretia Chapman, M-CMCP.

108 "The translator of the above . . . He is the lady's slave": July 25, 1831, letter, Mina (Washington) to Lucretia Chapman, M-CMCP.

109 "extensive robbery," "horse and carriage . . . cake basket," "You say in your last letter . . . Duke of England," "perfectly happy," "But no, Lino . . . happy this side of the grave" and "Lucretia": July 31, 1831, letter, Lucretia Chapman (Andalusia) to Mina (Washington), M-CMCP.

CHAPTER 7 DEPARTURES

111 Philadelphia's police force: *Report of Committee on Police,* p. 1.

111 The hardships of work in nineteenth-century print shops: See the reminiscences of Horace Greeley and William Dean Howells, cited in Larkin, *The Reshaping of Everyday Life,* pp. 41–42.

112 One of his underlings, thinking the widow's letter insignificant... discarded it: *Philadelphia National Gazette,* May 1, 1832.

112 A peculiar web of underlined words... narrow margins: An original of Lucretia's July 31, 1831 letter to Lino, which shows her emphatic style and distraught-looking handwriting, can be found among the papers in M-CMCP.

113 "I've been to New Orleans"; "I went all the way on the railroad"; and "Traveled night and day—at the rate of *thirty* miles an hour": TLC, p. 50 (italics added).

113 "Leave me": TLC, p. 40.

113 "What's the matter... believed it"; "The chain you gave me is not gold"; "If your affections are so slender... might have been deceived himself"; "I ran under the arcade... umbrella": TLC, p. 40.

114 "I was up all night... go home the next day": TLC, p. 51.

114 "My sister is not at all satisfied with this conduct" and "We had better be separated then—I find I have more wives than one to please": TLC, p. 40.

114 "The sooner, the better"; "Remember, Mrs. *Chapman,* before I go I must tell you something [italics added]"; "What is it"; and "I cannot tell you... I will tell you": TLC, p. 40.

115 "something between ourselves": TLC, p. 40.

115 Lino's request that the letter not mention their marriage: TLC, p. 87.

115 The Winslows' purchase of wilderness for the purpose of farming: Holton, *Winslow Memorial,* p. 74.

115 Brewster's prosperity: Schneider, *The Enduring Shore,* p. 224.

116 Elijah Cobb's history: Cobb, *Elijah Cobb,* pp. 8–9, and Schneider, *The Enduring Shore,* pp. 171–75 and 252.

117 "I saw Robertspiers head taken off by the [infernal] Machine": Cobb, *Elijah Cobb,* p. 9. Cobb's terseness about the death of Robespierre, a man he had actually met, is remarked upon by the editor of the captain's memoir, Ralph D. Paine.

117 Lino and the high sheriff of Barnstable County: *Philadelphia Saturday Bulletin,* Nov. 5, 1831.

118 "I understand that a person calling himself Mina spent some time in your house" and "He said he was going to the north": TLC, p. 49.

118 "I have in my possession . . . suffered from his impositions": TLC, p. 49.

119 "I'd supposed from his account . . . traveled night and day at the rate of thirty miles an hour" and "There *is* no railroad to New Orleans": TLC, p. 50.

119 A railroad train started running to New Orleans in November 1831: see *Chronicle of America,* Chronicle Publications, Mt. Kisco, N.Y., n.d., entry for November 1831.

119 "From my knowledge of the character of this man . . . that he administered it"; McIlvaine's surprise at Lucretia's sudden paleness; "Did anything occur . . . that I suspected"; and "No, I saw nothing of the kind. Lino was Mr. Chapman's kind nurse during his illness": TLC, p. 49.

120 McIlvaine takes note of Lucretia's reaction; "I have no knowledge further . . . to the north"; "If it is possible . . . punished for his crimes"; and "a mystery upon my mind": TLC, p. 50.

120 Lino's courtship of Lucretia's niece: TLC, p. 52; see also *Philadelphia Saturday Bulletin,* Oct. 22, 1831.

121 "Dear Madam": TLC, p. 53.

121 The details of Lino's letter to Lucretia from Brewster: Sept. 1, 1831, letter, Mina (Brewster, Mass.) to Lucretia Chapman (Andalusia), M-CMCP; see also TLC, p. 53.

122 "nearly a hundred ladies of the first families": *Philadelphia Saturday Bulletin,* Oct. 22, 1831.

122 Ballroom etiquette of the day: *The Laws of Etiquette,* pp. 57 and 113.

123 Cotillions: Americans, observed Fanny Trollope in 1832, in her *Domestic Manners of the Americans,* "call their dances cotillions instead of quadrilles" (p. 130). Today, many of the figures of the cotillion, including the grand chain, the ladies' chain, and the promenade, are still danced by square and contra dancers. See Elizabeth Aldrich, *From the Ballroom to Hell, Grace and Folly in Nineteenth Century Dance* (Evanston, Ill.), pp. 141–45.

123 Lino's ball costume: *Philadelphia Saturday Bulletin,* Oct. 22, 1831.

123 "I have been deceived and injured by Lino Espos y Mina": TLC, p. 50.

124 McIlvaine's thoughts: TLC, p. 50.

124 "I cannot promise . . . rescue you from those consequences";
"Fictitious"; "Did Mina palm upon you any other documents or
papers"; "For what purpose was this paper obtained": TLC, p. 51.
125 "Señor Mina's health is fragile . . . no means of claiming my rights to his
properties": TLC, p. 52.
125 "I want to obtain a divorce from Mina"; "I can offer you no opinion on
this"; "You must give me that paper . . . forgery committed in
Pennsylvania"; "Will these communications get me into trouble"; and
"You have come to me voluntarily . . . It is for you to decide whether the
papers should be left or not": TLC, p. 51.
126 Lucretia's agitation: TLC, p. 51.
126 Deputy attorney general: At the time, instead of a judicial district's
electing a district attorney as prosecuting officer, the attorney general of
the state appointed a deputy to fulfill this function. See *Philadelphia
Saturday Bulletin,* March 6, 1928.
126 He had a case to turn over to him . . . possibly of murder: TLC, p. 51.
126 *Philadelphia National Gazette* article: Interestingly, the story had
already appeared the day before in a New York newspaper.
126 "A Villain Arrested": *Philadelphia National Gazette,* Sept. 17, 1831.
127 "I hear Lino's been arrested in Boston! On suspicion of poisoning
William"; "Is it possible"; "I hear you married him"; "Of course not";
"Was my name in the paper"; "Oh, Lucretia. How could you have been
so imprudent as to marry that man"; and "It must be a fact. Or they
wouldn't dare to publish it": TLC, p. 36.
127 "I thought he was very rich. I thought it was best for me—and for the
children": TLC, p. 51.
128 "Mrs. Chapman, I shouldn't be surprised if the fellow had poisoned
your husband": TLC, p. 39.
128 "Do you think so, my dear? The police have intimated the same thing";
"Hearsay is not proof"; "Are you going somewhere"; "On a short trip.
I'm going to town to sell some books"; "Don't you think you are wrong
to go off at a time like this? It looks like running off"; and "I'm not
running off. I'm just going a short way to sell some books and get some
money. I'm badly off for money": TLC, p. 39.

CHAPTER 8 FRIENDS AND FOES
131 Brown's appearance: See his portrait in Jackson, *Encyclopedia of
Philadelphia,* p. 343; see also DPB, vol. 1, p. 119.

131 Brown's autobiographical work: see DPB.

131 "Hortensius was a lawyer—Cicero an orator, the one is forgotten, the other immortalized": DPB, vol. 2, p. lv.

131 If you asked *him,* David Paul Brown: My introduction of David Paul Brown is drawn from DPB's "Biographical Memoir," a lengthy tribute that is more autobiographical than biographical, for it consists chiefly of passages written by Brown himself and quotations from his speeches and from remarks he made to friends. I've used Brown's words, condensing them somewhat, as he was even wordier than he sounds here, and tried to give the flavor of his voice.

132 The story of the composition of *Sertorius:* DPB, vol. 1 p. 70.

132 "Composing upon all fours . . . profitable": DPB, vol. 1 p. 70.

132 Legal work had made him even richer: In DPB, p. xxxi, Brown says he made one hundred thousand dollars in his first fifteen years of law practice—i.e., 1816-1831. Very few lawyers earned this much at that time. "A typical income seemed to be something less than $1,000 a year in 1810 or 1820," writes Friedman in *A History of American Law,* p. 306. But there were, he points out, a few big moneymakers, one of whom was the extraordinary Daniel Webster, who "usually earned over $10,000 a year after 1825; in 1835-36, he earned over $21,000 in fees."

132 He spent money as fast as he earned it . . . was *his* spur: DPB, vol. 1, pp. 32, 120.

132 When he was a child . . . made himself master of all within: DPB, vol. 1, p. 120.

132 His early days as a lawyer and orator . . . eager to enjoy his erudition and his passion: DPB, vol. 1, pp. 40-49.

134 The very essence of the term "gentleman": Anne Royall says of Brown, "He is in the prime of life, of middling size, handsome person, and elegant manners. . . . If the appellation of gentleman be confined to personal appearance, Mr. Brown well merits the epithet." Royall, *Mrs. Royall's Pennsylvania,* p. 60.

134 All our days are anxious . . . knowing no end: DPB, vol. 1, pp. 123-24.

135 The poor thing . . . had come inquiring after her fiancé's whereabouts on the day after his arrest: see McIlvaine's testimony, TLC, p. 52.

135 "I wish to make some confidential communications to you," "On what subject," "On the subject of Mr. and Mrs. Chapman," and "I don't wish to hear anything. Better keep it to yourself": STMC, p. 3.

136 "That he and Mrs. Chapman were married. And that before they were married she used to come to his room very often": STMC, p. 2.

136 "Mrs. Chapman came to me . . . Mr. Chapman's death": STMC, p. 3.

136 Blayney's spurning of Lino: STMC, p. 3.

137 "So you've intimated two or three times," "If you'll answer two questions for me, I'll listen to you," and "Nothing you say to me will appear against you if you're indicted for the murder of Dr. William Chapman": STMC, p. 3.

137 "Have you ever been in jail," "No," "Have you ever been a pirate," and "No": STMC, p. 3.

137 Reynell Coates: His first name is spelled "Reynell" in *The Trial of Lucretia Chapman*, but "Reynall" in Jackson's *Encyclopedia of Philadelphia*, and "Reynold" in Green's *A History of Bristol Borough*.

138 Coates's wife: Green, *A History of Bristol Borough*, p. 184.

138 The condition of William's face and body: TLC, pp. 55 and 57; see also *Philadelphia Saturday Bulletin*, Oct. 22, 1831.

138 The graveside autopsy: TLC, pp. 55 and 57.

139 "Have I missed anything? Should I cut further?", and "I'd compare it to pickled herring": TLC, p. 55.

140 "the smell of a dried Scotch herring": TLC, p. 59.

140 Collecting the mucus: TLC, p. 60.

141 "the '*Domestic News*' of every journal . . . which the public appetite demands with a gusto": cited in Reynolds, *Beneath the American Renaissance*, p. 173.

141 Orson Squire Fowler: Interestingly, in *The Dictionary of American Biography*, published in 1937, Fowler's theories are treated with scorn and only a few of the many books he published are noted. But in Appleton's *Cyclopedia of American Biography*, published in 1888, before eugenics fell into disrepute, Fowler's theories are treated respectfully and a great many of his books are listed.

141 "the disposition and mental powers of mankind are *innate*—are *born*, not created by education": O. S. Fowler, *Hereditary Descent: Its Laws and Facts* (New York, 1843), p. 4.

142 "mode of moving . . . tone of voice, manner of laughing, form of nose and mouth, color of eyes and teeth, and other peculiarities": O. S. Fowler, *Hereditary Descent: Its Laws and Facts* (New York, 1848), p. 23.

142 "intellectual superiority," "acquisitiveness" and "destructiveness": Fowler, *Hereditary Descent*, 1848 edition, p. xi.

142 "conscientiousness" and "benevolence": Fowler, *Hereditary Descent,* 1848 edition, p. xi.

142 Lucretia's disguise: *Barnstable Patriot,* Nov. 16, 1831.

143 "unequalled by any County Court House and jail in the state": *Bucks County Intelligencer,* January 1833, cited in Davis, *History of Doylestown Old and New,* p. 28.

147 The conditions of Lino's confinement, his relationship with Brown, his prison break, and the remarks he makes to the army officer who apprehends him are drawn from accounts of his escape in the *Philadelphia Saturday Bulletin,* Nov. 12, 1831, and Dec. 10, 1831.

149 Lucretia's stay in Greenfield, Pennsylvania: *Philadelphia Saturday Bulletin,* Nov. 19, 1831.

150 "An able Advocate . . . to aid him in pleading her cause": TLC, p. 86.

150 "Ah! From what a height I have fallen" and the quotations in the following two paragraphs are from Lucretia's letter to Cobb, printed in the *Germantown Telegraph* on Feb. 15, 1832. The letter was eventually widely reprinted.

151 "very wellbred and intelligent woman" and "imprudently": *Boston Morning Post,* Dec. 1, 1831.

151 Brown's account of Lucretia's visit to him: DPB, vol. 2, pp. 419–20. Page references to specific dialogue and thoughts from that account are cited below.

152 "striking," "slender," and "well-proportioned": DPB, vol. 2, p. 419.

152 "What service can I render you, Madam?": DPB, vol. 2, p. 419.

152 *"Mrs. Chapman"*: DPB, vol. 2, p. 420.

152 Who could have put such an idea into the editor's head . . . no idea: Brown writes in DPB, vol. 2, p. 419, that he was "apprized through the public journals" that it was understood, "from what quarter I am at a loss to ascertain," that Lucretia's defense would be entrusted to him. But it's highly likely he put out the word himself. According to Friedman in his *History of American Law,* "Almost all lawyers, then, were constantly seeking new business and were in constant need of advertisements for themselves . . . lawyers reached out for the public through notices ('cards') and the newspapers" (p. 309).

152 Delicately, oh as delicately as possible: DPB, vol. 2, p. 420.

152 Remember . . . if you perform your task feebly, the blood of the defendant may be upon you. Do not, therefore, allow a feverish desire for notoriety blind you to the difficulties and dangers by which you will

inevitably be surrounded, for the trumpet of fame cannot drown the small still voice of remorse: DPB, vol. 1, p. 82. Brown originally wrote this maxim, and several others, which he called "Capital Hints in Capital Cases," in 1850, setting them down for the edification of his sons, who had just been admitted to the bar.

153 Lucretia's trial was due to start in just a few short days: The concept of a speedy trial meant something in those days. Lucretia was arrested on Nov. 11, 1831. She visited Brown on December 10, 1831. She was indicted on Dec. 12, 1831. The first hearing in her case was on Dec. 14, 1831. And her trial commenced on February 14, 1832.

153 "a splendid mansion, in which wealth and taste are alike diffused": Royall, *Mrs. Royall's Pennsylvania*, p. 60.

153 He would be like the commander of a ship in a storm. . . . perish gloriously in the faithful discharge of his duty: DPB, vol. 2, p. lxxxvi.

154 He had assumed the responsibility of a cause upon whose outcome depended . . . the hopes and happiness of all who belonged to her: DPB, vol. 2, p. 420.

CHAPTER 9 PENNSYLVANIA V. LUCRETIA CHAPMAN, PART ONE

155 Brown's first expedition to Doylestown: DPB, vol. 2, pp. 420–23.

157 "Lucretia Espos y Mina . . . Commonwealth of Pennsylvania": TLC, pp. 3–4.

158 "Iago," "old Judas," and "a stripling of old Judas": Yerkes, "John Ross and the Ross Family," p. 377.

158 John Ross's difficult personality: *Book of Biographies*, p. 12.

158 "Dear Tom . . . acceptable": Yerkes, "John Ross and the Ross Family," p. 382.

158 Mary Ross: Yerkes, "John Ross and the Ross Family," p. 384; see also *Book of Biographies*, p. 12.

158 Intended soon to tell a jury: In his opening remarks, Ross would call Lucretia "wanton" and declare she was "possessed of no moral principle sufficient to restrain her" from committing murder: TLC, p. 18.

158 "Not guilty. . . Not guilty": TLC, p. 6.

159 McDowell's appearance, popularity and success as a lawyer: Davis, *History of Doylestown Old and New*, pp. 144–45; see also Caleb E. Wright, "Four Lawyers of the Doylestown Bar," p. 267.

159 "How would you be tried . . . By God and my country": TLC, p. 6.

159 A jury half composed of foreigners: although McDowell and Rush had informed the court that they might request such a jury (TLC, p. 6), in the end they did not do so.

159 "Are you ready for trial" and "Yes": TLC, p. 7.

160 "To urge an immediate trial . . . highest degree unjust": TLC, p. 7.

160 William B. Reed: *The Dictionary of American Biography,* 1935.

160 "We are ready to go to trial. . . . earlier than February": TLC, p. 7.

160 "January ninth": TLC, p. 8. For the purpose of narrative energy, in both this chapter and the next I have frequently put into Fox's mouth words that DuBois attributed merely to "the Court" or "the judges."

160 Judge Fox's appearance and background: for his solemn and aristocratic looks, see the portrait of him in Davis, *History of Doylestown Old and New,* p. 304; for his stint as deputy attorney general of Bucks County, see Pugh, "The Rodmans and the Foxes," p. 230; for his intimacy with and services to Andrew Jackson, see Davis, *History of Doylestown Old and New,* p. 36.

161 "January thirtieth" and "Case continued until Monday, February thirteenth": TLC, p. 8.

161 "if life was to be lost, it would not be without a [valiant] struggle": DPB, vol. II, p. 424.

161 Brown and McCall's roadside mishap and the one-day delay of the trial: TLC, p. 8.

162 "Mr. Speaker! Who can bear the thought of seeing a black speaker occupying that chair in which you are now seated": *Philadelphia National Gazette,* Feb. 21, 1831.

163 Crushing the ribs of one guard: Kenderdine, "The Chapman-Mina Tragedy," p. 459.

163 Lucretia and Lino's appearance and dress: *Germantown Telegraph,* Feb. 22, 1832.

163 "My application for separate trials is a mutual one . . . injustice would be done if both were tried together": TLC, p. 8.

163 "The mode and manner . . . granted separate trials": TLC, p. 9.

164 "If our application is refused . . . that it may not be granted": TLC, p. 11.

164 "We can't proceed"; "The prosecution . . . direct that they be allowed to have separate trials"; and "We would like to take up the case of Lucretia Chapman first": TLC, p. 12.

165 "a sort of moral torture": TLC, p. 14.

165 "the doors of the prison . . . the trouble of a trial": TLC, p. 14.

166 Quaker opposition to serving on juries deciding capital cases: In subsequent years many Bucks County Quakers would ask to be excused from serving on juries that decided capital cases. Thaddeus S. Kenderdine, writing in 1907, says, "In the several murder trials in Bucks County since [the Chapman-Mina trials] I doubt if there has been a single member [of the Society of Friends] on the jury," and explains the willingness of Quakers to serve on the Chapman and Mina juries as being due to "the public desire for the riddance of monsters so great": Kenderdine, "The Chapman-Mina Tragedy," p. 460.

166 "Opposition to capital punishment . . . have such scruples, others have not": TLC, p. 16.

166 The jurors: for the son of a delegate to the Constitutional Convention of 1790, see Davis, *History of Bucks County Pennsylvania,* vol. 2, p. 84, re Hartzell; for the organizer of a society that promoted farming, see Davis, *History of Bucks County Pennsylvania,* vol. 2, p. 353, re Watson; for the coal merchant, see Davis, *History of Bucks County Pennsylvania,* vol. 3, p. 124, re Yardley.

167 "Gentlemen of the jury . . . any other country": TLC, p. 17.

168 Lucretia's tears and the presence of the children in the courtroom: see *Philadelphia National Gazette,* Feb. 28, 1832.

168 Mercy's daughter and son-in-law, Mrs. and Captain Baker, are referred to by McIlvaine, TLC, p. 52.

168 "We shall lay before you a letter of Mrs. Chapman's . . . Blood, though it sleep a time, yet never dies": TLC, pp. 18–19.

169 "They went up to Bonaparte's" and "I saw Mina and Mrs. Chapman together often": TLC, p. 19.

169 "Under what circumstances?" This is a surmised question. Du Bois almost never recorded the questions put by the lawyers and judges, merely the answers witnesses gave to their questions. Here, and throughout the courtroom scenes that follow, I have had to infer the questions from the answers. Additionally, for dramatic purpose, I have at times put the questions into quotation marks, rather than presenting them, as DuBois did on the rare occasions when he bothered to include questions, as indirect discourse.

169 "Mina used to have fits . . . closed the windows"; "I don't think Mrs. Chapman treated her husband right"; and "She called him a fool on Sunday, as we were going to church": TLC, p. 19.

169 Brown's questions: TLC, p. 20.

170 "this plaguey trial": TLC, p. 67.

170 "His shirt wasn't worth anything": TLC, p. 22.

170 "He was a Spaniard": TLC, p. 20.

170 "They used to kiss each other" and "They sang love songs to each other": TLC, p. 21.

170 "They were often engaged in a private room by themselves": TLC, p. 22.

170 "Mrs. Chapman went up to Lino's room. . . . wearing her nightdress" and "His spells . . . soon over them": TLC, p. 21.

170 Mrs. Chapman said *she* had to have the horse . . . could do as she pleased: TLC, p. 66.

171 "She spoke pretty harsh sometimes": TLC, p. 21.

171 "She used to tell him she was ashamed of him . . . tired of him": TLC, p. 67.

171 "Was that why you left the Chapmans' employ?": Question inferred from Ellen's answer, which follows.

171 "I left because there were things going on . . . great deal of talk about Mrs. Chapman and her boarder": TLC, p. 21.

171 The woman's a human volcano . . . bent on total destruction: TLC, pp. 168–70.

171 "I have had no difference with Mrs. Chapman" and "Mrs. Chapman always had the chief management of the household": TLC, p. 21–22.

171 "You say . . . what room was that": As mentioned earlier, Du Bois was in the habit of writing down witnesses' answers and leaving out the questions to which the witnesses were responding. Thus, in this scene, Brown's questions are surmised from the answers Ellen gave him.

171 "The parlor"; "Religious service . . . much good did it do"; "What did you mean . . . did no good"; and "No. It just seems that way, seeing the way things turned out there": TLC, p. 22. I have adapted this line of Ellen's from Du Bois's statement on p. 22 that when Ellen was "asked by the Court what she meant by that last phrase [i.e., 'much good did it do,'], she said she had no fact to ground her opinion upon . . . except the way things had turned out."

172 "Was your employer in the habit of singing songs?" This is a surmised question, based on the answer that Ellen gives next.

172 "She was not in the habit of singing songs," and "She had a piano, and played and sung hymn tunes": TLC, p. 23.

172 "What hymns did she sing?": Again, this is a surmised question, based on the answer Ellen gives next.

172 "I can't tell the names of any of the songs" and "This court has already refused . . . former case": TLC, p. 23.

173 Sat down at Lucretia's right: TLC, p. 23.

173 Where else should the boarder have sat . . . nothing at all: these musings are drawn from the remarks Brown made about Esther Bache's testimony in his closing argument; see TLC, p. 170.

173 The pivot upon which the prosecution intended to rest its whole case: See Brown, TLC, p. 171.

174 Brown's thoughts regarding Boutcher: In his summation, Brown would make a pun about "quackery" and the poultry farmer's "long lamented *Quacks*" (TLC, p. 172). It was a pun that the *Philadelphia Saturday Bulletin* of May 5, 1832, would criticize as being in bad taste, and call an "ill-timed and misplaced" attempt at humor.

174 "Who brought the soup and uneaten chicken back to the kitchen": A surmised question, based on Ann's answer, which follows.

174 "Mrs. Chapman put it on the table and left it there": TLC, p. 25.

174 "Did Mrs. Chapman . . . the leftover chicken": Again, surmised, based on the answer that follows.

174 "I don't recollect that she said anything": See TLC, p. 25.

174 "Was it thrown out right away": Again, a surmised question, based on answer that follows.

174 "No, the chicken stood on the table . . . washed up the dishes": TLC, p. 26.

174 "Was anyone else in the kitchen while the chicken and soup were sitting out": Again, a surmised question, based on the answer that follows.

174 "The whole five of the children . . . being in the kitchen every day": TLC, p. 25.

175 "Did Mrs. Chapman clean the pot": Fox's question is surmised from the answer Ann gives next.

175 "I do not think she cleaned the pot": TLC, p. 25.

175 "Did she tell you to throw away the leftover food": again, a surmised question, based on the answer that follows.

175 "Mrs. Chapman gave me no directions to throw the soup or the chicken away": TLC, p. 25.

175 Poisoned chalice: Brown would use the phrase "poisoned chalice" and

argue that it was beyond belief that a mother would permit such an object to remain "in the very centre of her children" in his closing arguments, TLC, p. 172.

175 "Carolino Estradas was born . . . generous, and liberal": CEM, p. 5.

176 "A quarter of a pound of arsenic . . . gave it to him myself": TLC, p. 29.

177 "I saw no want of tenderness . . . unbecoming to a wife": TLC, p. 33.

177 "Might arsenic have accounted for Dr. Chapman's symptoms": A surmised question, based on the answer Phillips gives, which follows.

177 "If arsenic had been administered, it would, I think, have accounted for some of the symptoms . . . But neither am I prepared to say that natural causes and natural disease might not produce the same symptoms": TLC, p. 33.

177 "At present, the aspect of affairs . . . so strong a case as was expected": *Germantown Telegraph,* Feb. 22, 1832. The story was actually written earlier; its dateline is Feb. 17, 1832.

178 When the trial resumed . . . suddenly sympathetic to her: The change is reported in the *Germantown Telegraph,* Feb. 22, 1832.

178 "She absented herself . . . thought right"; "I do not remember her saying she had no servant," and "I do not know if . . . reluctance to take the medicine": TLC, p. 34.

178 "There were between twenty and thirty that died that day and the next": TLC, p. 35.

179 "For him to describe these bones . . . miraculous organs": TLC, p. 70.

179 "this side of the grave": TLC, p. 48.

179 A clear reference to the pair's having committed murder: TLC, p. 124.

179 Brown, of course, viewed the words differently . . . one the jury might well appreciate: TLC, p. 151.

180 "Several letters were put in evidence today . . . sought after with great avidity": *Germantown Telegraph,* Feb. 22, 1832.

180 Murder trial books: see chapter six, "The Sensational Press and the Rise of Subversive Literature," in Reynolds, *Beneath the American Renaissance.*

181 He would make it a big book . . . *all* the romantic and seamy details: see Du Bois's "Advertisement," for his book, TLC, p. 1.

181 The publishing firm of G. W. Mentz & Son: Robert Cazden, *A Social History of the German Book Trade in America to the Civil War* (Columbia, S.C.), p. 81.

182 Brown's questions in this scene are, as explained earlier, surmised from Hopkinson's answers.

182 "Putrefaction might be retarded by dry soil"; "I never heard or read . . . belonging to arsenic"; and "Though I have never . . . terminate fatally": TLC, p. 56.

183 "No one can be certain . . . found in the body": TLC, p. 59.

183 "Chemical proofs . . . of its presence": TLC, p. 62.

183 "Smearcase and pork . . . sure to hurt him": TLC, p. 63.

184 "Other substances can produce . . . one may be deceived": TLC, p. 65.

184 Most trials at the time were exceedingly short . . . a few hours: Friedman, *Crime and Punishment in American History*, p. 245.

184 Ross's gold snuff box: Davis, "Half an Hour with the Old Taverns of Doylestown," p. 437.

185 The high constable had a sick child . . . official duties: TLC, p. 96.

185 "Your Honor, the stagecoach from Philadelphia . . . without his person"; "No further delays"; "May it please your Honors . . . staked upon the issue of your decision": TLC, p. 70.

CHAPTER 10 PENNSYLVANIA V. LUCRETIA CHAPMAN, PART TWO

187 Brown's strategy: DPB, vol. 2, pp. 432 and 436.

188 "Do you know what you have come here for"; "To swear to all I know"; "Do you know what will become of you if you do not tell the truth"; and "I will be cast into hell fire forever": TLC, p. 89.

188 "Pa was sitting in the rocking chair, nursing little John": TLC, p. 89.

188 "truckle bed": TLC, p. 91.

189 "Mary brought the chicken and soup upstairs"; "The soup was in a blue quart bowl. The chicken was on a plate, I think . . . Pa cut it himself": TLC, p. 91; "Pa tasted the gizzard, but it was tough. He gave the rest to me and I ate it" and "Pa ate only a few spoonsful of the soup, but ate very heartily of the chicken. I ate some of the soup myself": TLC, p. 90.

189 "Her character was more than moral"; "very religious"; and "If anything had happened . . . informed of it": TLC, p. 92.

190 "In the neighborhood of the ear": TLC, p. 92.

191 "I believe I am acquainted with the general character of Mrs. Chapman. From 1818 to 1829 . . . gradually getting worse": TLC, p. 96.

191 "Not in those exact words. I have said . . . to my personal knowledge, I

have never seen anything but what was right"; "She lived in my
mother's house and behaved herself remarkably well . . . I never heard
anything to the contrary"; "I am speaking of a police report"; and "I
can't say I ever heard a good police report": TLC, p. 96.

193 "the lower jaw falls . . . the eyes are cast down, half-shut" and "the eyes
open, but with the eyebrows considerably drawn down, the mouth
pouting out, mostly shut, and the lips pinched close": Moore, John
Hamilton, *The Young Gentleman and Young Lady's Explanatory
Monitor,* New York, 1813, p. 320.

193 "as husbands and fathers, knowing the loveliness of domestic love,
appreciating the sanctity of domestic obligation" and "a more
unnatural, a more revolting crime than that which blasts all these, and
blurs the purity of woman's fame": TLC, p. 118.

194 "in whose bosom the flame of impure passion brightens, that there is a
summary mode by which she can remove the only check to licentious
indulgence, and suggest means and materials for the completion of the
gloomy edifice of crime": TLC, p. 99.

194 "In the moral law of God the first great prohibition was, 'Thou shalt not
kill,' the next, 'Thou shalt not commit adultery'—and the interval
between the two points on the scale of human depravity is small,
indeed": TLC, p. 118.

194 "little creatures from five to ten years of age"; "to lisp from their slender
summits entreaties for Divine mercy"; and "The mercy this wretched
woman does not dare to ask, she has brought these innocent children to
ask for her": TLC, p. 128.

194 "thunder of *that* voice, the lightning of *that* eye": TLC, p. 115.

195 "filled as they are with disgusting effusions of passion": TLC, p. 116.

195 "the wealth she supposed the seducer to possess . . . the rank and
honors with which she believed him to be clothed": TLC, p. 112.

195 "Why is Mary Chapman not produced": TLC, p. 127.

196 Brown's indisposition on the morning of his summation: TLC, p. 155.

196 Brown's maxims: DPB, vol. 1, p. 83.

197 "One thing that speaks volumes . . . more than twelve months": TLC,
p. 144.

197 "Left upon the wide theater . . . and promoting their happiness": TLC,
p. 149.

197 "however, if fate should decree this speech to be my last . . . hapless,
helpless, friendless and forlorn": TLC, p. 155.

197 "the storm, the tempest, the whirlwind of prejudice . . . the leprous distillment of pernicious rumor," and "the sacred ermine of justice to be stained or polluted by the blood of the guiltless": TLC, p. 156.

197 "should it affix crime to a mother's name . . . stigmatize their memory when dead": TLC, p. 157.

198 "dumb witness . . . small, it is true, but with a giant's strength": TLC, p. 161.

198 Vipers and liars: TLC, p. 168.

198 "Was she to join in the general cry . . . fidelity is the brightest jewel that adorns the female character": TLC, p. 178.

199 "She was the teacher of a large and highly respectable seminary . . . That she should shrink from it, therefore, was natural—was excusable": TLC, p. 177.

199 "return to your own domestic circle, to your own firesides . . . And thereby give them to understand how frail and feeble is the tenure of human happiness—human character—and human life": TLC, p. 180.

199 "Powerful": *Philadelphia National Gazette*, Feb. 28, 1832.

199 "fame for energy and eloquence": *Philadelphia Saturday Bulletin*, March 3, 1832.

199 Mary Ross: Yerkes, "John Ross and the Ross Family," p. 385.

200 "the ground upon which you stand is holy; the moment you passed the threshold of this sanctuary of justice . . . every passion or feeling of excitement which you may have heretofore imbibed": TLC, p. 182.

201 "any woman who would compel [her husband] to make the bed . . . of a savage or a demon": TLC, p. 192.

201 "the wife who can defile . . . taking the life of that husband": TLC, p. 194.

201 "gained a niche in the temple of infamy," and "She has inscribed her name upon the darkest page of guilt . . . until oblivion shall have wiped her name from the scroll of time": TLC, p. 206.

202 Thomas Ross's singularity and his career: see Yerkes, "John Ross and the Ross Family," p. 385.

202 "persevering zeal": *Philadelphia Saturday Bulletin*, March 3, 1832.

202 "able": *Philadelphia National Gazette*, Feb. 28, 1832.

202 "masculine intelligence and habits": TLC, p. 117.

203 Judge Fox's charges: According to the *Philadelphia National Gazette*, Feb. 28, 1832, Fox's charges seemed to lean decidedly against Lucretia.

203 "Not guilty": TLC, p. 213.

204 Lucretia's triumphal departure from Doylestown: DPB, vol. 2, p. 440.

204 "The Creator who, in his infinite wisdom, foresaw that gold would be the cause of many evils to man . . . prime mover of all the horrid circumstances which followed": CEM, p. 36.

CHAPTER 11 "YESTERDAY I WAS A WONDER"

207 "My father, my parents, all will reward and favor you and take you away from your mother and you will be in the bosom of my family as a daughter": Jan. 13, 1832, letter, Mina (Doylestown Jail) to "My Dear Mari," M-CMCP.

207 He hadn't mailed the letter: After his conviction, Lino entrusted the letter to Thomas Ross and asked him to have it delivered to Mary. Ross refused to do so until after the execution, saying that he "feared it would be believed and would contribute to his release." This information is contained in a paragraph of writing in a different hand from Lino's at the top of his letter to "My Dear Mari," cited in the note above.

208 "flower that would have bloomed in the genial rays of the morning sun of love"; "fall"; and "scorching": CEM, p. 29.

208 "succeed in overcoming her scruples of delicacy": CEM, p. 31.

208 "That very evening, Miss Wilson was sacrificed at the shrine of pleasure": CEM, p. 31.

209 "not Miss Wilson, but Mrs. Lucretia Chapman" and "at a place called Andalusia about thirteen miles from Philadelphia": CEM, p. 33.

209 "another person of my own age": STMC, p. 11.

209 "chère amie in Philadelphia": Philadelphia Saturday Bulletin, May 5, 1832. The Bulletin's reporter states that Lino told him this story "previous to his conviction."

210 The hanging in Lancaster: Philadelphia National Gazette, April 24, 1832.

210 Lino's nonchalance and his picking his teeth: Germantown Telegraph, May 9, 1832.

210 "Yes. It is a proper question and I will allow it to be asked"; "Am I to understand your Honor to say that you have decided contrary to the opinion you gave in the former trial?" and "Yes, contrary to my own opinion": Germantown Telegraph, May 9, 1832.

211 "The death of Mr. Chapman was caused by a most deadly poison that

the day before he was taken ill the individual at the bar purchased in Philadelphia": *Germantown Telegraph,* May 9, 1832.

212 "Any declaration a man makes that is drawn from him by the offer of favor or by threats cannot be given in evidence. But the question is, did you actually promise the defendant favor": See STMC, p. 2. For purposes of clarity, I've adapted this quotation from the Court's original statement, which was, "Any declaration a man makes that is drawn from him by the offer of favor or by threats cannot be given in evidence. . . . The question therefore now is whether this promise of Mr. Blayney comes within the rule of law."

212 "The defendant's confession cannot be given in evidence" and "It is a statement made by Mina with a view of shielding himself. There was no admission of his having participated in the murder": STMC, p. 3.

212 "That was not a promise of favorable treatment": See STMC, p. 3. The quotation is slightly adapted from the original, "this was not a confession drawn from the prisoner upon promise of favor."

212 "You *must* tell us what he said": Du Bois reports simply the court's ruling, and follows the ruling with Blayney's testimony. For dramatic purpose, I've given Fox a directive to Blayney, one which prompts the testimony that follows.

212 "I asked Mina whether he had a medicine chest," and "He said he had, and had left it in the Boston jail . . . Mrs. Chapman then come and kiss and hug me and say, 'Lino, I want you to marry me' ": STMC, p. 3.

213 "clear" and "powerful": *Philadelphia Saturday Bulletin,* May 5, 1832.

214 "exciting interest": TLC, p. 2.

214 "Take the prisoner back for the night," and "Return him tomorrow for sentencing": STMC, p. 7.

214 Lino's flippancy: *Philadelphia Saturday Bulletin,* May 5, 1832.

214 "The Irishman was hanged and the American was not": Trollope, *Domestic Manners of the Americans,* p. 222.

215 Judicial review: It was not until 1855 that Congress gave the Supreme Court discretionary ability to grant appeals, not until 1891 that appellate courts were created.

215 "My name is Carolino . . . before I am ordered to be executed": STMC, p. 9.

216 "Is it necessary for the prisoner to be here as we present arguments as to why he should have a new trial" and "There is no such necessity,

if you are willing to argue the motion in his absence": STMC, p. 8.

216 "The High Constable made a compact with the prisoner. It *was* a promise of favor. It amounted to an offer of immunity from prosecution": See STMC, p. 8. The quotation is adapted from the original, which is, "The compact or promise of secrecy between Blayney and the prisoner was insisted upon [by Rush] to be a promise of favor, inasmuch as it amounted to an immunity from prosecution."

216 "We have not changed our opinion since the trial"; "We do not think that the statement or confession made by the prisoner to Blayney was obtained under any promise of favor whatever. It was at most a promise to keep secret a confession which Mina wished to make"; and "upon the condition that his declaration that he was neither a convict nor a pirate should turn out to be true": STMC, p. 8.

216 "We still think we were right, and therefore the motion for a new trial is refused": STMC, pp. 8–9.

217 "I move the prisoner be brought up for sentencing"; "Motion granted"; "Mr. Espos y Mina, do you have anything to say as to why the sentence of death should not be passed on you"; "The prisoner has drawn up a paper. We think it best if we read his words"; and "My name is Carolino. I was baptized in the Roman Catholic Church. I have in the island of Cuba, a daughter four years old": STMC, p. 9.

217 Fox's agitation: It was noted both by the *Germantown Telegraph,* which reported on May 9, 1832, that "the presiding judge [was] in much agitation and distress," and by Du Bois, who remarked that Fox shortly was to display "a difficulty of utterance which showed how largely he partook of the feeling which seemed to pervade the multitude," STMC, p. 9.

217 "It is necessary before I die, that I should execute some legal papers, in order to secure some property to my daughter" and "I pray the Court to grant me at least a few months of existence, a few months before I am ordered to be executed"; "These matters will be laid before the Governor who will no doubt grant the request which you make"; and "Lino Amalia Espos y Mina . . . And may God have mercy upon your soul": STMC, p. 9.

218 "Back out! Back out at once": *Germantown Telegraph,* May 23, 1832.

218 Forced to scamper away: *Germantown Telegraph,* May 23, 1832.

219 She did it . . . slipping arsenic into his glass: *Philadelphia Saturday Bulletin,* May 5, 1832.

220 The artist from Philadelphia: His name was E. Wellmore.

220 "He is a native of Cuba . . . connections are respectable": *Philadelphia Saturday Courier,* May 26, 1832.

220 "He is the *illegitimate* son of a very rich gentleman of Cuba": *Philadelphia Saturday Bulletin,* May 26, 1832.

220 "Unnatural" child: According to the *Gemantown Telgraph,* June 20, 1832, Lino "complained bitterly of certain editors, whom he alleged had done him serious injury, in calling him an illegitimate son, or 'unnatural' as he expressed it."

220 Robert DeSilver's background: See John Tebbel, *A History of Book Publishing in the United States* (New York & London, 1972), vol. 1, pp. 384–85. The titles of the books published by DeSilver were made known to me by Richard Layman of the Columbia, South Carolina, publishing firm of Bruccoli Clark Layman, Inc.

221 "the most delicate ear, to make it . . . of the community": CEM, p. 26.

221 *Never* forgave injuries and delighted in revenge: TLC, p. 85.

221 "as freely as it pleased him in her presence, and when her punishment would be sufficient to abandon her and return to Cuba": CEM, p. 38.

221 "Her body [was] lacerated and torn over its whole surface by the blows of her mother": CEM, p. 39.

222 "purchased [a] phial of poison from a doctor in the vicinity and . . . a promise of secrecy on his part as to his having sold it": CEM, p. 42.

222 "official" and "Mrs. Chapman called upon a physician in the city a short time previous to the illness of her husband and . . . gave the Physician a fee for the information which she obtained": *Germantown Telegraph,* June 6, 1832.

223 "My children and I have suffered unparalleled affliction. If you would convey us on more moderate terms than the usual ones, it would be an act of holy charity"; "What's your name"; "Lucretia Chapman," "*Mrs.* Chapman"; "All the wealth in the world would not induce me to take you aboard"; and "The way of the transgressor is hard": *Germantown Telegraph,* June 20, 1832.

223 "The governor writes a very good hand": *Doylestown Democrat,* May

22, 1832, as cited on p. 28 of a handwritten document entitled, "The
Chapman-Mina Murder Trial," written by George MacReynolds and
included among the papers in M—CMCP. MacReynolds, a former
librarian of the Bucks County Historical Society, may have prepared the
document for a lecture or publication.

223 "In what shape does the Evil One appear"; "In the shape of that
cricket"; and "Be sure to call and see me again": *Germantown
Telegraph,* June 20, 1832.

224 Lino's attempt to serve an arrest warrant on McDowell: *Germantown
Telegraph,* June 20, 1832.

224 "My dear Thomas . . . stronger than any other pleasure": May 16, 1832,
letter from Mary Ross to Thomas Ross (Jenkinstown), M-CMCP.

225 "But I am entirely innocent of Mr. Chapman's murder. I am innocent of
everything except a love of mischief": *Germantown Telegraph,* June 27,
1832.

225 "I am not even really married to Mrs. Chapman. . . . In order to get her
money": adapted from the *Germantown Telegraph*'s report on June 27,
1832, that Lino "boldly asserted that his marriage with Mrs. C. was a
mere trick to obtain her money."

226 Law office: The old Ross law office, which was next to the jail and
courthouse, has been moved from its original site, but it is still intact
and is now part of a private home in Doylestown.

226 "I hereby certify . . . United States of America": TLC, p. 40.

228 Ross's visits to Lino and to Onderdonk: My account is based on the
Germantown Telegraph article of June 27, 1832.

228 Lino's ballad: CEM, pp. 46–48.

229 Lino's *Soneto:* CEM, p. 48.

229 "Robbed her of the inmost jewel of her soul": CEM, p. 39.

229 Lino's suicide attempts: See "An Account of the Execution and the
Dying Declaration of Mina," CEM, pp. 49–50; see also *Germantown
Telegraph,* June 27, 1832.

230 The largest body of uniformed men . . . since the Revolution:
Kenderdine, "The Chapman-Mina Tragedy," p. 465.

230 The first hanging in Bucks County since 1693: Kenderdine, "The
Chapman-Mina Tragedy," p. 462.

230 Doylestown on the eve of Lino's execution: *Germantown Telegraph,*
June 27, 1832.

230 "I myself used to be a soldier . . . One in particular nearly proved fatal"

and "My own reflections after the interview were by no means pleasant or agreeable . . . A similar instance, I believe, can scarcely be found on record": *Germantown Telegraph*, June 27, 1832.

231 "I am innocent of murder . . . ready to die": *Germantown Telegraph*, June 27, 1832.

231 "It's cruel of you . . . like a soldier": *Germantown Telegraph*, June 27, 1832.

232 The military men were lacking in spit and polish: *Germantown Telegraph*, June 27, 1832.

232 Morris serves as the hangman: "An Account of the Execution and the Dying Declaration of Mina," CEM, p. 49.

232 Tuljeaux translates: "An Account of the Execution and the Dying Declaration of Mina": CEM, p. 49.

233 "You thirst for my blood . . . I am strong and not feeble" and "Farewell, my friends . . . He die innocent": *Germantown Telegraph*, June 27, 1832.

233 the penultimate prisoner to be publicly executed . . . in Pennsylvania: see Negley K. Teeters, "Public Executions in Pennsylvania 1682 to 1834," *Journal of the Lancaster County Historical Society*, Spring 1960.

234 Organs and skeletons of executed prisoners: Thomas M. McDade, *The Annals of Murder* (Norman, Okla.), p. xxxiii.

234 The experiment on Lino's body: *Philadelphia Saturday Bulletin*, June 30, 1832.

235 Lit out for the West . . . second career as an actress: *Philadelphia Gazette and Universal Daily Advertiser*, November 14, 1834.

EPILOGUE

237 "How she has fallen . . . the finger of scorn is pointed at her and she is greeted with hisses and general disaffection": The Philadelphia man wrote these words on the flyleaf of a copy of Du Bois's book which he gave to a brother as a gift. The inscribed copy is in the possession of the American Antiquarian Society.

238 One 1909 commentator: The commentator is Kenderdine. See his "Chapman-Mina Tragedy," p. 461.

238 William, Jr.'s history: Kenderdine, "The Chapman-Mina Tragedy," p. 461.

240 "Everybody knows that Maryland is a Slave State": Magill, "When Men Were Sold," p. 514.

240 "Everybody is nobody! Common report does not pass before a court of justice": Magill, "When Men Were Sold," p. 514.

241 "with human feelings [even] if he was a judge": Magill, "When Men Were Sold," p. 512.

241 Morris's history: Kenderdine, "The Chapman-Mina Tragedy," p. 464.

241 Du Bois's history: *American National Biography*, p. 950.

241 "Mina Flood": Lichtenwalner, *Bensalem,* p. 311.

Bibliography

PRINCIPAL SOURCES

BOOKS AND UNPUBLISHED MATERIAL

Brown, David Paul. *The Forum, or Forty Years Full Practice at the Philadelphia Bar,* 2 volumes. Philadelphia, 1856.

Chapman, Mr. and Mrs. William. *United States Institution for the Treatment of Cases of Defective Utterance Such as Partial Speechlessness, Stuttering, Stammering, Hesitancy, Weakness of Voice, Mis-Enunciation, Lisping, Etc., Etc.* Philadelphia, 1826.

Du Bois, William E. *The Trial of Lucretia Chapman,* Philadelphia, 1832.

——. *Supplement to the Trial of Mrs. Chapman: The Trial of Lino Amalia Espos y Mina.* Philadelphia, 1832.

Mina, Carolino Estradas. *The Life and Confession of Carolino Estradas de Mina.* Philadelphia, 1832.

Mina-Chapman Murder Case Papers. Spruance Library, Bucks County Historical Society, Doylestown, Pa.

DOCUMENTS

Baggage of William Chapman. Baggage Entries, 1799–1856. Records of the Port of Philadelphia, National Archives and Records Administration, Mid-Atlantic Region, Philadelphia, Pa.

Bensalem Township Census, 1820 and 1830. National Archives and Records Administration, Mid-Atlantic Region, Philadelphia, Pa.

Commonwealth v. Edward Winslow, 1814–1818. April term, Supreme Judicial Court, Boston, Mass.

Documents Pertaining to the Incarceration and Pardon of Edward Winslow, 1820–1823. Commonwealth of Massachusetts, Archives Division, Boston, Mass.

Documents Pertaining to the Incarceration of Mark Winslow, 1826.
Commonwealth of Massachusetts, Archives Division, Boston, Mass.

Naturalization Records, Philadelphia, 1789–1880. Genealogical Society of
Pennsylvania.

Passenger and Immigration Lists, Philadelphia, 1800–1850. Genealogical
Society of Pennsylvania.

Petition for Sale of Lucretia, William, Abigail, and John Chapman's Real
Estate. Orphans' Court files, Spruance Library, Bucks County Historical
Society, Doylestown, Pa.

NEWSPAPERS

Barnstable Patriot (Massachusetts), 1831–1832.

Boston Morning Post, 1831–1832.

Bucks County Intelligencer (Pennsylvania), 1831.

Germantown Gazette (Pennsylvania), 1831.

Germantown Telegraph (Pennsylvania), 1831–1832.

Philadelphia Aurora General Advertiser, 1813–1817, 1826.

Philadelphia Gazette and Universal Daily Advertiser, 1831–1832, 1834.

Philadelphia National Gazette and Literary Register, 1831.

Philadelphia Poulson's American Daily Advertiser, 1813, 1817, 1831–1832.

Philadelphia Public Ledger, 1831–1863.

Philadelphia Saturday Bulletin, 1817, 1831–1832.

Philadelphia Saturday Courier, 1832.

Relf's Philadelphia Gazette, 1813, 1817.

SELECTED ADDITIONAL SOURCES

Appleby, Joyce. *Inheriting the Revolution: The First Generation of
Americans.* Cambridge, Mass., 2000.

Banner, Stuart. *The Death Penalty: An American History.* Cambridge, Mass.,
2002.

Battle, J. H. *History of Bucks County, Pennsylvania.* Philadelphia, 1887.

*Book of Biographies: Biographical Sketches of Leading Citizens of Bucks
County, Pennsylvania.* Buffalo, N.Y., 1899.

Buck, William J. *A History of Bucks County.* Doylestown, Pa., 1855.

Cobb, Elijah. *Elijah Cobb, A Cape Cod Skipper,* with a foreword by Ralph D.
Paine. New Haven, Conn., 1925.

Davis, W. W. H. "Half an Hour with the Old Taverns of Doylestown." In *A Collection of Papers Read Before the Bucks County Historical Society*, vol. 2. Riegelsville, Pa., 1909.

———. *History of Bucks County Pennsylvania: From the Discovery of the Delaware to the Present Time*. Doylestown, Pa., 1876.

———. *History of Bucks County Pennsylvania: from the Discovery of the Delaware to the Present Time*. Pipersville, Pa., 1905.

———. *History of Doylestown Old and New*. Doylestown, Pa., 1904.

Dickens, Charles. *American Notes* [1842], with an introduction by Christopher Hitchens. New York, 1996.

A Digest of the Laws in Force Relating to the Police of the City of Philadelphia, with Some Account of the History of the Police Forces of the Same, from the Year 1682, to the Present Time. Philadelphia, 1851.

Dubois, Mary L. "Old Doylestown." In *A Collection of Papers Read Before the Bucks County Historical Society*, vol. 3. Riegelsville, Pa., 1909.

Elson, Ruth Miller. *Guardians of Tradition: American Schoolbooks of the Nineteenth Century*. Lincoln, Neb., 1964.

England, Joseph W., editor. *The First Century of the Philadelphia College of Pharmacy, 1821–1921*. Philadelphia, 1922.

Friedman, Lawrence M. *Crime and Punishment in American History*. New York, 1993.

———. *A History of American Law*. New York, 1985.

Gall, Ludwig. *The Travels of Ludwig Gall*. In "Pennsylvania Through a German's Eyes: The Travels of Ludwig Gall, 1819–1820," by Frederic Trautman, *Pennsylvania Magazine of History and Biography*. January 1981.

Green, Doron. *A History of Bristol Borough, in the County of Bucks, State of Pennsylvania*. Bristol, Pa., 1911.

Grund, Frederic. *The Americans in Their Moral, Social and Political Relations*. London, 1837.

Halttunen, Karen. *Confidence Men and Painted Women*. New Haven, Conn., 1982.

———. "Domestic Differences: Competing Narratives of Womanhood in the Murder Trial of Lucretia Chapman." In *The Culture of Sentiment: Race, Gender and Sentimentality in Nineteenth Century America*, edited by Shirley Samuels. New York, 1992.

———. *Murder Most Foul: The Killer and the American Gothic Imagination*. Cambridge, Mass., 1998.

Hamilton, Thomas. *Men and Manners in America.* Edinburgh, 1833.

History of Philadelphia . . . with an Historical Account of the Military Operations of the Late War, in 1812, 13 & 14. Philadelphia, 1839.

Holton, David-Parsons. *Winslow Memorial.* New York, 1877–1878.

Ierley, Merritt. *The Comforts of Home: The American House and the Evolution of Modern Convenience.* New York, 1999.

Jacobs, James Ripley, and Glenn Tucker. *The War of 1812: A Compact History.* New York, 1969.

Jackson, Joseph. *Encyclopedia of Philadelphia.* Harrisburg, Pa., 1931.

Jones, Ann. *Women Who Kill.* New York, 1980.

Kemble, Frances. *Journal by Frances Anne [Kemble] Butler.* London, 1835.

Kenderdine, Thaddeus S. "The Chapman-Mina Tragedy." In *A Collection of Papers Read Before the Bucks County Historical Society,* vol. 3. Riegelsville, Pa., 1909.

Kittredge, Henry C. *Cape Cod: Its People and Their History,* Boston, 1968.

Larkin, Jack. *The Reshaping of Everyday Life, 1790–1840.* New York, 1969.

The Laws of Etiquette, by a Gentleman. Philadelphia, 1836.

Leigh, Jane. *Facts in Relation to Mrs. Leigh's System of Curing Stammering, and Other Impediments of Speech.* New York, 1826.

Lewis, George Albert. *The Old Houses and Stores with Memorabilia Relating to Them and My Father and Grandfather.* Philadelphia, 1900.

Lichtenwalner, Muriel V., editor, *Bensalem.* 1984.

Magill, Edward H. "When Men Were Sold: Reminscences of the Underground Railroad in Bucks County and Its Managers." In *A Collection of Papers Read Before the Bucks County Historical Society,* vol. 2, Riegelsville, Pa., 1909.

Marryat, Frederick. *Diary in America* [1839], edited and with a foreword by Jules Zanger. Bloomington, Ind., 1960.

Martineau, Harriet. *Society in America,* 3 volumes. London, 1837.

Mayfield, John. *The New Nation, 1800–1845.* New York, 1982.

McClellan, Elisabeth. *History of American Costume, 1607–1870.* New York, 1937.

McNealy, Terry A. "Andalusia," *Bucks County Town & Country Living.* Spring 1998.

———. "Historic Hulmeville," *Bucks County Town & Country Living.* Winter 1996.

Miller, Douglas T., compiler. *The Nature of Jacksonian America.* New York, 1972.

Miller, Perry. *The Life of the Mind in America*, New York, 1965.

"Memoir of Elias Durand." Pamphlet from the Collection of the Philadelphia College of Pharmacy, author and date unknown.

Nelson's Biographical Dictionary and Historical Reference Book of Erie County, Pennsylvania, vol. 1. Erie, Pa., 1896.

Nye, Russel Blaine. *The Cultural Life of the New Nation*. New York, 1960.

Oberholtzer, Ellis Paxson. *Philadelphia: A History of the City and Its People*. Philadelphia, 1912.

Peirce, Charles. *A Meteorological Account of the Weather in Philadelphia from January 1, 1790 to January 1, 1847*. Philadelphia, 1847.

Pennsylvania Archives, 6th series, vols. 7 and 8. Harrisburg, Pa., 1874–1935.

Philadelphia Directories. 1813–1828.

Philadelphia in 1824: A Brief Account of the Various Institutions and Public Objects in This Metropolis. Philadelphia, 1824.

Picture of Philadelphia, or A Brief Account of the Various Institutions and Public Objects in This Metropolis, Philadelphia, 1835.

Pugh, Marshall R. "The Rodmans and the Foxes," in *A Collection of Papers Read Before the Bucks County Historical Society*, vol. 3. Riegelsville, Pa., 1909.

Report of Committee on Police to the Select and Common Councils. Philadelphia, 1837.

Reynolds, David S. *Beneath the American Renaissance: The Subversive Imagination in the Age of Emerson and Melville*, Cambridge, Mass., and London, 1988.

Rowson, Susanna. *Charlotte Temple* [1797], edited and with an introduction by Cathy N. Davidson. New York, 1986.

Royall, Anne. *Mrs. Royall's Pennsylvania, or Travels Continued in the United States*. Washington, D.C., 1829.

Rush, Benjamin. "Female Education," in *The Philadelphia Book, or Specimens of Metropolitan Literature*. Philadelphia, 1836.

Schneider, Paul. *The Enduring Shore: A History of Cape Cod, Martha's Vineyard, and Nantucket*. New York, 2000.

Tepper, Michael, editor. *Passenger Arrivals at the Port of Philadelphia, 1800–1819*. Baltimore, 1986.

Tevis, Julia. *Sixty Years in a School-Room: An Autobiography of Mrs. Julia A. Tevis*. Cincinnati, 1878.

Thackara, William Wood. *Diary of William Wood Thackara*. In "William

Wood Thackara, Volunteer in the War of 1812," by Anne Castrodale, *Pennsylvania Magazine of History and Biography.* July 6, 1967.

Thoreau, Henry David. *Cape Cod* [1857]. Peninsula Press edition, Cape Cod, Mass., 1997.

Trollope, Fanny. *Domestic Manners of the Americans* [1832], New York, 1997.

Tyler, Alice Felt. *Freedom's Ferment: Phases of American Social History from the Colonial Period to the Outbreak of the Civil War.* New York, 1962.

Vicery, Eliza. *Emily Hamilton, a Novel, Founded on Incidents in Real Life.* Worcester, Mass., 1803.

Wainwright, Nicholas B. "Andalusia, Countryseat of the Craig Family and of Nicholas Biddle and His Descendants," *Pennsylvania Magazine.* January 1977.

Walker, Joseph E. "A Soldier's Diary," *Pennsylvania History.* October 1945.

Waln, Robert. *The Hermit in America on a Visit to Philadelphia.* Philadelphia, 1819.

Watson, John F. *Annals of Philadelphia.* Philadelphia, 1830.

Wilson, Thomas. *Picture of Philadelphia for 1824, containing the "Picture of Philadelphia for 1811, by James Mease, M.D," with all its improvements since that period.* Philadelphia, 1823.

Wolf, Edwin II. *Philadelphia: Portrait of an American City.* Philadelphia, 1990.

Wright, Caleb E. "Four Lawyers of the Doylestown Bar," in *A Collection of Papers Read Before the Bucks County Historical Society,* vol. 1. Riegelsville, Pa., 1909.

Wright, Frances. *Views of Society and Manners in America* [1821], edited by Paul R. Baker. Cambridge, Mass., 1963.

Yerkes, Harman. "John Ross and the Ross Family," in *A Collection of Papers Read Before the Bucks County Historical Society,* vol. 2. Riegelsville, Pa., 1909.

The Young Lady's Book: Manual of Elegant Recreations, Exercises and Pursuits. Boston, 1830.